'At a time when free thinking and a democratically legitimate, diverse culture are increasingly under threat worldwide, this book provides a scientifically sound wake-up call to preserve open thinking not only in our culture and society, but also within our psychoanalytic community. With their consistent plea for an opening and fluidity of psychoanalytic theory and practice in the realm of sexuality and gender, the authors repeatedly touch on the original field of psychoanalysis. At the same time, their multi-layered message is: we need resistance to arbitrariness in our psychoanalytic concepts, but also resistance to normative restriction in the diversity of innovative theories on socially new, often still incomprehended forms of sexuality and gender. This is an excellent book that cannot be pigeonholed into any psychoanalytic cliché, but opens up creative spaces for thought and life.'

Dr. med. Heribert Blass, *IPA President*

'The paradox at the heart of psychoanalysis–without resistance, there can be no cure; yet when resistance calcifies, the analytic process stalls–shapes every treatment, implicating both analyst and analysand. With candor and precision, the ten essays in this volume—authored by a distinguished group of international clinicians—trace the evolving contours of resistance as it intersects with gender, embodiment, and the enduring question of sexual difference. It is, unmistakably, essential reading for the contemporary psychoanalyst.'

Patricia Gherovici, *PhD, psychoanalyst, Sigourney Award winner and author of* Transgender Psychoanalysis

Working Psychoanalytically with Gender Diversity and Sexualities

Working Psychoanalytically with Gender Diversity and Sexualities considers and challenges expectations about psychoanalytic work with LGBTQIA+ patients.

The book is organised into three parts, starting with a theoretical review, which includes a discussion of the relevance of the Oedipus complex, resistance to infantile sexuality, the conquest of otherness and challenges in maintaining neutrality. Secondly, the contributors approach an ethical dimension, with chapters describing different moments in the way in which psychoanalysts engage with ethical responsibility in the face of gender and sexual diversity. The third part of the book considers an ontological dimension, that incorporates fluidity as a condition of the subject as an object of study and includes factors such as race and generational status, emergence of stigmas and a particular focus on the concept of helplessness. The contributors offer insight into countertransferential reactions and responses in clinical work, ensuring that analysts can work with these patients without preconceptions standing in the way.

Extending an opportunity to air conflicting psychoanalytic views and rethink established psychoanalytic concepts, this book will be a key reading for psychoanalysts and psychotherapists in practice and in training. It will also be of interest to academics and students of psychoanalytic studies and gender studies.

Frances Thomson-Salo, PhD, is an adult and child psychoanalyst, European co-chair of the IPA Sexual and Gender Diversity Studies committee, and member of the International Journal of Psychoanalysis Board. She was an Associate Professor, Department of Psychiatry, University of Melbourne, specialising in infant mental health.

Marco Posadas, RSW, MSW, PhD, is a psychoanalyst based in Toronto, and inaugural chair of the IPA Sexual and Gender Diversity Studies Committee. He received the 2018 Sue Fairbanks Excellence in Psychoanalytic Knowledge Distinguished Lecturer award, the 2022 Distinguished Social Worker for Toronto award, and is the 2024–2025 Antoinette Calabria visiting scholar for the Psychoanalytic Center of the Carolinas.

Silvia R. Acosta, PsyD, PhD, is an Argentinian psychoanalyst, member of the SPP and the APC, a member of the IPA Sexual and Gender Diversity Studies Committee, and a co-founder of the FEPAL Working Party on drive constellations and subjectivation processes. She has published psychoanalytic articles and teaches on sexual and gender diversity in Europe and Latin America.

IPA Sexual and Gender Diversity Series
Series Editor: Leticia Glocer Fiorini

Recent titles in the Series include:

Polymorphisms
Sexual and Gender Migrations in Contemporary Psychoanalysis
Edited by Leticia Glocer Fiorini, Jean Marc Tauszik, and Silvia R. Acosta

Gender, Identifications, and Identities
Dialogues at the Edges
Edited by Frances Thomson-Salo, Luca Bruno, and Eva Reichelt

Working Psychoanalytically with Gender Diversity and Sexualities
Resistances to Differences
Edited by Frances Thomson-Salo, Marco Posadas, and Silvia R. Acosta

Working Psychoanalytically with Gender Diversity and Sexualities

Resistances to Differences

Edited by Frances Thomson-Salo, Marco Posadas, and Silvia R. Acosta

Routledge
Taylor & Francis Group

LONDON AND NEW YORK

First published 2026
by Routledge
4 Park Square, Milton Park, Abingdon, Oxon OX14 4RN

and by Routledge
605 Third Avenue, New York, NY 10158

Routledge is an imprint of the Taylor & Francis Group, an informa business

British Library Cataloguing-in-Publication Data
A catalogue record for this book is available from the British Library

ISBN: 978-1-032-87187-5 (hbk)
ISBN: 978-1-032-87186-8 (pbk)
ISBN: 978-1-003-53133-3 (ebk)

DOI: 10.4324/9781003531333

Typeset in Palatino
by KnowledgeWorks Global Ltd.

Contents

List of contributors   *ix*
Series preface   *xii*

Introduction   1
MARCO POSADAS, SILVIA ACOSTA, AND FRANCES THOMSON-SALO

PART I
Theoretical and technical changes within
psychanalysis: Gender and sexualities   5

Introduction   7
ÂNGELA VILA-REAL

1 The Oedipus complex: An expanded approach on sexual
   and gender polyphonies   11
   LETICIA GLOCER FIORINI

2 Psychosexuality and the problem of (mis)representation:
   A mentalising perspective   19
   LIZ ALLISON

3 Encountering otherness: On the ability (and inability) for
   psychic movement within sexual states of mind   30
   ANAT SCHUMANN

4 Shapes of gender identity: Three stories with impact   47
   DOMENICO DI CEGLIE

PART II
Psychoanalytic ethics and depathologising gender diversities and sexualities   59

Introduction: Intolerance as an unconscious response to violence in the analytic field   61
MARCO POSADAS

5   The many colours of the rainbow: Depathologising sexual diversity   65
SERGIO LEWKOWICZ

6   Towards a psychoanalytic ethics-based practice with transgender individuals   76
ALESSANDRA LEMMA

7   A history of reception: Falling apart as the ground for learning   94
OREN GOZLAN

PART III
In search of complexity   111

Introduction   113
NICOLAS EVZONAS

8   Gender fixed and fluid: Gender and suffering, gender and transformation   119
ADRIENNE HARRIS

9   Gender crossing as caesura versus gender crossing as cut   131
DANA AMIR

Eva Reichelt Discussion of Chapter 9   138
Elda Abrevaya Discussion of Chapter 9   142

10   On trying to pass off transphobia as psychoanalysis and cruelty as "clinical logic"   149
AVGI SAKETOPOULOU

Index   *160*

Contributors

Elda Abrevaya is a founding member and a training analyst of the Istanbul Psychoanalytical Association and a member of the Paris Psychoanalytic Society. She has been the Professor at the University of Puerto Rico and is co-editor of the book *Homosexualities: Psychogenesis, Polymorphism, and Countertransference* (Routledge, 2015).

Silvia Acosta, PhD, analyst of the Asociación Psicoanalítica de Cordoba, member of the Sociedade Portuguesa de Psicanálise, Lisbon and of the IPA Gender and Sexual Diversity Studies Committee since 2017. Full professor for 15 years in doctoral and Master programmes in psychoanalysis at Universidad del Salvador, Argentina. Currently, co-director of Revista Portuguesa de Psicanálise.

Liz Allison, psychoanalyst, member of the British Psychoanalytical Society, Director of the Psychoanalysis Unit at University College London, member of the Editorial Board of Routledge's New Library of Psychoanalysis, Associate Member of the International Journal of Psychoanalysis Editorial Board, and co-editor of the Karnac book series *Developments in Psychoanalysis*.

Dana Amir, PhD, is a clinical psychologist, supervising and training analyst, Israel Psychoanalytic Society, full professor, vice dean for research and head of the interdisciplinary doctoral program in psychoanalysis at Haifa University, and editor in chief of *Maarag*. She is the author of six poetry books, two memoirs in prose and four psychoanalytic non-fiction books. She is the winner of many literary and academic prizes, including five international psychoanalytic awards.

Domenico Di Ceglie is a Lifetime Honorary Consultant Child and Adolescent psychiatrist at the Tavistock Centre, in 1989 founding the Gender Identity Development Service at St. George's Hospital, London, which transferred to the Tavistock Centre in 1996. Previously, he was an Honorary Senior Lecturer, University College Londo, and has published widely about his work.

Nicolas Evzonas, PhD, was a clinical psychologist, psychoanalyst and Associate Professor of Clinical Psychology at the Université de Paris Cité, and a consultant to the European subcommittee of the IPA Sexual and Gender Diversity Studies committee.

Leticia Glocer Fiorini, MD, a training and supervising analyst, is a member of the Argentine Psychoanalytic Association, and current chair of the IPA Sexual and Gender Diversity Studies Committee. She is a Professor of Gender Studies at the University of Buenos Aires, and was a past APA President and past Chair of the IPA Publications Committee. Her paper, "The Feminine Position: A Heterogeneous Construction" won the Celes Cárcamo Prize.

Oren Gozlan, PsyD, a psychoanalyst in Toronto, is a member of the IPA Committee for Sexuality and Gender Diversity Studies. In 2015, he won the American Academy & Board of Psychoanalysis annual book prize, in 2022, the Ralph Roughton Award (APsaA), and in 2023, the Canadian Psychoanalytic Society Miguel Prados Prize for "Gender in Deep Time."

Adrienne Harris, PhD, faculty and supervisor, is a member of the NYU Postdoctoral Program in Psychotherapy and Psychoanalysis, faculty and training analyst at the Psychoanalytic Institute of Northern California, and on the Editorial Boards of *Psychoanalytic Dialogues, Studies in Gender and Sexuality, Psychoanalytic Perspectives* and the *Journal of the American Psychoanalytic Association.*

Alessandra Lemma, BSc., MA, MPhil, MSt, is a Chartered Clinical and Counselling Psychologist, Psychoanalyst and Fellow of the British Psychoanalytical Society, a Visiting Professor in the Psychoanalysis Unit, University College London and a Consultant at the Anna Freud National Centre for Children and Families. She has worked in the National Health Service for 35 years treating adults and adolescents with mental health problems.

Sergio Lewkowicz, psychiatrist, is a training and supervising psychoanalyst of the Porto Alegre Psychoanalytic Society, and a former president and chair of the Institute of the Porto Alegre Psychoanalytic Society, where he teaches regularly. He is a member of the IPA Gender and Sexual Diversity Studies committee, and professor and supervisor for psychoanalytic psychotherapy in the Psychiatry Department of the Medical School of the Federal University of Rio Grande do Sul.

Marco Posadas, PhD, is a psychoanalyst, the inaugural Chair of the first IPA Gender & Sexual Diversity Studies Committee and recipient of the Ontario Association of Social Workers 2013 Inspirational Leader award, and 2022 Distinguished Social Worker for Toronto. He delivered the 2018 Sue Fairbanks Lecture at Sue Fairbanks Psychoanalytic Academy, and is the 2024/2025 Antoinette Calabria visiting lecturer, Psychoanalytic Center of the Carolinas.

Eva Reichelt is a psychiatrist and psychoanalyst in Berlin, member of the German Psychoanalytical Association and a member of the IPA European Committee on Sexual and Gender Diversity Studies.

Avgi Saketopoulou, PsyD, is on the faculty at the NYU Postdoctoral Program in Psychotherapy and Psychoanalysis, and also teaches at the New York Psychoanalytic Institute and the William Alanson White Institute. Her work has received the annual *JAPA* essay prize, and she is co-author of the IPA's first Tiresias Prize.

Anat Schumann, clinical psychologist, training psychoanalyst of the Israel Psychoanalytic Society. She teaches in various psychoanalytic programs, including the IPS and the Psychoanalytic Psychotherapy Program, Faculty of Medicine, Tel-Aviv University and was awarded the 27th Frances Tustin International Prize (2024) for *Encountering Otherness: On the Ability (and Inability) for Psychic Movement within Sexual States of Mind.*

Frances Thomson-Salo, PhD, training adult and child psychoanalyst, European co-chair of the IPA Sexual and Gender Diversity Studies Committee, Fellow of the International Journal of Psychoanalysis College, former Committee on Women and Psychoanalysis Chair, and Associate Professor, Department of Psychiatry, University of Melbourne for 20 years. She has written/edited 18 books, including *Engaging Infants: Embodied Communication in Short-Term Infant-Parent Therapy* (2018) and *Infant Observation: Creating Transformative Relationships* (2014).

Ângela Vila-Real, PhD, psychologist and psychoanalyst is a member of the Portuguese Society of Psychoanalysis and teaches psychoanalytic candidates and psychology students on topics of gender and sexuality. Founder of IA-Identidades e Afectos, she is co-editor of "Género, relações, processos e transformações", 2019), co-author of "Ter duas mães: dinâmica da triangulação em filhos de casais de lésbicas" (2019) and co-editor of "Atas das Jornadas Trans" (2023).

Series preface

IPA Sexual and Gender Diversity Studies Committee

With this volume we continue the Sexual and Gender Diversity Series project, edited by the IPA's Sexual & Gender Diversity Studies Committee. The aim of the series project is to explore, expand and update psychoanalytic thoughts focusing on today's sexual and gender migrations. This objective is part of the Committee's mandate to present debates and controversies in the psychoanalytic field in order to better understand contemporary changes on subjectivities.

This applies to the review of epistemological, theoretical and clinical tools in the psychoanalytical field focusing on changes which demand continuing to develop new concepts and to reconsider others. By confronting them we might find agreements and disagreements which should be worked through in an open dialogue. In this frame, our perspective is to grasp a contemporary and present point of view on these topics. At the same time, there are crucial axes of psychoanalysis from Freud's onwards that should be maintained.

There is a complex fabric, which includes different psychoanalytic theories, different clinical approaches, as well as different cultures in the same or diverse latitudes. Certainly, throughout this proposal, a necessary intersection runs between psychic reality with otherness and culture.

All these facts lead to set out relevant ideas and themes that were and are discussed by several psychoanalytic theories as well as by gender and post-gender theories. This approach inevitably includes the clarification of the logical and epistemic perspectives from which different proposals are read today. Listening to other viewpoints inevitably guides us to a better listening of our patients, especially of what is new and original, meaning a space of freedom both to analysts and to patients.

In this context, concordances can be found, but also divergences that should be sustained in tension in the perspective of exploring which are the effects of the crucial changes that are part of current societies. Indeed, this implies an extra work for the reader to illuminate these contradictions in a fruitful way. In this way, our purpose has been to go beyond a unique, uniform line of thought, in order to sustain differences which each reader might process creatively, and surpass as well.

The S&GDS Committee's objective is to share these ideas with the psychoanalytic community and with professionals of other disciplines with the aim of generating a productive interchange between the text and the reader. We assume the challenge of displaying these debates that involve significant contributions to thinking about nowadays construction of subjectivity.

Lastly, our special acknowledgement to the authors for their outstanding contributions as well as to the Psychoanalytic International Association for their support in undertake this project.

Leticia Glocer Fiorini
Series Editor

Introduction

Marco Posadas, Silvia Acosta,
and Frances Thomson-Salo

The book aims to consolidate new conceptual, technical, and epistemological developments in recent years and represents a retrospective on sexual and gender diversity studies that we hope will enrich exchange with other disciplines. The chapters provide a sense of the breadth of ideas presented in different scientific events across Europe, of which the first was the International Psychoanalytical Association Study Day called Contemporary Psychoanalytic Perspectives on Gender and Sexualities, held in Brussels in 2019 at the European Psychoanalytic Federation House. It was part of the academic and institutional policy of the Committee to disseminate and expand knowledge and include authors to deepen the discussion and transmission of psychoanalytic developments in theories and practice. Those presentations are integrated with papers presented at subsequent scientific events.

One of the first issues identified were the resistances that began emerging and this became an inspiration for this book. The word "resistance" comes from the Latin *resistentia*, from the verb *resistere,* which means to stand firm, to oppose and to persevere, its root, *stare,* meaning both "to stand" and "to take a stand". The book is titled *Working Psychoanalytically with Gender Diversity and Sexualities: Resistances to Differences* to evoke the tension produced by antagonistic positions when they become rigid. This allowed us to include several different angles from which we can understand the reactions to certain differences, and conceptual and technical tensions in the psychoanalytic field. Such tensions regarding the issue of sexual and gender diversity, express the need to take a stand, to differ,[1] to resist, as well as to repair.

Psychoanalytic clinical work with a gender perspective represents an area of reflection and theoretical construction that has been in existence for the last 60 years. Within the psychoanalytic framework, it has generated movements that seek to understand new power dynamics, relationships and associated mental health suffering. It has also given rise to new subjective expressions and experiences linked to sexualities and bodies. This impacts family configurations that diverge from what has been labelled a traditional heteronormative model that prioritises hegemonic masculinity.

DOI: 10.4324/9781003531333-1

It is not just about sexual diversities nor theorising about gender poly-morphism; it also encompasses the emergence of transformative potential, brought about by the integration of technology into our lives, our families, kiniship, and the way we love.

Those authors who, a couple of decades ago, began to express their dis-sent and resistance to the rejection and pathologisation characterised by a relational scenario where relational formats that challenge traditional configurations proliferate. A significant portion of descriptive and diagnos-tic categories have been subjected to scrutiny, prompting a growing desire to comprehend and grasp the nuances of these phenomena. Thinking psychoanalytically about gender diversity and sexualities can provide guid-ance in confronting the formidable resistances that arise in the face of estab-lished theoretical frameworks. These resistances extend beyond the limits of theory to encompass the inherent uncertainty associated with a subject that defies conventional norms of knowledge. It is here where singularity is situated at a considerable distance from established theoretical tenets. This subject, as an ontologically diverse object of knowledge, demands a profound ethical and technical responsibility from us.

To resist is a multiple act where resistances can both oppose change and initiate and survive change. While resistance in singular evokes tension and standstill, we see the plural resistances as dynamic and plural, and in the service of the survival of the psychic life of the subject. Resistances help a person persist, stand up, and demand reflection on the necessity for change. The necessity for change is not only an invitation to innovation, but also an expression of respect for the subject of our practice. This respect is situated in a temporal and cultural context that is ethically oriented towards the existence of differences with hospitality and curiosity. Considering Freud's initial proposition within our theoretical field, namely that every action corresponds to a reaction and that every questioning is confronted by an opposing force, this book includes some contemporary psychoanalysts who have creatively theorised while navigating these resistances.

Now, we nominate *differences* in the plural, but what do we want to emphasise? In the face of the vast and largely unexplored field of uncon-scious phenomena that psychoanalysis does not yet fully understand, diversity and adaptability of psychoanalytic models have become increas-ingly necessary, and their clinical value more evident. The tendency to resist and oppose revising the theoretical canons is strained by the need to revitalise what is labelled as divergent. This seems to be the unusual nature of psychoanalytic knowledge.

The aim is to consolidate current knowledge in the psychoanalytic field, related to expressions of sexual diversity, gender expansivity and creativity, modes of jouissance, and singular forms of psychic suffering. Moreover, it is essential to determine the ultimate objective of the psychoanalytic en-deavour. If psychoanalysis is to be considered a theoretical model, a clinical technique, and a field of research, a closer look to the conditions that give rise to subjectivity invites a revision of the scientific rigour of our postulates and a consideration for the plasticity and flexibility necessary to create and use our formulations.

In this book, the various ways of conceptualising differences are organised into three distinct axes: a theoretical review, an ethical dimension, and an ontological dimension that incorporates fluidity as a condition of the subject as the object of our study. In the first part, Ângela Vila-Real introduces the works of Leticia Glocer, Liz Allison, Anat Schuman, and Domenico Di Ceglie. Leticia Glocer outlines an analysis of the continued relevance of the Oedipus complex in the context of contemporary relational world. Liz Allison, in turn, highlights the resistance to include infantile sexuality and the processes of mentalisation emerging from it as evidence that the anchoring or unanchoring of the sex-gender unit is the product of a complex drive integration. Anat Schumann describes the conquest of otherness as a distinctive trajectory that shapes an object configuration, articulating the feminine and the masculine from the perspective of psychic bisexuality. Domenico Di Ceglie examines the challenges associated with maintaining neutrality towards patients, particularly pubescent individuals, acknowledging the complexities that they present for transferential dynamics.

In the second part, Marco Posadas introduces chapters by Sergio Lewkowicz, Alessandra Lemma, and Oren Gozlan that provide different moments in the way in which psychoanalysts engage with the ethical responsibility of the psychoanalyst in the face of gender diversity and sexualities. Sergio Lewkowicz opens up the dialogue about violence targeting LGBTQI+ people in Brazil, and countries that criminalise sexual and gender diversity. He highlights the world tendency to pathologise differences and sexual diversities. Alessandra Lemma presents a perspective from England where given the rise in visibility and access to treatment of trans people, the moment demands caution when thinking about gender transitioning in general, and in children in specific. Alessandra Lemma uses a psychoanalytic approach to carve out a space to think about important cases and findings that can help an analyst to experience the complexity of psychoanalytic ethics when working with transgender people. Lastly, Oren Gozlan suggests entering gender as an unknown experience that provokes anxiety in the analyst. In line with Chase Joynt's documentary, *Framing Agnes* (2022), Gozlan uses the famous case of Agnes as starting point to push against psychoanalytic theories of gender, and to further understand transference dynamics.

In the third and final section, Nicolas Evzonas contextualises and frames the work of Adrianne Harris and Dana Amir, which is discussed by Eva Reichelt and Elda Abrevaya, and finally, that of Avgi Saketopoulou. Adrianne Harris's approach to the processes of gender subjectification and sexuality is one that treats these as a fluid and flexible field, which also imports a powerful component of suffering. Consequently, her work is characterised by a pronounced ethical stance, which connects analytical procedures to practices guided by an ethic of care. Additionally, she indicates that the forms of diversity under consideration and their ramifications extend beyond the immediate subjectivity under examination to encompass other factors such as race and generational status. She discusses the emergence of stigmas as a result of resistance and the ethical considerations associated with them, with a particular focus on the concept of helplessness as proposed by Laplanche. Dana Amir puts forward the concept of "caesura" as an alternative to the notion of the "cut". This epistemological position, derived from Bionian notions, enables us to transcend the limitations of gender binarism. Dana Amir's concept of caesura incorporates the notions of both cut and continuity, suggesting a mode of psychoanalytic thought that encompasses diversity as a condition of the object. Eva Reichelt and Elda Abrevaya examine the nuances of Amir's work, elucidating its ramifications. Avgi Saketopoulou addresses the inherent tension between the analytic model and transphobic elements embedded in certain postulates. In this vein, she proceeds to deconstruct, rework and propose alternatives within the analytic field that have the potential to impact the awareness of the analytic work, which is not exempt from prejudices that demand responsibility and rigorous research. She puts forward her own theoretical and clinical coordinates in an approach model that takes such complexities into account.

Considering the inherent limitations of any attempt to categorise the vast and multifaceted domain of sexual and gender diversity, in the hope that this endeavour will prove enlightening and constructive, contributing to the evolution of a psychoanalytic discourse that is at once rigorous, flexible, and receptive to diverse perspectives and differences.

Note

1   Badiou A. (1999). La scène du deux. De l'amour. Flammarion.

Part I

Theoretical and technical changes within psychanalysis

Gender and sexualities

Introduction

Ângela Vila-Real

The difficulties

This is very difficult as it is compounded by resistances of various orders, as Glocer Fiorini points out in her chapter, "The Oedipus complex: an expanded approach to sexual and gender polyphonies". The approach to sexuality has been a source of scandal from the outset. It continues to be so, not only about child sexuality, but also new sexualities. Added to this is the issue of new identities or subjectivities, which for a long time triggered feelings of strangeness and rejection in some psychoanalysts. Is it the analyst's ideological issues, theoretical issues or even personal issues that are responsible? Glocer Fiorini refers to the fact that the psychoanalytic theoretical body is not broad enough to include an understanding of new subjectivities. In addition to highlighting a wide range of social changes that make new realities evident, she raises many pertinent questions for the psychoanalytic world. These range from the construction of the Oedipus-castration theory to family organisations, identifications, notions of feminine and masculine, and even the new ideals that guide our lives and our psychic organisations. We therefore need to make a vast number of theoretical reformulations.

Reformulation of fundamentals

I highlight two conceptual reformulations from which everything else must necessarily be rethought: the notion of the subject and the notion of development. Glocer Fiorini places the notion of the subject at the forefront. The subject, as it begins to be represented today, is not constituted as a unitary organisation, but as a "weaving of psychic multiplicities". The idea of totalisation and completeness, more compatible with binary organisation, gives way to the idea of existence characterised by the tension between heterogeneous variables, resulting in a subjectivity put into perspective by theories of hypercomplexity (Morin, 1990). This is also evident in clinical work, which makes previous theories insufficient. Glocer Fiorini proposes thinking about the production of sexualised subjectivity from at least three variables: sexuality/desire, the body and gender. These variables, being heterogeneous, configure a subjectivity even though their interrelationships can never be harmonious. The idea of synthesis is absent as variables

DOI: 10.4324/9781003531333-3

in contradiction must remain in tension. The new subject is characterised, not by stability, but by the possibility of change and by a fragile stability.

The other issue concerning development is the evidence of contexts in which children and young people are exposed to multiplicities and variabilities in terms of time, rhythms of life, structure, dynamics, and family configuration. Their variations make standardisations difficult, make us rethink the theoretical status of the Oedipus-castration complex and invalidate linear causality. This type of causality excludes the multiplicity that we observe in life and in our clinical work.

The work with children and adolescents has evidenced what came to be called gender dysphoria, but today, based on clinical findings, we look at it differently. An increasing number of children and adolescents presenting with atypical gender identities has disturbed our perception of what a child is. Although the notion of gender is established early on, the refusal of some children to accept the gender assigned to them seems incompatible with our ideas of childhood immaturity and dependence. Added to this are the questions raised by the pubertal body with its changes in configuration, the appearance of secondary sexual characteristics, the intensification of impulses, menarche, etc., which make it more present and impossible to ignore by the child or young person and others. Trans adolescents tell us that the crucial period for awareness of gender is the pubertal process. However, they are diverse and there are more and more who do not place an absolute need for body alteration by surgical means. In fact, as di Ceglie points out in his chapter, "Shapes of Gender Identity: Three stories with an impact", the majority of children and adolescents who identify with an atypical gender do not maintain this identity reference in late adolescence. The administration of puberty blockers, as we know, has raised ethical concerns among clinicians who feared irreversible consequences in the adolescent development process. However, we still do not clearly understand the relationship between body change and the psychic process of adolescence. We do not know how or to what extent the pubertal outburst triggers something more than the triggering of autonomy and individuation in relation to family objects. Do puberty blockers also block the preadolescent process? Or does the administration of blockers only block puberty while maintaining the evolution of adolescence regardless of the body?

In addition, we are increasingly seeing patients who are non-binary and, therefore, do not intend to undergo surgical body changes. They demand from us a different reflective investment as they exclude themselves from the binary reference. The examples given by di Ceglie are witness to the diversity of these individuals and show the need for restraint on the part of the clinicians involved.

Polymorphous sexuality

The realm of psychoanalytic theory and research has shifted its focus from the centrality of the Oedipus complex and castration as the cornerstone of identity formation, object choice, and social relations based on symbolic sexual value, towards a new emphasis on polymorphous sexuality and Freud's formulations in his Three Essays (1905). The Oedipal reference, representing a family configuration, a relational matrix, and a cultural inscription, is generally seen as leading only to a dualistic outcome. However, the very starting point for this complex organisation is, from birth, the binary sexual division, as is now widely recognised.

Liz Allison, in her chapter, "Psychosexuality and the problem of (mis)representation: a mentalizing perspective", while highlighting the crucial role of maternal mirroring in enabling children to regulate their emotions and states of excitement, also draws attention to the pervasive lack of recognition and mirroring of infantile sexuality. This oversight hinders children's ability to acknowledge and process sexual arousal as an internal reality, consequently impeding the development of a sense of otherness. Allison acknowledges the resistance to Freud's theory and to the concept of infantile sexuality, as evidenced by his observation that "emotional factors make people confused and forgetful" (Freud, 1920, 34). This resistance stems from deeply ingrained beliefs that sexuality only awakens during puberty, that there is an inherent attraction between the sexes, and that the ultimate goal of sexuality is sexual union. Freud categorised these beliefs as "ready-made ideas" that continue to shape our understanding of sexuality, even if we are not fully conscious of them. Furthermore, Allison goes beyond disconnecting impulse from object and questions the very unity of the sexual drive, which is portrayed as fragile and prone to fragmentation into components that are often labelled "perverse" but which Freud asserted exist in all human beings. This blurring of distinctions blurs the boundaries between self and other, disrupting both otherness and the sense of self. This is a question that has been raised in relation to homosexuality, which should be completely distinct from heterosexuality, had the idea of psychic bisexuality not emerged in psychoanalysis.

Psychic bisexuality

Psychic bisexuality is currently a pivotal concept in understanding internal dynamics and relationships with others. The notion originates from Freud's (1901) clinical observations, leading him to formulate the idea of psychic bisexuality as a universal and innate condition linked to biology. However, it has evolved towards a relational justification based on identification with both parents, thus referring to the primal scene and the Oedipal configuration. The shift in focus to the primitive states of the mind with authors like Winnicott (1966), Tustin (1981), or Kristeva (1982) leads to another understanding related to an earlier period and a more primitive relationship where the mother-infant interaction and differentiation are placed in the foreground. It is in this context that Anat Schumann develops her conception of psychic bisexuality in her chapter, "Encountering otherness: On the ability (and inability) for psychic movement within sexual states of mind". Her description of psychic bisexuality as a creative movement between masculine and feminine in both men and women has many diverse implications. Masculine and feminine are not taken at their descriptive objectal or configurational value, but as psychic elements. These are conceived as distinct and separate, not linked to the body, and yet they are contained and allow for a fluid movement between them. There is, therefore, a distinction and a relationship between the two that would manifest itself through the representations male/female, me/not-me, self/other, container/contained. Here is based on the ability to maintain and contain the confrontation with otherness inside and outside the self. This implies the existence of a conception of internal functioning in which there are differentiated and even contrasting elements that relate to each other in a fluid way, allowing for the relationship with the other. They are therefore conjugated in the process of abjection that takes place when the first confrontation with reality and differentiation in relation to the object occurs, the first of which is the maternal one.

Thus, acceptance of the other would depend on the harmony of the abjection process in relation to the primary object. This delicate process can lead to the introjection of the primary object as strange, but on the contrary to its integration into the psyche as a feminine part.

Abjection and the therapeutic relationship

All authors, in one way or another, contemplate theoretical and clinical difficulties in their chapters. This is a common concern when we delve into the issues of gender diversity and sexualities. Freud (1905) was already aware of how sexuality is always disruptive. Allison addresses the fact that sexuality is difficult even for analysts in whose training it is poorly reflected, especially since object relations theory has tended to eliminate sexuality from psychoanalytic discourse.

Glocer Fiorini has written of the resistance that arises when, in the face of these issues, it becomes necessary to question our body of theories as if they constituted a threat to the psychoanalytic edifice. There is also resistance resulting from the ideology or blind spots of psychoanalysts who, in their clinical work, does not see or reject components of themselves. Sometimes, it happens that the difficulty of accepting the stranger provokes in the therapist a regression to a functioning marked by the split attitude of "us versus them" that makes progress impossible. Di Ceglie, like Allison, emphasises the need for an attitude of neutrality towards patients, especially pubescents, who may change over the course of development and should have the freedom to do so. Accompanying these young people with the necessary neutrality was one of his conclusions from his experience with adolescents and families. But the attitude of neutrality is not easy, especially when patients call on our psychic bisexuality or the difficulty of thinking and containing homosexual sexuality or even forms of sexuality that we feel as very disruptive.

Anat Schumann's theorisation of psychic bisexuality and the process of establishing otherness is of great help in understanding these difficulties. The question that arises, in general, is always to know the limits of analysts in their relationship with their patients, but for an analyst, due to the way in which psychic bisexuality has been established in him or her, it may become particularly difficult to accept the patient's difference regarding sexuality and even more so regarding gender.

These issues, and our activity in general, make it necessary to constantly investigate both external reality and our own inner selves.

1 The Oedipus complex

An expanded approach on sexual and gender polyphonies

Leticia Glocer Fiorini

In recent decades, sexual and gender diversities have become increasingly visible. They depart from standing norms of the social contract, and although they have always existed, they are acquiring growing acknowledgement and legality. These presentations represent movements of resistance that challenge established norms and, in fact, coexist with cultural and social tendencies rejecting them. Both tendencies cohabit in current societies, resulting in fruitful debates but also in violent confrontations.

It is important to promote discussions on these issues, which generate conflicting positions among psychoanalysts. We recognise the difficulties involved in establishing an open debate in which each one can listen to the other's words, recalling Bakhtin's concept of the 'dialogic'. As this author (Bakhtin, 1984) posited, based on his studies of Dostoyevski´s *oeuvre*, there is a polyphony of voices inhabiting subjectivity, and I take this concept to apply it to psychoanalysis. This notion encompasses both patients and analysts and certainly directs us to rethink theory. Ignoring it leads to crucial resistance regarding the analytic process.

It is well known that multiple voices, desires, identifications and fantasies exist in each subject and psychoanalysis puts them on display. This multiplicity, which was recognised since Antiquity, can be verified through myths, literature and philosophy, among other disciplines that have studied them. They also imply questioning differences in classical binarism.

There is an almost infinite series of mixtures, transformations and identifications between the masculine and the feminine (Zolla, 1981) that run through the history of culture. We will mention the double beings described by Plato in the ancient world before the Greeks, among which there were three types: Man/woman (the classic androgynous), man/man and woman/woman. These beings were separated as punishment by Zeus and so they were always looking for their other half. The most valued double beings were man/man, which can be interpreted as an attempt to include homosexuality, of strong social and cultural importance in Ancient Greece, especially among men. We also highlight the Greek myths of Hermaphroditus, of Cenis and Ceneus, of Tiresias, as well

DOI: 10.4324/9781003531333-4

as some versions of Narcissus being alternately male or female, among others (Méantis, 1964).

In Hindu metaphysics, the polarity of being, represented by Siva and Sakti, becomes pure unity on a higher level and merges into the androgynous Ardhanarisvara. Among shamans, the phenomena of trance and transformation into the other sex were common. The lamas identified themselves with their goddesses in a hallucinatory way. Similar experiences are described in Tantrism, Taoism and Buddhism. In addition, it is of interest to note the frequent presence of mixed figures such as Christ in a breastfeeding attitude or female Christ, as described in the iconographies of the Middle Ages. Zolla also points out that in mystical love songs around the world, the poet loses his sense and groans like a woman. This tradition ranges from Siberian shamans to Chinese Taoist poets through Iran, Arabia, Provence, to the Florentine poets of the Dolce Stilnovo, who called themselves women.

The two aforementioned tendencies coexist in the present: The strict separation of the sexes accentuated in Modernity and the sexual variants that Postmodernity (also considered as Late Modernity) brings with it. The first tendency is part of the consensus of meanings of an era that sustains a set of practices and social relations, which are nowadays confronted by the second tendency. These sexual and gender variants, even when they tend to erase the strict male–female polarity, have not substantially modified the permanence of the ancestral equating of the feminine with the enigmatic other, despite important changes in the female condition in important social strata of the West. Again, both conditions coexist in today's societies and they represent the struggle between the androcentric preeminence and the resistance against it.

In the field of literature and essays, we also find rigorous descriptions of devalued women's position in Western societies. De Beauvoir (1987), in *The Second Sex*, describes the equation between otherness and women. Virginia Woolf, through her writings, sheds light on the frequent location of women as objects of study in a masculine world. In *A Room of One's Own* (Woolf, 1993a), she refers acutely to the cultural and social inequalities of women, and in *Orlando* (Woolf, 1993b), to gender and sexual transformations.

In short, both from the field of sexual and gender diversity and from the prevailing conceptions of women and the feminine, the concept of sexual difference is questioned. As I said elsewhere (Glocer Fiorini, 1998, 2017), this subject includes two perspectives. One refers to the aim of non-discrimination. This issue includes groups affected by discrimination: Sexual and gender migrations, women, as well as ethnic, religious and racial groups, among others. However, I stress that non-discrimination is not enough for psychoanalysis, although indispensable. It is the first step.

The second step, which is crucial for psychoanalysts, is the need to rethink certain established psychoanalytic concepts, which may be an obstacle to clinical approach. This is a major challenge. We should add that each psychoanalyst's available ideology, personal beliefs, and explicit and private theories regarding sexual and gender diversity converge on this point. Their thoughts with respect to the masculine–feminine dualism and its impact on countertransference determine fundamental differences in clinical work. If they are not reviewed, the negative influence on the analytic process may become eternal and unchangeable. We recall many cases of homosexuality forced to be renounced because the psychoanalyst's clinical approach considered that they failed to fit into the norm.

This chapter aims to contextualise and historicise our psychoanalytic approach, taking into account its key axis: The unconscious, infantile sexuality, the drive, the field of desire, and transference, although different theoretical currents give these categories diverse interpretations. Rethinking certain theoretical categories does not tear down the psychoanalytical edifice, which is already well established. Nevertheless, other points may be rethought or expanded without biases to expand listening. If not, our clinical practice may fail, since these subjectivities will inevitably be considered 'abject' and excluded from social ties.

In this context, we should stress Freud's contributions to the exploration of the polyphony of voices, already mentioned. His work shows us the plurality of paths of desire, the multiple fantasies and identifications that inhabit subjectivity, as well as the contingency of the object choice. This polyphony is based on one of his crucial papers: 'Three Essays on the Theory on Sexuality' (Freud, 1905), where he describes the multiplicity and anarchy of the drive agency.

We will approach the polyphonies of sexuality and gender focussing on the intersections of clinical, theoretic and meta-psychological perspectives understanding that none of these approaches can be analysed separately. Only a view that grasps the crossings among these perspectives can go beyond the 'paradigm of simplicity', as Morin (1990) proposed. Even more, confrontations among different epistemologies are also at stake.

My points of departure were the following:

a *desire* always exceeds accepted norms,
b assigned *gender* is a complex category that may be part of identity but may also be experienced as something foreign to the ego or may contradict biological sex,
c *bodies* alone define neither sexual identity nor object choice,
d the *object of desire* is contingent, which does not mean that it is arbitrary, and
e *ideals* of masculinity and femininity vary historically.

This panorama opens at least three paths: One is the way of thinking on these polyphonies: Binary and non-binary logics are in play and complexity (Morin, 1990) to approach this challenge. The other is the relation of the drive and unconscious desires with gender mandates. The third one illuminates the mechanisms by which culture and current discourses about sexual and gender migrations permeate subjectivity.

Following these thoughts, I will focus on the Freudian Oedipus complex, its contributions, but also its limits. There are several angles to focus on that encompass non-normative subjectivities, women's condition and, last but not least, subjectivity in general.

The Freudian Oedipus complex: Apertures and dead ends

The Oedipus complex was thought of by Freud as a necessary tool to clarify how the anarchic field of the drive is organised and how both sex and gender are constructed. Freudian discourse regarding the Oedipus complex proposes to explain the process by which a boy or a girl is inserted into a symbolic context of social bonds (Freud, 1923, 1924). Freud uses the Oedipus myth to explain this insertion into culture by envisioning an exogamic resolution that includes heterosexual object choice, prohibition of incest and the formation of the superego.

Freud draws upon the myth to explain through what mechanisms the field of the drive, chaotic and anarchic, is organised within the context of social bonds. Inevitably, the patriarchal organisation of society puts a wedge: The issue of reproduction of the human species equated with the sexual division of labour leads to the inequality between the masculine and the feminine position and does its job. In this framework, it is worth including the subtle performative mechanisms that determine how 'difference' is psychically registered. In this line of thought, when he develops his proposal, he is taking the boy as a model. In the boy's phallic phase, the vision of female genitals joins the threat of castration. In other words, the threat of castration acquires value when the perception of female genitals is interpreted as a lack. Therefore, *difference is interpreted as castration in the frame of punishment for his incestuous wishes.*

The issue is that this infantile sexual theory, created by Freud (1909) based on his interpretation of the boy's experience – the little Hans case – is thereafter established as an adult theory, and moreover, as the psychoanalytic theory on sexual difference (Laplanche, 1980). In this way, the interpretive and imaginary character of infantile sexual theories is lost. Although Freud himself posited that this theory was false, the risk is that if we fail to consider this imaginary character, it proceeds to function as if it were a proven truth.

Furthermore, is the Oedipus complex enough explanation to understand sexualities and gender that go out of the norms? We have two lines of thought concerning this question. One is to reconsider that the complete Oedipus complex described by Freud is much more adequate to understand both the feminine and sexual/gender diversity than the positive Oedipus complex. The other is to rethink and/or expand the notions that are implied in the Oedipus complex. Following this second line of thought, we can include another point of view to analyse other itineraries of desire and gender as well as changes in the feminine position. I recall Deleuze's proposal (1972) on this topic thinking about an expanded Oedipus complex, beyond the nuclear family (mother/father/son). His perspective describes a porous, trans-familial Oedipus. In my view, both options can be used whenever necessary, though not schematically, for a clinical approach.

This approach involves several concepts to be explored:

- The masculine/feminine dichotomy. In this context, I argue the standing ideals regarding the masculine-feminine pair. Indeed, these ideals respond to social discourse and practices deeply rooted in culture and language, strongly impacting on each subjectivity by means of the ego ideal. We should remember that they embody androcentric conceptions of social and family relations. In other words, thinking simply in terms of a masculine-feminine polarity falls short regarding sexual and gender migrations in clinical work, and leads to impasses impossible to overcome.
- The complex relation between desire and gender, which includes concordances and discordances. Another point to be considered: Do analysts utilise contributions from gender and post-gender theories? In general, American psychoanalysis differs from French psychoanalysis and their zones of influence share their positions. This debate focuses on whether gender is a category that should be used in psychoanalysis or not. In brief terms, I consider that gender perspective should be utilised in psychoanalysis, always intersecting with the domain of sexuality and desire. Furthermore, taking into account that the vast majority of newborns are assigned to one or another gender (or in rare cases to none), we must recognise *social gender and subjective gender. The last one is based on identifications. In this frame, gender mandates influence the paths of desire but, at the same time, desire always goes beyond gender mandates. This conflict is part of the construction of subjectivity.*
- The implicit and explicit notions of desire that emerge from the Oedipus complex. For the little girl, the notion of desire is based on a substitution of penis envy by the desire for a child. For the boy, there is no specific explanation, but in general, it is considered as emerging from lack. In other publications, I included another notion of desire as a poietic, originally productive desire, which certainly includes lack, void and deserts, as Deleuze, interviewed by Parnet, posited (Deleuze & Parnet, 1987).
- A review of the 'paternal' function: Its connotations and insufficiencies. In this context, it is worth to include how we conceptualise the notion of family, mainly the maternal and paternal functions usually assigned to mothers and fathers, according to their gender and biological sex. This is a crucial issue that concerns the construction of subjectivity in children raised by non-conventional families outside accepted normative canons. If homosexuality is considered a perversion, would the children raised by homosexual couples be considered perverse? My approach is to think

in terms of functions (caregiving and symbolic functions) which may not coincide with traditional mothers and fathers and may be independent of gender or sexual characteristics of their bodies. In this frame, I proposed to think in terms of third-party symbolic functions, which may be performed by the mother, father or other significant subjects, in order to avoid the androcentric connotations of naming it 'paternal'. This means that all of them can perform this symbolic function because they are performing a third-party function based on their own symbolic possibilities (Glocer Fiorini, 2013, 2017).

This proposal does not ignore the importance of real parents, but it is a question of contemplating the symbolic construction of subjectivity as broadly as possible without it depending strictly on each person's sexual choice or gender. Thinking only about acceptance of a masculine or feminine identity or a heterosexual position is insufficient.

It is in this context that I include the discussion about whether the Oedipus castration complex and its ideal resolution are enough to analyse 'non/conventional' subjectivities. Of course, we work with the Oedipus complex as a clinical fact but, in my view, it is not a universal category since it contemplates only a normative, dualistic outcome for the construction of subjectivity. *It is a narrative that describes accurately the paths of desire and gender mandates in androcentric cultures.* This limitation may become an obstacle since it is insufficient for analysis of the multiple paths of desire and gender that we encounter in our times, plus new types of family organisation. And, as it was pointed out above, we should also focus on the Oedipus' limits to understand 'conventional' binary subjectivities.

All the points mentioned above are interlinked: We cannot think about one of them without including the others. They also involve the feminine position very strongly. Following this line, I consider that 'horror of femininity' is also related to the rejection of other forms of sexuality that de-center the masculine/phallic traditional model.

In this framework, I proposed (Glocer Fiorini, 2017) to make a distinction between the category of 'difference' as a symbolic agent and sexual/gender differences.

Focusing on the construction of subjectivity through the paradigm of hyper-complexity

As I proposed in previous publications (1998, 2017, 2024), dualistic thinking is insufficient to think about the complexity of the psyche. Binary thought cannot be eliminated – it is part of language – but it should be included within more broadly encompassing complexities such as thinking in a triadic way or, yet, with more variables in play. For this reason, I propose to think about the production of sexed subjectivity, including at least three variables: *Sexuality/desire, body, and gender,* pierced through by current discourse and crossed by unconscious determinations. They are heterogeneous variables whose interrelations are never harmonious, defining a singular subjectivity for everyone. The fourth is *otherness*.

Currently, we may use theories of hyper-complexity to think about this issue. For instance, we find a necessary tool in Morin's contributions (1990) that allows an approach based on the coexistence in tension of heterogeneous variables. Furthermore, they are not necessarily resolved into any surmounting dialectic synthesis. This way of thinking goes well in order to comprehend the construction of subjectivity. In addition, this approach implies working at intersections. Theoretical centers are extremely difficult to move, except at their borders. In philosophy, Trías (1991) said: 'being' is constituted at the *limes,* which means limit or border. This limit or frontier is the place where the new, the event, may be worked on; in Badiou's terms, whatever does not fit into our previous schemas (Badiou,1999).

Distinguishing 'difference' from sexual difference

Finally, these questions include the way of thinking about the category of sexual difference since its access and recognition are usually considered indispensable for the symbolic construction of subjectivity. This is a crucial point for revision if we are considering sexual and gender diversity.

In this context, my proposal (Glocer Fiorini, 2017, 2024) is that access to a symbolic world depends on the way each subject assumes a network of differences: Anatomical difference (always signified by culture and language), gender difference, psychosexual difference, linguistic and discursive differences. This multiplicity of differences, pierced through by inter and trans-subjective variables, determines how subjectivity is constructed, beyond sexual orientation. Symbolic difference refers to recognition of otherness as a fundamental element in the understanding of the construction of subjectivity.

In addition, difference as distinction (Heidegger, 1969) exceeds the network of differences we have just mentioned although all these notions are related. On the contrary, the category of difference is a symbolic agent that exceeds that network. This perspective greatly expands the concept of 'difference' and, if psychoanalysts choose only one variable as a master key, the analytic itinerary may be highly restricted.

To end, I highlight that the riddle of sexual difference is 'difference' itself, an 'empty slot', which is filled in with narratives that are often constructed and projected onto the feminine. This concerns the interpretation of sexual and gender diversity as well as the feminine and masculine positions and changes the way to think about them.

These thoughts lead us to the concept of subject with which we work. I consider the concept of subject a fabric of psychic multiplicities, unlike conceptions that propose a unitary, totalising, and harmonious notion of the subject. In this sense, I adopt Castoriadis's proposal (1984) of psychic *magma,* pointing out that this concept is not an indiscriminate, eclectic, or chaotic condition but enlightens the multiplicity of psychic inscriptions and their movements. As Guattari (1995) said: heterogeneous universes inhabit subjectivity.

References

Badiou, A. (1999). *El ser y el acontecimiento*. Buenos Aires: Manantial.
Bakhtin, M. (1984). *Problems of Dostoyevski's Poetics*. Edited and translated by Caryl Emerson. Minneapolis: University of Minnesota Press. [(1993) *Problemas de la poética de Dostoievski*. Buenos Aires: Fondo de Cultura Económica].
Castoriadis, C. (1984). *Psychoanalysis: Project and Elucidation*. In *Crossroads in the Labyrinth*, Translated by K. Soper and M. H. Ryle, 133. Cambridge: MIT Press. [(1992). *El psicoanálisis, proyecto y elucidación*. Buenos Aires: Nueva Visión].
De Beauvoir, S. (1987). *El segundo sexo*. Buenos Aires: Siglo Veinte.
Deleuze, G., and C. Parnet. (1987). *Dialogues*. Translated by H. Tomlinson and B. Habberjam. London: Athlone. [(1980). *Diálogos*. Valencia: Pre-Textos].
Deleuze, G.-Guattari, F. (1972). *El AntiEdipo*. Barcelona: Barral Ed. 1973.
Freud, S. (1905). *Three Essays on the Theory of Sexuality*. London, *S.E.*, 7: 125–245.
Freud, S. (1909). *Análisis de la fobia de un niño de cinco años*. Buenos Aires: Amorrortu.
Freud, S. (1923). *The Ego and the Id*. London, *S.E.* 19: 3–66.
Freud, S. (1924). *The Dissolution of the Oedipus Complex*. London, *S.E.*, 19: 171–179.
Glocer Fiorini, L. (1998). The Feminine in Psychoanalysis: A Complex Construction. *Journal of Clinical Psychoanalysis* 7: 421–439. [(1994). La posición femenina: una construcción heterogénea. *Revista de Psicoanálisis*, 51(3):587–603.]
Glocer Fiorini, L. (2013). Deconstruyendo el concepto de función paterna. Un paradigma interpelado. *Revista de Psicoanálisis*, LXX (4):671–681.
Glocer Fiorini, L. (2017). *Sexual Difference in Debate. Bodies, Desires and Fictions*. London: Karnac. [(2015) *La diferencia sexual en debate. Cuerpos, deseos y ficciones*. Buenos Aires: Lugar Editorial].
Glocer Fiorini, L. (2024). *Deconstructing the Feminine: Subjectivities in Transition*. London: Routledge, 1st edition 2007. [(2001) *Lo femenino y el pensamiento complejo*. Buenos Aires: Lugar Editorial, 2a Edicion, 2020].
Guattari, F. (1995). *Chaosmosis: An Ethico-aesthetic Paradigm*. Bloomington, IN: Indiana University Press. [(1996). *Caosmosis*. Buenos Aires: Manantial].
Heidegger, M. (1969). *Identity and Difference*. New York: Harper and Row. [(1988). *Identidad y diferencia*. Barcelona: Anthropos].
Laplanche, J. (1980). *Problématiques II: Castration-symbolisations*. Paris: PUF.
Méantis, G. (1964). *Mitología griega*. Buenos Aires: Hachette.
Morin, E. (1990). *Introducción al pensamiento complejo*. Barcelona: Gedisa, 1995.
Trías, E. (1991). *Lógica del límite*. Barcelona: Destino, 1991
Woolf, V. (1993a). *Un cuarto propio y otros ensayos*. Buenos Aires: A.Z. editora.
Woolf, V. (1993b). *Orlando*. Buenos Aires: Sudamericana.
Zolla, E. (1981). *Androginia*. Madrid: Debate.

2 Psychosexuality and the problem of (mis)representation

A mentalising perspective

Liz Allison

Freud described psychoanalysis as a method of investigation, but historically, when psychoanalysts have tried to investigate and discuss sexuality, there has been a widespread tendency for description to shade into prescription, especially when the phenomena being considered challenge social norms. Drawing on the theory of mentalising and its account of the social construction of our sense of ourselves, I will explore the challenges of talking about sexuality to ourselves, to our colleagues and to our patients, and reflect on how we can navigate between the Scylla of inappropriate, dogmatic and alienating certainty and the Charybdis of anxious and anxiety-provoking silence.

In his 1920 preface to the fourth edition of the *Three Essays* (1905, 134), Freud pondered the strength of the resistance to the picture of human psychosexuality that he had drawn in this book, which seemed to him to arouse the most indignant reactions of any of his works. He reflected that "emotional factors make people confused and forgetful." This observation often comes to my mind when I think about the dismaying ways in which psychoanalysis has engaged with homosexuality over the years, which only in very recent times have led to public apologies from organisations such as the American Psychoanalytic Association and the British Psychoanalytic Council. I want to make room for us to consider the possibility that the astonishingly persistent certainty that homosexuality is a problem, a pathology, a disorder, etc., can be thought of as a response to unacknowledged confusion and uncertainty about an area of our personal experience which for developmental reasons remains extremely difficult to think about.

Freud's rhetorical strategy in the *Three Essays* is to unsettle the reader. Freud's ambition was not to arouse conviction but to stimulate thought and to upset prejudices, and he certainly achieves the latter aim in the *Three Essays*. What I would like to add to this is that the overall trend of the subsequent history of psychoanalytic thinking about sexuality serves to remind us that the upsetting of prejudices, while potentially salutary, also has the potential to lead to backlash when a violent emotional reaction

DOI: 10.4324/9781003531333-5

derails the capacity to think. Freud (135) opens the first essay with the popular assumption that the sexual drive:

> is generally understood to be absent in childhood, to set in at the time of puberty in connection with the process of coming to maturity and to be revealed in the manifestations of an irresistible attraction exercised by one sex upon the other; while its aim is presumed to be sexual union, or at all events actions leading in that direction.
>
> (Freud, 1905, 135)

He then proceeds methodically to demonstrate that, in fact, all these assumptions are untenable. In the first essay, his comprehensive review of activities commonly labelled perverse (including various forms of homosexuality, whose diversity he is careful to emphasise) leads him to the conclusion that:

> No healthy person, it appears, can fail to make some addition that might be called perverse to the normal sexual aim; and the universality of this finding is in itself enough to show how inappropriate it is to use the word perversion as a term of reproach.
>
> (Freud, 1905, 160)

Although Freud is clearly still writing within a heteronormative frame of reference, he pushes this frame to breaking point. His most challenging observations often appear not within the frame but, as it were, in the margins, in the footnotes of the text. For example, despite the implication of the passage just quoted that the normal sexual aim is heterosexual, in the footnotes, he puts this norm in question: "the exclusive sexual interest felt by men for women is also a problem that needs elucidating and is not a self-evident fact based upon an attraction that is ultimately of a chemical nature" (146). According to Freud there is no essential connection between instinct and object; they are merely soldered together. Furthermore, "the" sexual instinct turns out to have, at best, a provisional and precarious unity. Freud concludes the first essay with a speculation that "perhaps the sexual instinct itself may be no simple thing, but put together from components which have come apart again in the perversions" (162). The second essay develops this theme, showing that manifestations of the sexual instinct that are commonly labelled perversions in adults are found prior to the establishment of so-called normal sexuality in all of us. This includes homosexual object choice: "all human beings are capable of making a homosexual object choice and have, in fact, made one in their unconscious" (145). Freud also suggests that "without taking bisexuality into account I think it would scarcely be possible to arrive at an understanding of the sexual manifestations that are actually to be observed in men and women" (220).

Sadly, the psychoanalytic literature is replete with confused and forgetful reactions to the emotional stimulus of Freud's perspective on homosexuality (and on psychosexuality considered more broadly) as set out in the *Three Essays*, which in keeping with the spirit of many of his other early works demonstrate how phenomena that have tended to be pathologised and located in denigrated others can be shown to exist in so-called "normal" individuals. We've already heard from Bergler; another infamous example is Charles Socarides, who was still being invited to lecture on homosexuality in the UK as late as the mid-1990s (Newbigin, 2013). Socarides' (1968) book *The Overt Homosexual* shows that he had read Freud quite closely, and yet he persists in identifying homosexuality as a "serious illness," an emotional disorder which caused symptoms and suffering that he believed psychoanalysis could and should seek to cure, although he was also disturbed by the fact that gay people often seemed surprisingly untroubled by the pain and suffering that one would expect a "serious illness" to cause:

> Of all the symptoms of emotional origin which serve simultaneously as defenses, homosexuality is unique in its capacity to produce for limited intervals a utilization of profound psychic conflicts and struggles for the purpose of attaining a pseudo-adequate equilibrium and pleasure reward (orgasm), permitting an individual to function however marginally and erratically.
>
> (Socarides, 1968, 4)

If we take the pejoratives out of this statement, we can see that Socarides is grudgingly acknowledging that gay people could achieve psychic equilibrium, experience pleasure, and function well, despite his pathologisation of homosexuality. Confused thinking indeed. To give one further illustration, the following is a passage where Socarides is practically quoting from the *Three Essays* at the beginning and yet has managed to renaturalise heterosexuality by the end by means of a teleological argument:

> Homosexuality, the choice of an object of the same sex for orgastic satisfaction, is not innate. There is no connection between sexual instinct and the choice of sexual object. Such an object choice is learned, acquired behavior; there is no inevitable genetic or hormonal inborn propensity toward the choice of a partner of either the same or opposite sex. However, the *male-female design* is taught and exemplified to the child from birth and culturally ingrained through the marital order. This design is anatomically determined as it derives from cells which in the evolutionary scale underwent changes into organ systems and finally into individuals reciprocally adapted to each other. This is the evolutionary development of man. The male-female design is perpetually maintained, and only overwhelming fear can disturb or divert it.
>
> (Socarides, 1968, 5–6, italics in the original)

I don't think this passage tells us much about homosexuality, although it may tell us something about overwhelming fears experienced by its author when confronted with phenomena that disturb his sense of the proper order of things, so perhaps we can part company with Dr. Socarides at this point. Socarides is an extreme example, but his work does illustrate the temptation to drift into moralising that talking about sex produces. One reason for this may be the tendency to treat talking about sex as manifest content which needs to be interpreted in terms of object relationships of a supposedly deeper nature, as noted by Andre Green in some reflections on the diminishing amount of attention paid to sexuality by psychoanalysts. Green (1995, 873) wrote:

> …it frequently happens that when we listen to the material presented by some colleagues during meetings, the manifest presence of sexuality - either through dream material or unconscious fantasy, or even in the reports of the patient's life and relationships with others - is interpreted in a way which bypasses the sphere of sexuality to address object relationships of a supposedly deeper nature, in a way which intentionally refuses to pay attention to the specific sexual aspects that are very often supposed to be a mere defence.

The more that sexual feelings and behaviours are interpreted as manifestations of the vicissitudes of object relationships, the more they start to be conceptualised and judged as more or less ethical modes of relating to the other. However, I suggest that we need to resist the temptation to moralise and remind ourselves that psychoanalysis arguably begins as a genealogy of morals, in which sexuality plays a fundamental role. Considering human psychosexuality exclusively through the lens of object relations theory effaces the developmental histories of the constitution of the self, the object and the sexual drive itself. By seeking to describe the processes that allow what appears to be an identity to be constructed, Freud's work problematised both sexual and gender identities along with the nature of the sexual drive. Originally he conceived these processes mainly in intrapsychic terms, but in his later work he increasingly recognised the role played by interpersonal experience as he began to develop the ideas that would form the basis for object relations theory.

Many analysts since Freud have addressed the question of the role played by the other in the constitution of a sense of self or identity. Here, I would like to draw on the work of my colleagues at UCL, Peter Fonagy and Mary Hepworth, to think further about the role played by the caregiver in the constitution of the self and sexuality and the specific vulnerability that this early experience leaves us with, which may tempt us to retreat from confrontation with the enigma of our own sexuality to what might feel like the surer ground of evaluating the quality of our patients' object relations (Fonagy, 2008; Fonagy & Allison, 2015; Target, 2007). Building on the work of Bion, Winnicott and attachment theorists, who all in different ways consider the impact of significant others on the developing self, they have set out a theory of self-development which understands the capacity for self-representation and affects regulation to develop out of the matrix of early experience with the caregiver.

To summarise very briefly and schematically, in order to make sense of his early constitutional self-states, when he will frequently be overwhelmed by needs, wishes and feelings that he is unable to deal with by himself, the baby looks to the caregiver for assistance. In the terms of Freud's definition of drive, we could say that the demand made on the mind for work in consequence of its connection with the body has initially to be met by turning to the other. As well as meeting the baby's needs, the caregiver helps him to develop representations of his inner world through their marked mirroring (where their reflecting back of what they understand the baby to be feeling is modulated, for example, by a trace of irony, to help the baby understand that what the caregiver is conveying refers to his own state rather than theirs). In this way, if things go well, the infant gradually learns about his mind, understands that there is a distinction between his picture of the world and the reality it represents, and comes to appreciate the otherness of the other's mind (he knows that he cannot know what the other is thinking or feeling). This lays the foundations for the ability to understand both his own and others' behaviour in terms of their thoughts and feelings, that is, to mentalise, even when emotions are running high.

If the caregiver is unwilling or unable to perform this mirroring function for the infant, this can sow the seeds of later difficulties. In the case of neglect, where there is simply no response to the infant's emotional display, the infant doesn't have access to the tools he needs to develop a picture of his own mind and the minds of others. There is no representation on which he can build. If mirroring of the infant's affect takes place but is not marked, he is likely to experience his affects as dangerously contagious, so that the caregiver's response feeds the arousal state rather than having a soothing effect. If the caregiver's response is incongruent with the arousal state (for example, if distress is understood and reflected back as aggression) then the infant will internalise this misrepresentation to create what has been described as an "alien self". In all cases, if the infant is not helped to construct a self-representation or helped to manage his affects by developing the capacity to think about them, he will find it very difficult to constitute and sustain an experience of himself as a coherent agent who is separate from but related to a world of objects, and keeping the capacity to mentalise online will be very challenging, especially in interpersonally stressful situations. These early difficulties may be the seeds of problems such as borderline phenomena (identity diffusion, affect dysregulation) and dissociative states in later life.

Although much of their work links these kinds of early difficulties to specific forms of psychopathology, Fonagy and colleagues have also proposed that infantile sexuality is an area where the caregiver's mirroring function routinely and perhaps appropriately fails. While caregivers are often aware that sexual excitement can occur in their infants, a survey study found that by far the most common response to this was to ignore or look away from its manifestations. Freud was of course acutely aware of the discomfort aroused by his work drawing attention to infantile sexuality and the universality of the wish to look away. He prefaced the fourth edition of the Three Essays with the remark that "If mankind had been able to learn from a direct observation of children, these three essays could have remained unwritten" yet he maintained throughout his life that "Enough can be seen in the children if one knows how to look" (Freud, 1933). The trouble is that one does not know how to look.

This even seems to be the case for psychoanalytically trained observers. As Fonagy (2008) notes, the psychoanalytic infant observation studies that candidates in almost all British psychotherapy and psychoanalysis training programmes are required to produce are remarkably silent on the subject of sexuality. I am suggesting that this may be partly because our experience of our own sexuality remains profoundly enigmatic. Unlike almost all other forms of emotional arousal, Fonagy suggests that "sexual excitement is unmirrored and never achieves second-order representation" (Fonagy, 2008, 23). This means that in this particular area of experience, an experience of containment or even a sense of ownership of these feelings cannot be achieved. If the caregiver ignores the infant's arousal, this may result in intensification rather than containment of the feelings. If any kind of reflection of the infant's sexual excitement does occur, this is likely either to be rather obscure, clouded by discomfort, or to lack markedness, so that the caregiver seems excited herself. In either case, the caregiver's response will not be experienced by the infant as faithful to his own affects and experiences. The consequence of this is that although the infant takes the caregiver's responses as though they mirror his own experience and identifies them as his own, the mismatch means that they are simultaneously also experienced as not his own, as alien. Fonagy suggested that "Sexual arousal can never truly be experienced as owned' and that it will always be felt to be an externally imposed burden unless we can find someone to share it with."

In adolescence and adulthood, the incongruence of the experience of sexual excitement creates a pressure to find someone into whom it can be projected. The core of the accompanying fantasy is the other's experience of the encounter rather than one's own.

Dan, the adolescent presented in Fonagy's 2008 (24) paper on sexuality, reported his first experience of intercourse in the following way:

> One aspect of the experience had felt quite shocking to him. He found that as he had penetrated Beverly he was not thinking of himself but of her having him inside her. He said it was weird. As he found himself focusing on Beverly's excitement, he lost control of his own.

The fact that the object is sought in order to rid the self of feelings that cannot be digested or metabolised seems to suggest that the crossing of a boundary is fundamental to the experience of sexual pleasure. Over time the experience of the partner is gradually reinternalised through a process that consciously feels like getting to know one's partner but at another level involves arriving at a more integrated sense of oneself. This can be conceptualised as a continuation of the process of infantile affect mirroring. As the urgency of the need for externalisation is diminished, libido appears to reduce, at least with that partner, and in its place, a powerful attachment relationship rooted in the experience of having been accurately mirrored develops.

In the meantime, while the burden of psychosexuality drives the individual to find new objects, the relationships thus established initially are areas where prementalising modes of subjective experience hold sway as the boundary between self and other is felt to disappear. I am suggesting that this should not be conceptualised as an evasion of the reality of the otherness of the other or loss of the capacity to sustain awareness of this. Rather, it is part of a developmental process that is ongoing well into young adulthood and perhaps even beyond. While we might attain a provisional mastery of the capacity to mentalise by middle childhood, the biological upheavals of adolescence require us to consolidate this capacity in the face of new challenges: relationships with our changing bodies and with new objects. The fact that our early relationships with our caregivers leave us with this area of experience that remains profoundly enigmatic acts as a powerful force propelling us towards these new challenges. While it may at times appear that our first clumsy attempts at sexual relationships preclude genuine concern for the other, they are the matrix out of which – in optimal circumstances – concern develops. However, this is not to say that sexuality is something that could or should ultimately be mentalised away. The body does not cease to make demands on the mind for work, and in order to do this work we will always need to be involved with others as well as reflecting on that involvement.

For developmental reasons, then, our sexuality remains, for most of us, an area of uncertainties, mysteries, and doubts. In an 1817 letter often quoted by psychoanalysts, the poet John Keats noted the difficulty of remaining in such a state without giving in to "irritable reaching after fact and reason" (quoted in Bion, 1970, 327). The claims of so many post-Freudian psychoanalytic writers about sexuality to certainty about what is normal, natural and healthy – a certainty that I don't think Freud himself entirely shared and in places definitely undermined – can perhaps be read as examples of such irritability in the face of a troubling enigma. The enigma of sexuality becomes less bothersome if it can be represented as a problem for certain denigrated others with whom the observing subject has nothing in common. Bion (1970, (327–8) suggested that Keats' formulation could be used to help the analyst guard against a common (though commonly unobserved) fault in the analyst's work: "The fault lies in the failure to observe and is intensified by the inability to appreciate the significance of observation." According to Bion, what gets in the way of observation is memory, desire and understanding. Rushing to make sense of what we observe in others in relation to our own experience, to what we think ought to happen, or to frameworks of understanding that we are already in possession of, can lead to misrepresentations that might sometimes be comical but can also be tragic and dangerous. Following a conversation he once had with Andre Green, Bion was fond of quoting Maurice Blanchot's aphorism, "La reponse est la malheur de la question." In a 1976 paper, *Emotional Turbulence*, he illustrates the question's misfortune by describing a joke illustrated in Punch magazine: "A small boy draws an adult's attention to a lark singing in the sky. He states, 'Hi, mister, there's a sparrer up there an' 'e can't get up an' 'e can't get down an' 'e ain't 'arf 'ollerin'."

Bion describes this as an example of a comically simple answer to a question. It should be noted that it is also an example of pathologising an experience that has been misunderstood. He goes on:

> If it is true that the human being, like nature, abhors a vacuum, cannot tolerate empty space, then he will try to fill it by finding something to go into that space presented by his ignorance. The intolerance of frustration, the dislike of being ignorant, the dislike of having a space which is not filled, can stimulate a precocious and premature desire to fill the space. One should therefore always consider that our theories, including the whole of psychoanalysis, psychiatry, medicine, are a kind of space-filling elaboration not in essence dissimilar to the belief that the lark in the sky is "a sparrer that can't get up and can't get down and ain't arf ollerin". In other words, the practicing analyst has to decide whether he is promulgating a theory or a space-filler indistinguishable from a paramnesia.

The small boy's misrepresentation of the skylark is amusing, but Bion considers that the promulgation of such space-fillers is a very serious matter:

> I would, without alarm, draw attention to a situation which is now one of urgency. It is a question of whether the paramnesias, the answers that are immediately comprehensible, that can be used to fill up the space of our ignorance, mislead us into extreme danger, whether the powers of the human mind match its destructiveness. So far the human being has survived and preserved a capacity for growth.

Returning to Freud, we can perhaps illustrate this tendency in the analyst towards precocious and premature desire to fill the empty space of ignorance by considering his case history of "Dora", whose precipitate departure from analysis he was honest enough to recognise had to do with failures on his part as well as resistance on hers. Many illustrations of a heteronormativity which is disturbing at times can be drawn from this case; for example, Freud's claim that when Herr K invited Dora, aged 14, to his office, he arranged for her to find him there alone, and then kissed her forcefully without her consent:

> This was surely just the situation to call up a distinct feeling of sexual excitement in a girl of fourteen who had never before been approached. But Dora had at that moment a violent feeling of disgust […] I should without question consider a person hysterical in whom an occasion for sexual excitement elicited feelings that were preponderantly or exclusively unpleasurable […] instead of the genital sensation which would certainly have been felt by a healthy girl in such circumstances.

As we know, this is the case that forced Freud to recognise the power of transference, which he acknowledges that he did not succeed in mastering in good time. At the time the treatment took place, he understood the transference in terms of Dora's assumed heterosexuality:

> … it was clear that I was replacing her father in her imagination, which was not unlikely, in view of the difference between our ages […] the transference took me unawares, and, because of the unknown quantity in me which reminded Dora of Herr K., she took her revenge on me as she wanted to take her revenge on him, and deserted me as she believed herself to have been deceived and deserted by him.

However, in a footnote to this passage Freud proposes a different understanding:

> The longer the interval of time that separates me from the end of this analysis, the more probable it seems to me that the fault in my technique lay in this omission: I failed to discover in time and to inform the patient that her homosexual (gynaecophilic) love for Frau K. was the strongest unconscious current in her mental life […] Before I had learnt the importance of the homosexual current of feeling in psychoneurotics, I was often brought to a standstill in the treatment of my cases or found myself in complete perplexity.

Elsewhere in the case history he states, "I have never yet come through a single psycho-analysis of a man or a woman without having to take into account a very considerable current of homosexuality." However, despite knowing this in theory, specific understanding of Dora did not seem to be available to him until he opened his mind to the possibilities both that Dora's most intense desires might *not* be for a man such as himself and perhaps also that she might at times have a maternal transference to him.

Freud (1956, 146–147) once told another of his female patients, the poet H. D., that he found such transferences difficult to deal with:

> I must tell you (you were frank with me and I will be frank with you), I do not like to be the mother in the transference - it always surprises and shocks me a little. I feel so very masculine.

What I think this suggests is that in order to listen well to people whose experiences do not correspond with our own – people of different races, different genders, different sexual orientations, and so on – we also need to be able to listen to ourselves and notice our responses so that we can wonder about what they might mean. The poet, Rainer Maria Rilke, famously wrote, in his *Letters to a Young Poet*:

> I want to beg you, as much as I can, dear sir, to be patient toward all that is unsolved in your heart and to try to *love the questions themselves* like locked rooms and like books that are written in a very foreign tongue. Do not now seek the answers, which cannot be given you because you would not be able to live them. And the point is, to live everything. *Live* the questions now. Perhaps you will then gradually, without noticing it, live along some distant day into the answer.

It would be easy and not inappropriate to offer this advice to a patient embarking on analysis. However, perhaps it is also advice that the analyst would do well to heed. In fact, it is arguably Freud's advice to clinicians in his 1912 paper *Recommendations to Physicians Practising Psycho-Analysis*, which sounds as simple as the requirement for the patient to say whatever comes to their mind, yet may be equally challenging:

> It consists simply in not directing one's notice to anything in particular and in maintaining the same 'evenly-suspended attention' (as I have called it) in the face of all that one hears […] For as soon as anyone deliberately concentrates his attention to a certain degree, he begins to select from the material before him […] if he follows his expectations he is in danger of never finding anything but what he already knows; and if he follows his inclinations he will certainly falsify what he may perceive. It must not be forgotten that the things one hears are for the most part things whose meaning is only recognised later on. […] If the doctor behaves otherwise, he is throwing away most of the advantage which results from the patient's obeying the 'fundamental rule of psychoanalysis'. The rule for the doctor may be expressed: 'He should withhold all conscious influences from his capacity to attend, and give himself over completely to his "unconscious memory".' Or, to put it purely in terms of technique: 'He should simply listen, and not bother about whether he is keeping anything in mind.

When faced with the mystery of another person's sexuality or gender identity, perhaps especially when their orientation is not congruent with our own, the inevitable reminders of what remains somewhat mysterious in our own experience may make it particularly difficult to stay with the uncertainty in order to accompany them on their journey. Historically, an irritable clinging to supposed sexual norms has been preferred over the imaginative leap required to understand both other sexualities and the complexity of our own, because making this leap inevitably involves a certain amount of disturbance. If we are nevertheless able to tolerate this, it may have a salutary impact on the patient's experience of our listening. However, I would like to suggest in conclusion that the kind of listening required to do justice to the experience of patients whose experiences differ in important ways from our own not only is but also must remain a work in progress. When we begin to think we have arrived at the answers, we are no longer living the questions, and our capacity to continue to do this is important not only for the patient's growth, but also for our own.

References

Bion, W. R. (1970). Attention and Interpretation: A Scientific Approach to Insight in Psycho-Analysis and in Groups. In C. Mawson (ed.) *The Complete Works of W. R. Bion*, vol 6, pp. 211–330. London: Karnac.

Bion, W. R. (1976). Emotional Turbulence. In C. Mawson (ed.) *The Complete Works of W. R. Bion*, vol 10, pp. 113–122 (first of Four Papers). London: Karnac.

Doolittle, H (1956). Tribute to Freud; with unpublished letters by Freud to the author.

Fonagy, P. (2008). A Genuinely Developmental Theory of Sexual Enjoyment and Its Implications for Psychoanalytic Technique. *Journal of the American Psychoanalytic Association* 56:11–36.

Fonagy, P. & Allison, E. (2015). A scientific theory of homosexuality for psychoanalysis. In Lemma, A. & Lynch, P. (eds) *Sexualities: Contemporary Psychoanalytic Perspectives*, pp. 125–137, London: Routledge.

Freud, S. (1905). *Three Essays on the Theory of Sexuality*. S.E., 7:123–246.

Green, A. (1995). Has Sexuality Anything to Do with Psychoanalysis? *The International Journal of Psychoanalysis* 76:871–883.

Newbigin, J. (2013). Psychoanalysis and Homosexuality: Keeping the Discussion Moving. *British Journal of Psychotherapy* 29:276–291.

Rilke, R. M. (1929). *Letters to a Young Poet*.

Socarides, C. W. (1968). *The Overt Homosexual*. New York: Grune & Stratton.

Target, M. (2007). Is Our Sexuality Our Own? A Developmental Model of Sexuality Based on Early Affect Mirroring. *British J of Psychotherapy* 23:517–530.

3 Encountering otherness

On the ability (and inability) for psychic movement within sexual states of mind[1]

Anat Schumann

I will suggest several psychoanalytic reflections on the ability (and inability) for psychic movement within sexual states of mind, in relation to the capacity to tolerate *otherness* in the psyche. Following the concept of *psychic bisexuality* as described by Freud, Winnicott and Tustin, as well as Kristeva's elaboration on the concept of *abjection*, various psychic scenarios in which the *sexual difference* may represent the traumatic encounter with the "not-me" are discussed. This overwhelming encounter with otherness may give rise to the *splitting* of psychic bisexuality, which may affect the individual's sexual states of mind at different levels of integration.

At the schizoid-paranoid level, an encounter with the unfamiliar or the "foreign", who unconsciously resonates with an introjected threatening "other", may lead to a persecutory withdrawal resulting in an "us versus them" dichotomy. This psychic scenario will be discussed in the case of homophobic phenomena as a state of dissociated psychic bisexuality, a detrimental manifestation of an incapacity to bear *otherness* in the mind.

At an earlier psychic level, a traumatic encounter with the primary "not-me" may be revealed through fetishistic sexual states of mind, when one is clinging to another while simultaneously effacing its wholeness and humanness. Through clinical illustration, I suggest listening to these compulsive sexualities as psycho-somatic states, involving sexualisation of an early traumatic encounter with otherness, in the absence of the capacity to represent it psychically. Finally, the significance of *neutral* and *unobtrusive analytic attitude* is emphasised, which may facilitate psychic movement within anxiety-ridden and rigidified sexual states of mind – as a fundamental aspect of self-reclamation.

Fear and hatred in the sexual spheres of the mind

In the 2022 Study Workshop of the European Committee of the IPA's Sexual & Gender Diversity Studies committee, Maria Juusela presented a paper which aimed to reflect on the pervasive pathologising of homosexuality in psychoanalysis. She presented a historic review of homophobic statements by leading psychoanalysts. Among others, she quoted Edmond Bergler

DOI: 10.4324/9781003531333-6

who, throughout his career, had published dozens of books and hundreds of papers and was considered a prolific and creative analyst. I will present several excerpts from his writings, featured in Juusela's paper:

> [I]t is striking how great is the proportion of psychopathic personalities among homosexuals. [...] how great is the proportion of homosexuals among swindlers, pseudologues, forgers, lawbreakers of all sorts, drug purveyors, gamblers, spies, pimps, brothel owners, etc.
> (Bergler, 1944, 272–273)

> Since every homosexual believes that he has a more or less artistic temperament, it is evident that he is rationalizing, in this way, another outstanding trait, that of *instability, unreliability, and the inability to stay with a specific task for an appreciable length of time*. Every homosexual is a prima donna [...] This bridges the gap to a sordid topic: the pronounced *tendency toward parasitism in the overwhelming majority of homosexuals*.
> (Bergler, 1956, 149; emphasis in original)

The only effective way of fighting and counteracting homosexuality would be the wide dissemination of the knowledge that there is nothing glamorous about suffering from the disease known as homosexuality, that the disease can be cured, and that this apparently sexual disorder is invariably coupled with severe unconscious self-damage (Bergler, 1956, 302).

During the discussion, the name of Felix Boehm came up, a psychoanalyst from Berlin, who explored and studied homosexuality in the 1930s. After the Nazis rise to power, Boehm joined the German Reich's Institute for Psychological Research, where he aided in the gathering of information leading to the persecution, imprisonment and torture of tens of thousands of German homosexuals, who were sent to concentration camps, where they were forced to wear a pink triangle (much like the yellow star Jews were compelled to wear). Many of them were executed by Boehm's authorisation.

Listening to these disturbing remarks, I wondered about the intra-psychic dynamics which could account for such manifestations of murderous hatred and racism towards "the other" – homosexuals, people of colour, Jews or any other receptacle for projections. I recalled a recent paper depicting the collapse into binary non-thinking in terms of "us and them" as the root of various racist views, laden with prejudice and a sense of moral superiority, associating this "non-thinking" with psychotic functioning related to the difficulty of tolerating the psychic pain involved in encountering the complexity of emotional reality, resulting in the creation of a simplified version of reality that would be easier to digest (Bergstein, 2022). These difficulties in encountering "the other" may be related to a temporary or continuous failure of the capacity for representation and symbolisation (alpha-function) in a group or in an individual. This failure reflects an "attack on linking", an attack on the ability to attribute meaning to perceived reality (Bion, 1962), as a way of avoiding the unbearable anxiety involved in encountering otherness, which undermines the self's boundaries and thereby threatens its cohesiveness.

Contemplating both Bergler's homophobia and the atrocities committed by Boehm, I wondered whether they were preoccupied with, and at the same time intensely anxious about, facing "the other" or "the foreign" within themselves. One may therefore ask, what element of *otherness* has been internally encountered to have become so unsettling?

Leaning on the psychoanalytic view of human psyche as inherently bisexual (Freud, 1905) and following Winnicott's (1966) and Tustin's (1981/2021) contributions to the concept of *psychic bisexuality*, homophobic manifestations may be perceived as related to the existence of a split-off, unmetabolised "feminine" element within a *dissociated* psychic bisexuality. This split-off internal "feminine" presence, both fascinating and threatening the sense of being, may give rise to the urge to attack and eliminate its "representatives" in external reality, in this case, the "homosexuals". Why does so-called homosexual sexuality stir up such overwhelming anxiety that may engulf thinking? And how might the religious prohibition on male homosexual practices, common to the three major monotheistic religions, be related to such deep and primordial fears?

Before addressing these sensitive issues, I wish to suggest some preliminary thoughts. As psychoanalysts, would we be able to consider sexual and gender-related states of mind without collapsing into persecutory, pathologising attitudes (as may have occurred with Bergler)? Or, on the other hand, are we prone to avoid any endeavours at psychoanalytic thinking in these areas, due to our fear of finding ourselves engaged in discrimination or even in some kind of "conversion" therapy? It seems that the ability for any psychic movement between these two poles of analytic "non-thinking", which cannot be taken for granted these days, is crucial for analytic inquiry into the spheres of sexual states of mind.

In this context, Bergstein (2022) notes that the collapse into dichotomous unthinking is not only characteristic of racism and totalitarianism but may also characterise indiscriminate adherence to other "isms". Bergstein suggests that analytic listening, which aspires to encounter psychic truth should be less focused on the *contents* of the verbal narrative and more attuned to its *psychic function* as either inhibiting or facilitating the ability for thinking and dreaming. I find this analytic principle to be most important when listening to sexual states of mind. Thus, it can be said that descriptive concepts such as "homosexual" or "heterosexual", while ostensibly denoting "facts", are of little value to psychoanalytic thinking (Bion, 1970; Meltzer, 1973), as they fail to encompass the polymorphous complexity of adult sexuality, including its infantile aspects which involve unconscious identifications embodied in internal objects, residues of early trauma and archaic modes of containing primordial anxieties (McDougall, 1986).

Returning to the phenomena of homophobia, Freud (1920) argued that sexuality is inherently traumatic. The primary psycho-physical encounter with infantile sexuality, which may be experienced as an external *otherness*, is inevitably overwhelming due to the intensity of the sexual drive, which always leaves an excess that cannot be represented in the psyche. Winnicott believed that the encounter with infantile sexuality is held and contained by the primary object, as "there is no id before ego" (Winnicott, 1962, 56). Therefore, according to Winnicott, encountering otherness is experienced as premature and traumatic when the primary mother-infant container collapses, due to internal and/or external circumstances. One way or another, while the encounter with sexuality is perceived as inherently or potentially unsettling, it seems that so-called homosexual sexuality, which might be experienced as a threat to the social order, may evoke another, more archaic fear, that of *"the feminine"*.

The concept of "the feminine" represents here the *internalised maternal otherness* in both men and women. Freud (1937), Winnicott (1986) and Kristeva (1982) all referred to "the feminine" as representing the unknown, the "alien", which may challenge the boundaries and threaten the autonomy of the self. It should be noted that, in this context, "the feminine" represents the encounter with the first maternal "other", the preliminary "not-me", and therefore is introjected into the bisexual psyche of both men and women.

Encountering "the Feminine" as "the Other" in men and women

Freud (1937) depicts two obstacles to working through the transference, which indicate that analysis has arrived at a point from which it is impossible to continue. With women patients, it is penis envy, and with men, it is the "struggle against his passive or feminine attitude to another male" (250). At the time, Freud saw both obstacles as rooted in the biological "bedrock" of the differences between the sexes. He attributed the man's "repudiation of femininity" (252) to castration anxiety, arguing that his striving towards masculinity was a result of his innate biological structure. Thus, the passive-feminine position in men, which presupposes the acceptance of castration, is adamantly repressed. While Ferenczi (1927) believed that a successful analysis would enable a man to embrace his passive wish towards another man, Freud (1937, 252) was more sceptical:

> At no other point in one's analytic work does one suffer more from an oppressive feeling that all one's repeated efforts have been in vain and from a suspicion that one has been 'preaching to the winds' [… than] when one is seeking to convince a man that a passive attitude to men does not always signify castration and that it is indispensable in many relationships in life.

Freud thus believed that castration anxiety is at the root of masculine re-sistance to the passive-feminine psychic position. It may therefore account for displays of homophobia in men in whom the repression of the internal "feminine" element is loose, so psychic bisexuality becomes unstable. What do we mean when we relate to the "repression of the female aspect" in men's psyche? To investigate this query, I will now elaborate more on the concept of *psychic bisexuality* – as an ongoing psychic movement between the "masculine" and the "feminine", which is related to the bisexual subjec-tivity in both men and women. Freud (1901) first coined the term "psychic bisexuality" as a universally innate condition that is actualised through the child's identifications with both parents in the two-fold, positive and negative, Oedipal situation. The outcome is an internal bisexual structure in which either the "feminine" or "masculine" aspect is repressed and be-comes unconscious[2] (Freud, 1923). How would we define the "masculine" element versus the "feminine" element in the psyche?

The attempt to clearly define and distinguish between the so-called "feminine" and "masculine" psychic elements has been undertaken by many psychoanalytic theorists. Freud (1905) and later Winnicott (1966), sought to go beyond the simplistic equating of psychic masculinity with activity and psychic femininity with passivity. Hence, Freud (1905/1915) proposes the *libido* as a masculine psychic element shared by both men and women, while Winnicott (1966) defines the "pure feminine element" in both men and women as the parental capacity to surrender to the m/other-infant unity. Winnicott thus believes in the capacity of men and women to hold within themselves a true and lively feminine element, which they have internalised through their own m/others, thereby becoming "good-enough m/others" as a manifestation of psychic bisexuality.

Either way, the masculine-feminine dichotomy is broadly seen as one of the first internalised dichotomies in human thinking, and, therefore, as a prototype for all subsequent binaries represented in the psyche (Amir, 2018). Hence, psychic bisexuality, in its broadest sense, becomes associ-ated with the ability to represent and contain distinct and separate ele-ments in the psyche: male and female, me and not-me, self and other. In this sense, it involves the very capacity to *encounter otherness*. In other words, an integrated psychic bisexuality, as opposed to a dissociated psychic bisexuality, is crucial for containing and bearing the encounter with any internal or external "other". This may mean that an integrated bisexual structure, which is linked to the ability to move freely between "masculine" and "feminine" elements in the psyche, may be related to a safe and gratifying encounter with the primary "other". However, when early environment is experienced as traumatic, related to external and/ or internal vicissitudes,[3] the essential bisexual condition may emerge as ruptured or split. In this context, Winnicott, Tustin and Kristeva all sug-gest turning our focus from the Oedipal phase to the sphere of primitive mental states.

Winnicott (1986) thought that every man or woman possesses an un-conscious fear of the "WOMAN" as an essence that reflects the primary encounter with the "not-me". The root of this fear he saw as related to the absolute human dependence on the primary object when physical and/or psychic separateness may be experienced as fatal. This primordial trepida-tion, manifested in different ways, varies in intensity from person to person and is associated with regression to the state of undifferentiated m/other-infant merger, which may threaten the autonomous existence of the self. Winnicott (1986), therefore, perceives the encounter with the "WOMAN" as one that often entails the fear of being dominated and perhaps, if I may add, also a regressive yearning to be dominated. In this context, Winnicott (1966) emphasises the essentiality of the good-enough maternal object, who provides the infant with an attuned environment, thereby alleviating the "anxiety of otherness" and facilitating the internalisation of a "pure femi-nine element" into an integrated psychic bisexuality. Nevertheless, when early environment is experienced as impinging on the infantile going-on-being, the primary femininity may be experienced as a *persecutory otherness* which is then incorporated into the self as a split-off "female" element – sometimes perceived unconsciously as a foreign-object implanted inside the body-self. In this sense, Winnicott (1966) believes that the fear of homo-sexuality has to do with a difficulty to move freely between the "masculine" and the "feminine" within a *dissociated* psychic bisexuality: "In the normal, where bisexuality is a fact, homosexual ideas do not conflict in this way" (Winnicott, 1966, 175–176).

In terms both similar to and different from Winnicott's, Tustin (1981/2021) addresses the "pathology of otherness" in the context of the early split she noted in the psychic bisexuality of autistic children. Tustin describes the primary "nipple-breast" bisexual object as evoking the initial registration of bisexuality in the infantile psyche, when the soft element, the breast, which represents "me", turns into the "feminine", and the hard, thrusting element, which represents the "not me", turns into the "masculine". According to Tustin, when an early encounter with "otherness" is safe enough, the hard nipple is experienced as harmoniously related to the soft breast, which leads to the integration of the "feminine" and "masculine" elements in the psyche. Nevertheless, when early encounter with the "not-me" is pre-mature and traumatic, the primary object is *split* into its "masculine" and "feminine" elements as a defence against the catastrophic dread involved in encountering otherness. In such traumatic scenarios, the autistic defence may involve a significant failure to integrate psychic bisexuality, which may be manifesting in concrete and rigidified sexual and gendered states of mind.[4]

Drawing on Freud's (1921) conceptualisation of primary and secondary identifications, and following Houzel's (2021) depiction of the three levels of psychic bisexuality integration (the container, the part-object and the whole-object), I suggest a distinction between *primary psychic bisexuality* that represents the rudimentary encounter with the not-me, akin to the archaic bisexualities described by Winnicott (1966) and Tustin (2021), and *secondary psychic bisexuality* which is consolidated through later introjective processes which may involve the m/other and father as objects discerned as "others" within the Oedipal scenes. The case of homophobic phenomena given below may illustrate a dissociation of the *secondary* psychic bisexuality.

Abjection – The primordial discerning of Otherness according to Kristeva

Kristeva (1982) explores the encounter with otherness by elaborating on the concept of *abjection*: "there looms, within abjection, one of those violent, dark revolts of being, directed against a threat that seems to emanate from an exorbitant outside [… but] it lies there, quite close, but it cannot be assimilated" (Kristeva, 1982, 1). The process of abjection refers to the *primordial discerning of otherness* from the primordial mental state that precedes the "me/not-me" differentiation. Kristeva suggests that this budding awareness of the "not-me" is experienced as formless dread, represented in unconscious fantasy as filth, disgust, humiliation and impurity. Abjection is described as an unsettling feeling of blending the foreign with the familiar, which seems to resonate with the dread of the "uncanny" (Freud, 1919). Kristeva (1982, 4) suggests that in this archaic mental state, when subjectivity is fluid and experienced as an undifferentiated blend of "me" and "not-me", the primary sense of otherness embodies the threatening encounter with the real, from which one can get away only by separating from the primary object or by expelling it:

> The abject confronts us … with our earliest attempts to release the hold of *maternal* entity even before existing outside of her … It is a violent, clumsy breaking away, with the constant risk of falling back under the sway of a power as securing as it is stifling.

How can *abjection* be related to the fear of homosexual sexuality, and to the strict biblical prohibition of male homosexual practices? Kristeva argues that the purification of the abject, representing the primordial other, the "feminine", is at the core of religious rituals aiming to separate the sacred from the profane: "the biblical text's basic concern with separating, with constituting strict identities without intermixture" (Kristeva, 1982, 93). The abject, perceived as impure, challenges the boundaries of the self and threatens individual identity. Therefore, the role of the religious rituals is to "create order", to keep things separate and thus ward off the wish for the archaic m/other and the fear of being engulfed by her. Through a close reading of the book of Leviticus, Kristeva illustrates how the biblical text deals with impurity and defilement as relating to the threatening reunion with the maternal other, "the feminine", stressing the fundamental prohibition on incest.[5]

Later, the biblical text shifts from discussing impurities of food and blood as representations of the "feminine abject", to the curtailing of sexual choice, which touches upon the unconscious anxiety concerning the effacement of differences between sexes and generations, which may represent the actualisation of the incestuous longing for the primordial mother. Hence, "...intercourse between same and same will have to be prohibited - neither promiscuity within families nor homosexuality" (Kristeva, 1982, 103). In this sense, Kristeva views homophobia as related to the primordial process of abjection, which embodies the danger of mixing with the *similar-other*, who might silently infiltrate and devour the self. For Kristeva, unlike Freud, this is an archaic anxiety that involves the pre-Oedipal mother, when the subject is "risking the loss not of a part (castration) but of the totality of his living being" (Kristeva, 1982, 64). In her view, the biblical text prohibits homosexual intercourse as it represents the incestuous wish involving the m/other, associated with any similar-other, which is distinguished from the different-other that is seemingly selected in the heterosexual object-choice.

The sexualisation of abjection – The case of Joseph

I will now turn from the anxiety of otherness as may be revealed in homophobic phenomena, which seem mostly paranoid-schizoid in nature, to the *sexualisation of abjection* – suggested as an autistic-contiguous protection against the traumatic discerning of otherness, the "intolerable terror of twoness" (Tustin, 1981/2021) evoked when encountering the primary not-me. This archaic anxiety may be evaded through auto-sensual maneuvers, which may manifest as compulsive sexual states of mind with fetishistic features. When one is clinging to an Other while simultaneously effacing its distinctiveness, wholeness and humanness, it may imply the existence of an *autistic enclave* within the psyche (Tustin, 1987).

Clinical illustration

While anticipating the coming birth of his first-born son through a shared parenting agreement, Joseph developed significant anxiety symptoms, manifested as compulsive sexual overwhelm with fetishist content, that recalled the symptoms that had first led him to start therapy with me, many years earlier. In an attempt to take in his anxiety and glean some of its underlying unconscious meanings, I listened to Joseph:

> I don't understand what's happening to me... I have no idea why it's coming back now. Everyone's so happy for me about the baby. I don't share their joy. I'm just scared. I'd prefer to have a baby who was created from someone else's genes. Not mine. It's hard to wrap my head around it.

It seems that Joseph was reacting with severe anxiety to the confronting of *abjection*, that terrifying admixture of the familiar and the alien embodied in the imagined encounter with his unborn son, simultaneously an unknown stranger and someone so close and familiar, carrying Joseph's genetic material, created out of his own body.

The *sexualisation of abjection*, manifested as a fetishist fantasy that occupied Joseph's mind at the time, seemed to reflect an auto-sensuous attempt to block out the intolerable dread of inter-mixing, evoked by the coming birth of his son - perceived as a similar-other threatening his self-cohesion. It seems that this unthinkable anxiety could only be evacuated by compulsive sexualisation, a concrete actualisation of both Joseph's yearning for a holding and soothing human other, and his need to efface the other's distinctiveness to protect himself from a painful awareness of his separateness.

McDougall (1986) describes psychosomatic and sexual archaic languages that may harbour an early registration of unrepresented traumatic vicissitudes. She coined the term "neosexualities" to describe the sexual solutions her patients created in order to bear a distressing encounter with others, echoing early object-relations, often experienced as traumatically excessive. In times of distress, in certain moments in life or within the transference relations, involving a repeated traumatic encounter with an early deficient or unattuned environment, experienced as an annihilating *otherness*.

In his need to reassure his sense of existence, Joseph repeatedly drifted into flights of fancy about living in an isolated fortress, surrounded by water, where "nobody comes, nobody goes". About a year into therapy, he broke up with his girlfriend and informed me that I would be next, since as long as he kept seeing me, he could not be sure that his thoughts were his own and not mine. This fear of the annihilating inter-mixing with the other's interiority kept growing in the transference as intimacy grew more significant. Joseph graduated and announced that he would not be coming to therapy anymore.

Some ten years later, these neosexualities, which frequently have fetishistic and/or sado-masochistic features, may attain a compulsive quality, as may have happened with Joseph, in an attempt to distract his attention away from anxiety, providing an illusion of control and impermeability and thereby blocking out the unbearable awareness of a differentiated otherness.[6]

Back to Joseph. He first came to see me, some twenty years before the birth of his son, suffering severe distress due to an obsessive "crush" on a male classmate, which had overwhelmed his mind and consumed his ability to function, to the extent of suicidal ideations. His obsession involved a fetishistic sexual fantasy that was occupying his mind. At the time, he was 26 years old, in his last year of engineering school and in a long-term relationship with his girlfriend since high school. I wondered, what kind of sexual state of mind was Joseph displaying? What sort of anxiety was defended by this compulsive erotisation, and why did it manifest with such intensity now, as Joseph was about to graduate and was thinking about proposing to his girlfriend?

Joseph came to therapy hoping to rid himself of the fetishistic fantasy that was already familiar to him from his masturbatory habits but was now intensified and fixated on an actual object – his classmate, whose physical closeness he obsessively sought, stalking him and probing into his life, all the while agonising and driving himself insane. His fetishistic obsession was focused on a smooth masculine shin, which he desperately desired to look at and "own it for himself". In his associations, he recalled himself at the age of 5-6, "shaving" his tiny shins with a razor blade, which he believed his mother used for shaving her body. He recalled an intense urge to imitate her in a way that may imply an "adhesive equation with the mother's body" (Tustin, 1981/2021, 13), denoting the wish *to be* the maternal object in order to eliminate its devastating separateness.

As previously mentioned, MacDougall (1995) describes compulsive neosexual scenarios that fulfill the function of substance abuse. Lacking an introjected safe-enough internal object, the individual seeks to use another person in a way that robs him of his humanness and otherness, as if he was an inanimate and replaceable object like many other addictive substances. The psychic void, which reflects the absence of a reliable internal object, is filled by a concrete and addictive sexual scenario, aimed to protect the psyche against unthinkable anxiety. For Joseph, it seems that acute distress had appeared towards the transition into adult life, specifically around the prospect of marrying his girlfriend, which may have aroused unconscious engulfment anxieties he couldn't contain in his psyche. In other words, when sexuality serves an anaclitic function, meaning that a person needs to use a human-other in the way he used to cling to his mother in infancy, he tends to adopt psychosomatic and sexual coping mechanisms in moments of distress. In Joseph's case, his compulsive sexualisation could be related to his inability to rely on mental functions such as thinking and dreaming, which drove an internal process presence of a good enough m/other, an otherness digested and contained in the psyche.

Joseph began therapy. The more a sense of stability was established within the transference, the more Joseph was able to begin mentalising his fetishist sexual fantasy, giving shapes and meaning to what was going on inside him. As his obsession gradually faded, the analytic process uncovered a fragile and vulnerable sense of self, which was threatened by any contact with a significant other, experienced as potentially overwhelming and diluting his sense of identity. Was it an innate sensitivity that rendered any infantile awareness of bodily separateness as traumatic rupture (Tustin, 2021)? Or was it the impact of an early environment that had been experienced as excessive in its presence or its absence? Or was it some combination of these? Either way, it seemed that Joseph's compulsive sexual arousal indicated rising levels of archaic anxiety. Winnicott (1989) might describe it as a "fear of breakdown", a catastrophic sensation revived in certain moments in life or within the transference relations, involving a repeated traumatic encounter with an early deficient or untuned environment, experienced as an annihilating *otherness*.

In his need to reassure himself of his sense of existence, Joseph repeatedly drifted into flights of fancy about living in an isolated fortress, surrounded by water, where "nobody comes, nobody goes". About a year into therapy, he broke up with his girlfriend and informed me that I would be next, since as long as he kept seeing me, he could not be sure that his thoughts were his own and not mine. This fear of the annihilating inter-mixing with the other's interiority kept growing in the transference as intimacy grew more significant. Joseph graduated and announced that he would not be coming to therapy anymore.

Some ten years later, Joseph called and asked for a meeting. It turned out that he had indeed locked himself inside a fortress. While enjoying considerable professional success, having established an impressive career, he nevertheless avoided any social or intimate relationships with either women or men, so as not to run the risk of having his compulsive sexual fantasy resurface and dominate his life: "that trauma back in the day was more than enough. Not happening again. I not getting close to anyone and I highly recommend you don't try me too much".

I heard his warning. Joseph resumed therapy. Once again, it seemed that the emergence of a safe-enough holding environment within the analytic process relieved his anxiety and enabled psychic growth. While traveling abroad, now in his late thirties, Joseph began actualising the fetishist fantasy that dominated his internal life. He often felt the need to vomit after these sexual encounters, expressing feelings of repulsion and disgust, as if he sought to expel "an other" invading his psychic interiors. In Kristeva's terms, this nausea seems to represent the dread of *abjection*, of that traumatic encounter with *otherness*, which is linked unconsciously with filth and disgust. In Tustin's terms, when the "male-hardness" of external reality is felt to penetrate the "female-softness", excitement is produced. In normal development, the mother will seem to hold her infant together so that he is not overwhelmed by the discharge of intense excitement. If the child does not feel held together, this panic seems to be experienced as a bodily explosion, in which "male hard not-me" things are expelled, reflecting the *splitting* of *psychic bisexuality*.

When Joseph would come back from his trips, he eagerly awaited our sessions, sharing his experiences in detail. I felt that he needed me to be a quiet and attuned "female-softness" presence, willing to be receptive to an "alien" and unknown male-hardness experiences, trying to metabolise and give them meaning within the transference relations. I said to him: "When you are waiting to come here and tell me about all that happened to you, maybe the nausea becomes more bearable". It appeared that Joseph's ability to modulate these limited sexual encounters with casual others maintained a sense of controllable, predictable world, that was crucial on his journey towards otherness, in the consulting room and beyond. However, he would repeatedly state that he had no interest in entering any sexual or emotional relationship with either men or women: "Don't you get any ideas… I have zero intentions to start dating anyone, let alone men". I replied: "You are asking me to keep my ideas in my own mind, not try to thrust them into your mind, to avoid any kind of intermixing which might put you at risk here".

Over the years, it seemed that Joseph's ability to make room in his mental fortress for the analytic mother was growing and so was his ability to "safely use the object" when engaging the outside world. In time, he developed an interest in various fields of knowledge and created some social ties while maintaining a "safe distance". He chose to build his family with a woman he met, through a "shared parenting" contract, which he linked in his associations to the analytic contract. The latter, which is based on a clearly defined and unchanging setting, seemed to enable a safe-enough analytic environment which may foster the internalisation of a "rhythm of safety" as a hard-stable-paternal aspect of the bisexual container (Houzel, 2004). It seems that in this analytic environment he could work through his traumatic early encounter with the primary object, "an other" experienced as taking over his body and mind. Over the last few years, I have occasionally suggested to him the more intense setting of psychoanalysis. His reply remains the same: "Anat, if a day comes when I am finally able to accept this offer of yours, that will mean that I no longer need it".

Through the case of Joseph, I sought to illustrate some psychic movements made possible within the transference relations in the analytic process. Joseph's nascent ability to make room for the analytic m/other within his psyche, to acknowledge both his need for the "other" and his anxiety of "getting lost" in contact with another, was followed by some psychic movements within his conscious and unconscious sexual states of mind, facilitating a more creative and lively sense of being. In anticipation of his son's birth, many years after he had first come to therapy, Joseph was again overwhelmed by a compulsive sexual need that may indicate a temporary recurrence of his deep anxiety in encountering the abject, the separateness of the other, a similar-other, this time his first-born son. In Winnicott's terms (1989), it seems that Joseph's growing ability to encounter the otherness of the analytic mother, allowed him to internalise a genuine and lively *pure* feminine element (as opposed to a *split-off* and persecutory "female" element), thereby restoring a continuous movement between "pure feminine" and "masculine" elements within the psyche, psychic bisexuality.

Concluding remarks

Why is it that in certain cases, as with Joseph, early trauma manifests specifically in the sexual areas of the mind? A deep discussion of this query will be beyond the scope of this chapter but briefly, I suggest that the "sexualisation of Abjection" is often related to early traumatic encounters with the not-me, involving *sensual* and *bodily* aspects of the mother-infant relation, beginning with innate vulnerabilities that render the primary encounter with the mother's physical separateness traumatic, as Tustin (2021) depicted in the autistic states, through an infantile environment experienced as untuned, invasive and excessive in a way that involves the physical aspects of mother-infant relation as described by Winnicott and his followers. According to Laplanche (1987), the sexual aspect of the mother's unconscious may permeate the emotional and physical care she provides her infant. When this maternal aspect is overwhelmingly excessive, it might become incorporated into the infant's interiority as a "foreign body", which may interfere with his sexual state of mind. And finally, sexual abuse in childhood, particularly in the case of incest, generates devastating somatic and emotional excess, which due to the inability to digest it psychically, may manifest as compulsive and repetitive scenarios within sexual states of mind.

What kind of analytic attitude might support the reclamation of the ability for psychic movement within sexual states of mind? From the cases of Joseph and others, two related main aspects come to mind: *analytic neutrality* and an *unobtrusive presence* (Balint, 1968). Laplanche and Pontalis (1967) define analytic neutrality as "one of the defining characteristics of the attitude of the analyst during the treatment", adding that "the analyst must be neutral in respect of religious, ethical and social values – that is to say, he must not direct the treatment according to some ideal" (Laplanche and Pontalis, 1967, p. 271). They add that Freud saw the establishment of secure transference as predicated on analytic neutrality. It seems that for Joseph, psychic change was made possible largely by the creation of safe and reliable transference relations within the analytic environment.

In the context of neutrality, Meltzer (1973) discusses the need for distinction between adult sexual life, which content is *not* the subject of psychoanalytic exploration – "what is adult and private is of no analytic concern" (Meltzer, 1973, 65) – and infantile sexual aspects that interfere with mature sexuality, often in an invasive and compulsive manner. Therefore, the focus of analytic concern is the sexual *state of mind*, with its underlying unconscious phantasies and identifications, and the sense of self, which oscillates between vitality and emptiness. In other words, does the subject encounter another person, a "not-me", in his sexual state of mind at a given moment? Or is the sexual scenario one that involves a partial or a dismantled object, when psychosexuality is reduced to the concrete and the corporeal, to the compulsive and the repetitious? On the importance of analytic neutrality, Meltzer adds:

Psychoanalysis has no aspiration to free people of [sexual] conflict [...] This is extremely important for an analyst to appreciate in order to avoid being drawn as mentor, mediator or judge into the patient's external relations. In no area is the pressure more severe than in connection with sexual life. (65)

This statement corresponds with Freud's (1935, 423–424) words in a letter to the "mother of a homosexual":

> What analysis can do for your son runs in a different line. If he is un-happy, neurotic, torn by conflicts, inhibited in his social life, analysis may bring him harmony, peace of mind, full efficiency, whether he remains homosexual or gets changed.

Regarding this same matter, MacDougall (1986, 277) notes on the "neosexual" solutions: "inventions capable of fulfilling such diverse func-tions … must be solidly constructed from infancy on and … will scarcely be modifiable in the years to come unless the experience of analysis leads to a richer erotic life". It can therefore be said that psychoanalytic listening is concerned neither with altering sexual object-choice or practice, nor with the removal of any sexual "symptom", but rather with facilitating creative psychic movement and the sense of being real and alive in general, and in particular within the sexual states of mind. For this purpose, psychoana-lytic listening should focus on early object relations, emphasising the pri-mary encounter with otherness, its traumatic residues and their derivatives in unconscious phantasy.

A neutral and reliable analytic attitude may be defined as grounded in an *internal bisexual position*, the pairing of the "feminine" and the "masculine" in their broader sense, embodying the unceasing challenge involved in encountering the other – the feminine, the unknown – within and outside of ourselves. Nevertheless, when analytic listening is saturated with "memory and desire", searching for the familiar and the known (Bion, 1970), clinging to ideals or social "isms", the analyst's bisexual position might be weakened, leading to the impoverishment of the creative analytic space that relies on it.

Following Bion, Sandler (2009) suggests that *bisexual movement* be-tween "feminine" and "masculine" psychic positions, between container and contained, is possible for the analyst when she allows herself to be "penetrated" by the patient's otherness, which introduces her to what she does not know and may have never known. It seems that the same applies in the complementary direction, as the patient's ability to make room in his mind for the therapist's otherness may facilitate bisexual movement within the psyche, a movement of creativity and aliveness. This is illustrated in the case of Joseph, where my encounter with his otherness allowed me to think new and unfamiliar thoughts – for example, about the actualisation of archaic sexual aspects as manifestations of psychic change within the transference relations, moving from adhesive or fetishistic object related-ness to human object usage. Hence, the aspiration is to maintain a *bisexual* or *binocular vision*, enabling a continuous movement between different per-spectives, between knowing and not-knowing, as much as possible.

The distinction suggested between *primary* and *secondary* bisexualities may fine-tune our listening and interpreting in areas of unrepresented mental states, embodied in the archaic sexual states of mind. Clinically, it seems that profound distress at the "archaic edge" of sexual states of mind requires a reliable and safe analytic environment willing to be receptive to excessive feelings of formlessness, emptiness and psychic deadness.

Winnicott (1971) described an infant who looks in his mother's eyes and does not see himself in her. The mother's face is not a mirror. It shows her mood, her needs, her anxieties, her being empty of herself. This is a *traumatic encounter* with a *significant other*. In such circumstances, the infant's subjectivity is prematurely permeated with foreign maternal materials. The core-self fades, the psychic existence does not develop, the body remains an empty cover. And in the analytic situation, when transitional space is saturated with the analyst's otherness, with her conscious and unconscious desires, with her theoretical or social ideals, her attempt to "help" the patients normalise their otherness or "perversion" – all of these may leave the patient staring at the beautiful reflection of his analyst, devoid of the gaze that would restore his own selfhood.

When the essential distress involves a traumatic encounter with *otherness*, a neutral and non-invasive analytic environment is required, being receptive to catastrophic experiences of psychic annihilation, willing to give back shapes and meanings which facilitate the capacities for thinking and dreaming. All of these may allow for profound psychic change in the analytic process. In the context suggested in this chapter, it is about creating movement within sexual states of mind, *reclaiming psychic bisexuality*.

Notes

1 A modified version of this chapter was awarded the 2024 Tustin Prize.
2 Freud found it difficult to define the factors that affect which parent the child ultimately identifies with, and resorted to the constitutional explanation, pointing to "the relative strength of the masculine and feminine sexual dispositions" (Freud, 33).
3 The encounter with early environment, the "not-me", could be experienced as traumatic in *internal* circumstances (innate hyper-sensitivity, excessive instinctuality and other constitutional factors which may mould unconscious phantasy) or *external* ones (environmental trauma in terms of excess of any kind, which may also affect unconscious phantasy).
4 This theoretical model may account for recent research findings correlating a diagnosis on the autistic spectrum with high prevalence of gender dysphoria (Kallitsounaki & Williams, 2023).
5 For example, the injunction to separate meat and dairy, through the verse "do not cook a young goat in its mother's milk" (Exodus, 23:19), alludes to the tabooed incest; The same holds true for biblical injunctions concerning menstruation, the birth of a male son, circumcision, etc.
6 It should be noted that the sexualisation of abjection may manifest in sexual states of mind at different psychic levels – neurotic, narcissistic or psychotic – in accordance with the individual's unique phantasmatic scenarios and the severity of traumatic residue revealed in the transference relations.

References

Amir, D. (2018). The Two Sleeps of Orlando: Transsexuality as Caesura or Cut. In O. Gozlan (ed.), *Current critical debates in the field of transsexual studies* (pp. 36–47). London & New York: Routledge.

Balint, M. (1968). *The Basic Fault*. London: Tavistock.

Bergler, E. (1944). Eight Prerequisites For The Psychoanalytic Treatment Of Homosexuality. *Psychoanal Review*, 31:253–286.

Bergler, E. (1956). *Homosexuality: Disease or way of life?* New York: Hill & Wang.

Bergstein, A. (2022). *Unknowability, complexity and the collapse to binary (un)thinking and 'isms': A contribution to the psychoanalytic understanding of prejudice.* Unpublished.

Bion, W. R. (1962). *Learning from experience*. London: Tavistock.

Bion, W. R. (1970). *Attention and interpretation*. London: Tavistock.

Ferenczi, S. (1927). The problem of termination of the analysis. In M. Balint (ed.), *Final contributions to the problems and methods of psycho-analysis*. London: Hogarth Press.

Freud, S. (1901) Letter from Freud to Fliess, August 7, 1901. *The Complete Letters of Sigmund Freud to Wilhelm Fliess*, 1887–1904 42:446–448.

Freud, S. (1905). *Three Essays on the Theory of Sexuality*. In J. Strachey (Ed.), *The standard edition of the complete psychological works of Sigmund Freud* (vol. VII, pp. 123–246). London, England: Hogarth Press.

Freud, S. (1919). The Uncanny. In J. Strachey (Ed.), *The standard edition of the complete psychological works of Sigmund Freud* (vol. 17, pp. 219–256). Hogarth Press.

Freud, S. (1920). Beyond the Pleasure Principle. In J. Strachey (Ed.), *The standard edition of the complete psychological works of Sigmund Freud* (vol. 18, pp. 7–64). Hogarth Press.

Freud, S. (1923). The Ego and the Id. In J. Strachey (Ed.), *The standard edition of the complete psychological works of Sigmund Freud* (vol. XIX, pp. 1–66). Hogarth Press.

Freud, S. (1935). Letter from Sigmund Freud to Anonymous, *Letters of Sigmund Freud 1873-1939*, 51:423–424.

Freud, S. (1937). *Analysis Terminable and Interminable*. In J. Strachey (Ed.), *The standard edition of the complete psychological works of Sigmund Freud* (vol. XXIII, pp. 209–254). London, England: Hogarth Press.

Houzel, D. (2004). The Psychoanalysis of Infantile Autism. *Journ Child Psychotherapy*, 30(2):225–237.

Houzel, D. (2021). *Splitting of Psychic Bisexuality in Autistic Children* [Lecture]. Frances Tustin Memorial Trust Lecture Series.

Juusela, M. (2022). *The Ideal Homosexual is Heterosexual, The Ideal Analyst Makes It So – Understanding the Generalized Pathologisation of Homosexuality within Psychoanalysis.* A paper given in the IPA SGDS committee study day, Vienna, 2022.

Kallitsounaki, A. and Williams, D. (2023). Autism Spectrum Disorder and Gender Dysphoria/Incongruence. *Journal of Autism and Developmental Disorders*, 53:3103–3117.

Kristeva, J. (1982). *The powers of horror: An essay on abjection*. Tr. L.S. Roudiez. New York: Columbia University Press.

Laplanche, J. and Pontalis, J.-B. (1967). *The language of psychoanalysis*. London: The Hogarth Press, 1973.

Laplanche, J. (1987). *New foundations for psychoanalysis*. Tr. D. Macey. Oxford: Basil Blackwell.

McDougall, J. (1986). *Theaters of the mind*. New York: Basic Books.

McDougall, J. (1995). *The many faces of eros*. New York: W.W. Norton.

Meltzer, D. (1973). *Sexual states of mind*. Perthshire: Clunie Press.

Sandler, P.C. (2009). *A clinical application of Bion's Concepts: Dreaming, transformation, containment and change.*

Tustin, F. (1987). *Autistic barriers in neurotic patients*. London: Karnac Books.

Tustin, F. (1981/2021). *Autistic states in children*. London and New York: Routledge Classics.

Winnicott, D.W. (1962). Ego integration in child development. In *The maturational processes and the facilitating environment* (pp. 56–63). London: The Hogarth Press, 1965.

Winnicott, D.W. (1986). *Home is where we start from: Essays by a psychoanalyst*. New York, NY: W. W. Norton & Company.

Winnicott, D.W. (1989). Fear of Breakdown. In *Psychoanalytic explorations* (87–95). London: Karnac.

Winnicott, D.W. (1966). On the Split Off Male and Female Elements. In *Psychoanalytic explorations* (pp. 168–192). London: Karnac, 1989.

Winnicott, D.W. (1971). *Playing and reality*. London: Tavistock Publications.

4 Shapes of gender identity

Three stories with impact[1]

Domenico Di Ceglie

This chapter, which was originally presented at the Tavistock Centre via Zoom on the 16th of February 2021, describes the early history and origins of the Gender Identity Development Service (GIDS) and its model of care and philosophy. Within the Centenary Events of the Tavistock, it seemed particularly appropriate to reflect on the foundations of a service which has a focus on the complex dynamics of identity development and, in particular, of gender identity. I will do this by briefly describing three cases which made a significant contribution to the construction of the original model through the use of "observation and imagination" in the words of Donald Meltzer, as well as of clinical experience and available empirical research.

Bonnard's "Young Women in the Garden" is one of the most extreme examples of a painting made over a long period of time. Having started work in 1921–3, Bonnard put the canvas aside for many years before revisiting and revising it in 1945–6. Resuming his work was part of an attempt to rediscover the original experience, bringing it into the present without losing its place in the past. In this chapter, I will use a similar approach to that of Bonnard to three children and young people whom I saw in the past and published. I will look at these cases from a new perspective applied to the case material: their impact on the creation of a model of care for children and adolescents with atypical gender identity development or gender diversity, in today's language.

Jennifer

Jennifer was 16 when she was referred in the 80s to the Adolescent Department of Tavistock Clinic following three suicide attempts. She had been assigned female at birth but perceived herself as a male. She presented very distressed with depressive episodes and several features, which at the time were considered borderline. Today, we would have looked more closely for the presence of autistic spectrum features as she had difficulties in communication and avoided eye contact. Recent studies have shown the presence of autistic spectrum features in some transgender people (di Ceglie et al.,

DOI: 10.4324/9781003531333-7

2014; Jones et al., 2012; Skagerberg et al., 2015). A large part of the session was spent in silence. At the time of the referral, Jennifer was still living in a female role, maintained her female name and wished to be addressed using a female pronoun. She was uncertain about physical interventions. Her mother, who had died just before Jennifer came to the clinic, had suffered depression after Jennifer's birth, and her father had been physically violent towards his wife during Jennifer's childhood, until they separated. During her psychotherapy sessions, she remembered episodes when her father, in fits of temper, had kicked her mother in the stomach. In one session, she admitted, not without a sense of embarrassment and shame, that she had identified with him, an experience that she could not explain. She loved her mother, and her main aim in life was to do something extraordinary that would have made her mother happy. There was no recollection that Jennifer herself had been physically abused by her father, but witnessing violence between her parents had been a traumatic childhood experience.

It is possible to hypothesise that the way Jennifer coped with the fear of damage to her mother, and possibly to herself, was to identify with a male, possessing the strength of a masculine body. Once established, this gave her a sense of survival and a sense of protecting in her mind the "damaged" mother. A female representation of herself had to be strongly avoided, as it was equated in her mind with being weak and damaged.

Another important factor also seemed to play a part. After the birth of two older sisters, her mother miscarried a baby boy. One year later, Jennifer was born. Jennifer seemed to feel that her mother had expected her to be a boy, and in one session, she alluded to her mother having "psychic qualities", as if she had been part of a magical experience in which she and her mother could read each other's mind. She had probably received, and made her own, her mother's wish that she had been a boy. Her mother probably never consciously expressed this wish, but possibly, it remained unconsciously active in the relationship between them.

Two years of psychotherapeutic exploration with this young person allowed the therapist, together with Jennifer, to make this partial reconstruction of her childhood relating to her atypical gender identity development. However, any attempts to explore this understanding further with Jennifer led to continuous interruptions of the therapeutic work, which may have indicated her extreme resistance and fears of having the foundation of her gender identity revisited.

Even if Jennifer retained some of this understanding, it certainly did not alter her gender identity development, the sense of who he was. His male gender identity seemed well-established and fixed. It formed very early in life, and it is likely that traumatic events played some part in it.

Towards the end of therapy, Jennifer was able to live in a male role with a male name and his well-being improved. He did not attempt suicide again. He settled into a job, and he was more able to establish relationships with other people. One might say that therapy had helped him to cope with his well-established gender identity in a better way, to make the transition to a male role and to give him a sense of hope (an important therapeutic aim). He was eventually referred to an adult gender identity service to explore further his perceived identity and the distress generated by the incongruence between his perceived gender and his sexual body. Physical interventions, aimed at harmonising his gender identity and his body, could also be considered in the adult service.

I became aware in working with Jennifer that I was fundamentally dealing with a developing identity and not a psychiatric condition, long before there was a legal recognition of these new identities in many countries. A question remains: what conferred continuity to his atypical gender identity development?

This case shows that the combination of an exploratory and accepting attitude could be a good approach in terms of promoting well-being. Here, the focus of the work was the amelioration of the associated psychosocial difficulties. I later realised that these are present in several cases. Reflection on this case led to the original formulation of the therapeutic aims in working with children with gender diversity and their families (di Ceglie, 1998).

The therapeutic aims were summarised as follows:

1 To foster recognition and non-judgemental acceptance of gender identity issues.
2 To ameliorate associated behavioural, emotional and relationship difficulties.
3 To break the cycle of secrecy.
4 To activate interest and curiosity by exploring the impediments to them.
5 To encourage exploration of the mind-body relationship by promoting close collaboration among professionals in different specialties, including paediatric endocrinology.
6 To allow mourning processes to occur.
7 To enable symbol formation and symbolic thinking.
8 To promote separation and differentiation.
9 To enable the child or adolescent and the family to tolerate uncertainty in gender identity development.
10 To sustain hope.

It is important to add to this list the need to combat stigma, which is often associated with the experience of atypical gender identity, and which is, at times, internalised by the individual experiencing gender diversity. It is also valuable to alleviate the feeling of shame that some children/adolescents and their families experience and enable them to develop skills in handling social interaction and dealing with possible hostility.

This therapeutic approach is developmentally based, is not prescriptive, addresses the young person's distress and aims at promoting well-being. It is not part of reparative/conversion therapy and has elements of affirmative therapy.

In one of the last sessions after two years of exploratory therapy, Jennifer said that perhaps this form of help had come too late and that her parents should have been aware of how she was feeling by the way she behaved as a child. She wondered why they had not sought help at that time. Jennifer's thoughts made me wonder why there was no service for children with these distressing experiences. This planted in me the seed for the creation of such a service. About three years after, GIDS was established in the Department of Child Psychiatry in 1989 at St Georges Hospital in South London. In 1996, the service was transferred to the Tavistock and Portman Trust (di Ceglie, 2021).

Max

Britton (1998, 11), in his book, *Belief and Imagination*, distinguishes between beliefs and fantasies and states: "Beliefs have consequences: they arouse feelings, influence perception and promote actions … Fantasies, conscious or unconscious, which are not the object of belief, do not have consequences: disavowal therefore can be used to evade these consequences".

Therapeutic exploration will help to clarify these two different states of mind. The following interaction illustrates the level of conviction of belief of a 13-year-old, assigned female at birth whose self-perception was of being a boy. This interaction occurred in a family session involving the mother, the stepfather, the young person called Max, a child psychotherapist colleague and myself. The session was recorded for a documentary in 1994.

The metaphor, which I use in the following clip, came to my mind after reading an article by Jan Morris, "On the sadness of living abroad". Here, Morris describes the psychological experience of some English people who had migrated to France. Today, we could call this experience "the migrant dysphoria". She writes:

> It is not just that I am sorry for the French, who are going to have to suffer the proximity of these cuckoos in the nest of the world; in a way I am sorrier for the English, who are going to turn themselves into expatriates. All over the world one sees them, the islanders, evading their heritage, looking for the London newspapers in the Spanish newsagent, talking about duchesses at the New England Tennis Clubs, and, above all, almost anywhere beautiful in France, visiting each other's houses, remembering old times, comparing Major with Thatcher, Gooch with Botham. How happy they always say they are! How sad they generally seem to me.
>
> (Morris, 1991)

The following section is the transcript of a clip from the documentary.

Female Therapist (FT):	What would you like to be called?
Max:	Now? It's certainly not Sarah.
FT:	What would you like us to call you?
Max:	I don't know.
Mother (M):	We just call Max, Max. But when I hear somebody else calling her, Sarah, or something, I just …
Max:	Why do you say 'her'?
M:	Sorry, sorry.
Father:	That's the hardest bit …
M:	It's the 'he' and the 'she' because it's really difficult and I feel weird calling Max 'her' or 'she'. Yeah. (To Max) I feel weird calling you it.
FT:	Is that the bit that hurts the most?
Max:	Yes. She says it all the time.
M:	I do. I do. Yeah.
FT:	But do you feel (hurt) with your mother or with everyone?
Max:	No, [Male Therapist] calls me it too.
FT:	Does it hurt the same?
Max:	Yes.
FT:	It hurts the same.
Max:	Yes.
M:	I know you'd rather be called 'he' but I do try, promise, we both do.
Male Therapist (MT):	But I think it is a difficult issue to tackle because it's a bit similar to an English boy, born in England, brought up in England, about 15, 16, who emigrates to France and then goes around and says to everybody that I'm French. That I want to be considered French. While his accent will show that he is not French. So this is …
Max:	No, that's not it though, because he wants to be, he isn't, but I am.
MT:	But that is one of the problems because, of course, what your body says is different from what you feel inside you are. Like in this person, what he would like to be is French and this is different from what his accent, at least, you know, no other features …
Max:	I don't want to be, I don't like to be … a boy.
FT:	You are a boy?
Max:	Yes.

An extract from another session shows further the strength of the conviction of this teenager and the difficulties in tolerating uncertainty or that the mother could have another point of view.

M: Max has asked us specifically on several occasions not to call him Sarah because we have called him Max since he was incy, and to say 'he' and not 'she'. And he's explained that it really, really hurts when someone says 'she'. And also it's ever so complicated if I introduce him as 'she' because people think I've gone mad so …

Max: You sound as if you're just doing it …

M: M. Because you've asked me to …

Max: Yeah, one of the reasons. Why aren't you doing it for you?

M: Also for me, because eventually if you do go ahead and have all the treatment I'm gonna have …

Max: Why do you say 'if'?

M: Well, all right then, 'when'. I'm gonna look pretty stupid if I'm the only person on the planet calling you 'she'.

Max: You sound as if you're just worried about what you do.

M: No, it's for you and for everybody. What you need to understand is that it takes some time for somebody like me to readjust and I do try, really, really, hard because the last thing I want is to upset you …

MT: The important point that you are making is that you feel that there should be no doubt about who you are …

Max: Yeah.

MT: … in this case you feel that you are a boy and there should be no doubt that you are a boy. And when you pick up any doubt about it, or that people are uncertain about it, that's very upsetting for you …

Max's perception of his male gender identity persisted until he was in contact with the service. At 18 he pursued further treatment in an adult service.

This case shows the value of a psychotherapeutic exploration in helping to distinguish between gender identity presentations, which are more solid and presentations which are more fluid and changeable. The material from this case, in particular, enabled the formulation of the so-called "atypical gender identity organisation" (AGIO).

The characteristics of the organisation are as follows:

a *Rigidity–flexibility or solidity–fluidity of the AGIO*

This refers to the capacity of the atypical gender identity organisation of the individual to remain unchangeable or, alternatively, along a continuum, to be amenable to evolution in the course of development. Organisations which are more rigid or solid will contribute to the persistence/continuity of the atypical gender identity development, while organisations which are more flexible or fluid will lead to shifts in gender identity development. In about 10–30% of pre-pubertal children, gender dysphoria persists into adolescence. After puberty, the persistence/continuity into adulthood is much higher.

b *Timing of the AGIO formation*

Atypical Gender Identity Organisations that develop very early in the child's life may be more likely to become solidly structured than organisations that develop later. The early onset of gender dysphoria is, in fact, one of the criteria for considering early pubertal suppression.

c *Traumatic events in childhood*

It can be hypothesised that in some cases, an AGIO may be formed as a psychological coping strategy in relation to a traumatic event in childhood. The earlier the trauma occurs, the more likely it is that the organisation will acquire unchangeable qualities.

d *Position on the paranoid-schizoid-depressive continuum*

The Klein-Bion model of psychological development posits a continuum from the paranoid-schizoid to the depressive position. An individual oscillates between these two positions or mental states. Precisely where the child's mental state resides along this continuum when an AGIO is formed is of significance. The hypothesis here is that if the AGIO is formed during a period of development within the mental functioning of the paranoid-schizoid position, it is more likely to become very structured, have the quality of a solid identity and therefore be less amenable to change. Alternatively, if it is formed within a mental functioning of the depressive position, it is likely that the organisation will have more fluid qualities (fluid identity) and be amenable to evolution.

Therapeutic exploration may be able to elucidate the characteristics of the organisation or the shape of gender identity of that individual and therefore guide management.

Martin

Martin was referred in the early 1990s to the GIDS at the age of eight when he was attending a primary school. The educational psychologist reported that his mother said that he had told her when he was seven that he wanted to be a woman when he grew up. He enjoyed dressing in women's clothing and, ever since he could walk, he liked to wear high heels and use tea towels to mimic long hair. He was very fond of Barbie dolls and his mannerisms and style of walking were feminine. At school, he played only with girls. He lacked confidence and was teased by other children, who called him offensive names. He suffered from symptoms of anxiety including stomach upsets, dizziness and headaches. His mother did not encourage his feminine behaviour but was supportive.

During his assessment at GIDS, we confirmed that Martin presented the features of a well-established gender identity disorder (gender dysphoria in DSM-5). His anxiety about attending school resulted in poor attendance, and he also experienced teasing in the area where he lived. He also had difficulties separating from his mother. At our service, we started working closely with the family, which consisted of Martin, his mother and his stepfather, and had meetings with the school staff to facilitate his attendance at school.

Two years later, Martin moved with his family to another town in England. Here, his wish to live in a female role became very intense and the parents agreed to let him live as a girl, expressed by dressing in female clothes and changing his name to Martina. In her new town, Martina became involved in individual therapeutic work with a community nurse in the local child and adolescent mental health service (CAMHS). A colleague and I continued to see the parents every two months to help them to reflect on the gender identity and other developmental issues involved and to be able to make more informed decisions with their child (parental counselling). The parents attended a group for parents of GD children for six months (di Ceglie & Coates Thümmel, 2006). We continued to hold regular professional network meetings, including the school staff, two or three times a year. Martina attended a small special educational unit in a female role, following careful preparation and discussions of the issues involved between the professional network (including us) and the family.

When Martina was 13, the Social Services Department called a child protection conference as the school had become concerned that parental attitudes could have contributed to the development of Martina's gender dysphoria. After an investigation and a child protection conference, no child protection issues were found. As a result of this conference, the mother was offered further supportive individual counselling by local services.

When Martina was 14, while waiting to be seen by our paediatric endocrinologist, as she was entering puberty, she unexpectedly announced to her mother that she no longer wished to be a girl, and she now felt happier about being a boy. From then on, Martina reverted to living as Martin. The next time I saw him, he had physically developed a lot and had the clear appearance of a boy. At the last professional/family network meeting, I asked Martin if he thought that his parents had made a wrong decision in allowing him to attend school in a female role and he replied without hesitation that it had been right because that was how he had felt at the time (di Ceglie, 2018b).

From this case, which I saw in the 1990s, I drew the following conclusion:

1 Pubertal development can sometimes, even in well-established cases of gender dysphoria, change the course of gender identity development.
2 A parental response, which goes along with the intense wishes of the child to live in the perceived gender identity and role, does not necessarily influence the course of gender identity development. However, maintaining an open mind facilitates the process of change if this occurs.

3 My professional role was to maintain a reflective approach in working
   with the family and the professional network, evaluating pros and cons,
   and to facilitate decision-making within the family regarding what was
   in the best interests of the child in that particular social context.

There is very limited research evidence to suggest which approach to
children living in their preferred gender role (social transition) during
childhood is best. Long-term follow-up studies have shown that only in a
small proportion (up to 30%) of pre-pubertal children presenting with the
features of gender dysphoria did the gender dysphoria continue through
adolescence and adulthood with or without any therapeutic intervention
(Cohen-Kettenis, 2001; Drummond et al., 2008; Green et al., 1987; Wallien
& Cohen-Kettenis, 2008; Zucker & Bradley, 1995). Steensma et al. (2011, 1)
suggest that among young people who changed:

> …the period between 10 and 13 years of age was considered to be
> crucial … Both persisters and desisters stated that the changes in their
> social environment, the anticipated and actual feminization or mascu-
> linization of their bodies, and their first experiences of falling in love
> and sexual attraction, had influenced their gender related interest,
> behaviour, feelings of gender discomfort, and gender identification.

My initial thinking about the management of gender roles and social
transition in childhood was based on a long-term observation of the case
described from the 1990s. Since then, I have seen several pre-pubertal children and found that the exercise of autonomy in decision-making on the
part of the parents and the child has been a helpful policy. The provision
of a therapeutic exploration, jointly with the family and a neutral professional, is helpful. The exploration would aim at enhancing the capacity for
autonomy in the family and, in this way, lead to better-informed consent
to what is in the best interests of the development of the child and, in particular, of their gender identity. The value of therapeutic explorations and
counselling with young people and their families could be seen from a new
vertex: "their role in the service of the ethical principle of autonomy and
better-informed decision-making". Long-term follow-ups and further research in this area can contribute to the continuous development of appropriate guidelines.

Conclusion

In this chapter, I have tried to show how reflecting overtime on case material, as Bonnard did with painting, can allow a process of "learning from
experience" in the words of Bion and contribute to the development of
models of care for different shapes of atypical gender identity. As clinical experiences and research evidence evolve, so will models of care. The

management of gender dysphoria in a number of young people may require for the young person and the family decision-making regarding hormonal intervention. There is a risk, in our digital age and current cultural climate, that the process of evaluation and assessment becomes rather mechanical and simplistic. The role of therapeutic exploration may promote the development of autonomy and better-informed decision-making in young people and their families.

I would like to end with a metaphor which stimulates a reflection on the nature of gender diversity in children. Recently, the Chinese artist Ai Weiwei created an installation at the Tate Modern in London, which he called Sunflower Seeds. This extensive mass of seeds (120 million) seen at a distance looks uniform and undifferentiated, but as one looks a bit more closely, the individuality of each seed becomes more and more evident. There are no two seeds which are the same. Ai Weiwei explained that each porcelain seed was individually painted by workers, who collaborated on the project, and not by a machine. Each seed required between three and six strokes according to the ability or the style of each collaborator. Therefore, the diversity of the seeds was the result of the creative process (di Ceglie, 2018a).

In a way similar to this work of art, children who present with atypical gender identity development, ("gender dysphoria" in DSM-5) all present differently within this category and not as part of a stereotype. It is, therefore, important to offer different types of help according to a range of diverse needs. "One size fits all" cannot be applied to this group, instead, as professionals and society, we should respond empathically and flexibly to the particular experiences and stories of each young person.

Note

1 This chapter was originally given at the IPA Study Day, Brussels, Belgium, 27–28 September, 2019. It was printed in Italian entitled "Forme dell'identità di genere: tre storie dall'impatto significativo" in *Rivista di Psicoanalisi*, 2020, LXVI, 1, pages 169–181; it was then published as Shapes of gender identity: three stories with impact, *Psychoanalytic Psychotherapy*, 2021 35(4), 383–395, https://doi.org /10.1080/02668734.2021.1990115, and is included here with kind permission of Rivista di Psicoanalisi.

References

Britton, R. (1998). *Belief and imagination*. London: Routledge.
Cohen-Kettenis, P. T. (2001). Gender Identity Disorder in DSM? *Journ Am Academy Child and Adolescent Psychiatry*, 40(4), 391.
di Ceglie, D. (1998). Management and therapeutic aims with children and adolescents with gender identity disorders and their families. In D. di Ceglie, and D. Freedman (eds.), *A stranger in my own body: Atypical gender identity development and mental health* (pp. 185–197). London: Karnac.
di Ceglie, D. (2018a). The use of metaphors in understanding atypical gender identity development and psychosocial impact. *The Journal of Child Psychotherapy*, 44(1), 5–28. https://doi.org/10.1080/0075417X.2018.1443151

di Ceglie, D. (2018b). Autonomy and decision-making in children and adolescents with gender dysphoria. In M. Shaw, and S. Bailey (eds.), *Justice for children and families – A developmental perspective* (p. 151). Cambridge: Cambridge University Press.

di Ceglie, D. (2021). The creation of a service for children and adolescents facing gender identity issues. In M. Waddell & S. Kraemer (eds.), *The Tavistock Century: 2020 Vision* (pp. 159–164). Bicester: Phoenix Publishing.

di Ceglie, D., & Coates Thümmel, E. (2006). An experience of groupwork with parents of children and adolescents with gender identity disorder. *Clinical Child Psychology and Psychiatry*, 11(3), 387–396. https://doi.org/10.1177/1359104506064983

di Ceglie, D., Skagerberg, E., Baron-Cohen, S., & Auyeung, B. (2014). Emphathising and systemising in adolescents with gender dysphoria. *Opticon 1826*, 16(6), 8. https://doi.org/10.5334/opt.bo

Drummond, K. D., Bradley, S. J., Peterson-Badali, M., & Zucker, K. J. (2008). A follow up study of girls with gender identity disorder. *Developmental Psychology*, 44(1), 34–45. https://doi.org/10.1037/0012-1649.44.1.34

Green, R., Roberts, C.W., Williams, R., Goodman, M., and Mixon, A. (1987). Specific cross-gender behaviour in boyhood and later homosexual orientation. *British Journal of Psychiatry*, 151, 84–88.

Jones, R., Wheelwright, S., Farrell, K., Martin, E., Green, R., di Ceglie, D., & Baron-Cohen, S. (2012). Female-to-male transsexual people and autistic traits. *Journal of Autism and Developmental Disorders*, 42(2), 301–306. https://doi.org/10.1007/s10803-011-1227-8

Morris, J. (1991, October 19). *On the sadness of living abroad*. The Independent, online only.

Skagerberg, E., di Ceglie, D., & Carmichael, P. (2015). Brief report: Autistic features in children and adolescents with gender dysphoria. *Journal Autism and Developmental Disorders*, 45(8), 2628–2632. https://doi.org/10.1007/s10803-015-2413-x

Steensma, T. D., Biemond, R., De Boer, F., & Cohen-Kettenis, P. T. (2011). Desisting and persisting gender dysphoria after childhood: A qualitative follow up study. *Clinical Child Psychology and Psychiatry*, 16(4), 499–516. https://doi.org/10.1177/1359104510378303

Wallien, M. S. C., & Cohen-Kettenis, P. T. (2008). Psychosexual outcome of gender dysphoric children. *Journal of the American Academy of Child and Adolescent Psychiatry*, 47(12), 1413–1423. https://doi.org/10.1097/CHI.0b013e31818956b9

Zucker, K., & Bradley, S. J. (1995). *Gender identity disorder and psychosexual problems in children and adolescents*. New York City: NY: Guildford Press.

Part II

Psychoanalytic ethics and depathologising gender diversities and sexualities

Introduction

Intolerance as an unconscious response to violence in the analytic field

Marco Posadas

Much has been said about the impact that psychoanalysts and psychoanalytic institutions have had in the lives of trans, queer and gender-expansive people (Saketopoulou & Pellegrini, 2023). Whether these are patients, clinicians, members of psychoanalytic institutes and/or psychoanalysts in training, harm has been done and it is important to acknowledge it. This is crucial work to continue building psychoanalytic theories and clinical knowledge that support our work as clinicians when working with LGBTQI+ patients and other marginalised communities. Throughout the four regions of the International Psychoanalytical Association (IPA), I am consistently asked the following question: how do we achieve institutional change that supports contemporary psychoanalytic clinical practice with the populations we serve? In Part II, there are three chapters with theoretical proposals that address these questions.

As an introduction to Part II, I would like to ground it in the psychoanalytic craft. Following the line of Bleger (1967), let me bring the focus to the analyst's technique and, more specifically, the use of countertransference as a clinical tool. I propose the use of the emergence of intolerance in the countertransference as an indicator for the analyst that the mentalisation capacities (Bateman & Fonagy, 2013) of both patient and psychoanalyst are at risk of collapsing. Having a blind spot in the countertransference, such as not being able to think when we experience intolerance in the analytic situation, operates as a bastion (Cassorla, 2005) in the mind of the analyst. It is behind that bastion in the analyst's mind where internalised prejudices hide.

Findings in countertransference research highlight the importance of a sophisticated management of intense emotions (Hayes, 2004; Hayes et al., 2011). That bastion, upheld by the analyst's internalised prejudices, sequesters our capacity to think about how to manage intense emotions in transference and countertransference dynamics. It limits our capacity to metabolise and detoxify the violence inherent in prejudices such as racisms and homotransphobia (Saketopoulou & Pellegrini, 2023). Furthermore, it obstructs our capacity to sustain silence by overriding the use of

DOI: 10.4324/9781003531333-9

the rule of abstinence with our anxiety. The flexibility necessary to think about the tensions in the countertransference for an effective psychoanalytic neutrality becomes stiff and brittle by clinical theories turned into dogmas. Without flexibility to think, the analyst runs the risk to identify with the superego, and unconsciously push towards normalisation/adaptation.

The bastion created by the belief that, as psychoanalysts, we are above the impact caused by prejudices in our theories and clinical practice. It puts us at risk of initiating or participating in an iatrogenic enactment (Chused, 1991; Jacobs, 1986). For this reason, working with racisms, homotransphobia (Saketopoulou & Pellegrini, 2023) and other types of prejudices (Young-Bruehl, 1996) in the psychoanalytic situation, demands rigorous attention to transference and countertransference dynamics. It helps us to know when we need to keep quiet as the voice of the analyst may not be necessary in the room; when we need to hold space for a long silence (the rule of abstinence),or when we need to say something to subtract what is useful from the intensity in our countertransference. As sophisticated and nuanced use of the countertransference helps to increase the effectiveness of our clinical interventions in the face of something that we have defined as intolerable for the analyst.

I propose to think of intolerance as an antagonistic response to the intolerability of the death drive. This can help us to think about the impact that intolerance can have on institutional life and on the development of psychoanalytic knowledge. This strengthens the analyst's capacity to symbolise and metabolise the violence that trans, queer and gender-creative patients survive. The impact that the psychoanalyst's prejudices have on their reactions, understanding and theoretical-clinical formulations when working with patients who are labelled in the analytic setting as intolerable can and must be researched (Posadas, 2023).

Both gender identity and its expression are fertile ground for intolerance. According to Mexico's National Human Rights Commission (2018), tolerance is defined as respect for differences in beliefs. Tolerant behaviour is defined as "an individual discernment to respect and accept the racial, political, sexual, and social differences of others" in the World Health Organization's 1995 Declaration of Principles of Tolerance (7). Therefore, thinking psychoanalytically, intolerance is the inability of the subject of the Unconscious to respect and recognise what is different in the environment and its surroundings. This inability includes not being able to recognise and respect differences within oneself. Intolerance is not being able to witness, legitimise and be present with what represents living difference as intolerable.

Borrowing the definition of tolerance from the French philosopher Ricoeur (1996a, 1996b) where he delimits it as an individual and collective virtue that is exercised in the space between intolerance and the intolerable, we can see a positive (+) added value prescribed to tolerance as a virtue. I find it necessary to think about the economic (libidinal) relationship between intolerance, the intolerable and tolerance to understand the power of intolerance in the psychoanalytic clinic, and its role as a countertransference indicator of internalised prejudices in the psychoanalyst. If intolerance with negative added value (-) serves as a countertransference indicator of the response to what we cannot tolerate in our clinic, then the intolerable is a form of plus de jouissance or an abject object that is experienced as too much or monstrous (+). Thus, tolerance would be the non-neutral but neutralised space, a remaining space of the difference existing between the metabolisation of the violence inherent in intolerance, and the violence of the intolerable (‡0). Unlike Ricoeur who defines tolerance as a virtue (positive value), tolerance from the psychoanalytic point of view is the ability to flexibly maintain psychoanalytic or anti-oppressive neutrality that goes hand in hand with the effectiveness with which we use the rule of abstinence, and our ability to remain silent when is needed even if it feels intolerable.

The analyst's ability to think intolerance in the countertransference strengthens their ability to metabolise violence, and not act it in the analytic setting. We act what cannot be put into words, in this case, intolerable violence for the analyst is usually projected onto an intolerable patient. This dehumanises the patient by labelling them as a monster (homotransphobia) or objectifying them (as is the case with anti-black and anti-indigenous racisms and white supremacy). The rule of abstinence and psychoanalytic neutrality are useful technical guides to prevent the repetition of trauma resulting from racist, homotransphobic and heteronormative actions of the psychoanalyst when they step out of their place and operate as an agent of the superego. Thus, reinforcing stereotypes informed by prejudice, and limiting the possibility of trans, queer and gender-creative patients to exist in our clinical settings. We stop listening to our patients when we expect to be convinced of our trans patients' pronouns, and/or when we benefit from the effects that white supremacy has on psychoanalytic work: the whitening of psychoanalytic neutrality, turning it into a white surface that leads us to violently eradicate the different in our patients.

References

Bateman, A., & Fonagy, P. (2013). Mentalization-Based Treatment. *Psychoanalytic Inquiry*, *33*(6): 595–613.

Bleger, J. (1967). Psycho-Analysis of the Psycho-Analytic Frame, *International Journal of Psycho-Analysis 48*: 511–519.

Cassorla, R.M. (2005). From Bastion to Enactment, *International Journal of Psycho-Analysis 86*(6): 699–719.

Chused, J.F. (1991). The Evocative Power of Enactments, *Journal of the American Psychoanalytical Association 39*: 615–639.

Hayes, J.A. (2004). The Inner World of the Psychotherapist: A Program of Research on Countertransference, *Psychotherapy Research 14*(1): 21–36.

Hayes, J.A., Gelso, C.J., & Hummel, A.M. (2011). Managing Countertransference. *Psychotherapy, 48*(1), 88–97. https://doi.org/10.1037/a0022182

Jacobs, T.J. (1986). On Countertransference Enactments, *Journal of American Psychoanalytical Association 34*: 289–307.

México Comisión Nacional de Derechos Humanos (2018). Los Derechos Humanos y la Tolerancia. Retrieved from https://www.cndh.org.mx/sites/default/files/documentos/2019-05/32-DH-tolerancia.pdf

Posadas, M. (2023). How do Psychoanalytic Mental Health Clinicians' Reactions, Understandings and Formulations Shape Their Work with Gender-Creative LGBTQ+ Clients? (Publication No. TBD) *[Doctoral Dissertation, Smith College School for Social Work]*. ProQuest Dissertations and Theses Database.

Ricoeur, P. (ed.) (1996a). *Tolerance between Intolerance and the Intolerable* (Vol. 176). Berghahn Books.

Ricœur, P. (1996b). The Erosion of Tolerance and the Resistance of the Intolerable. *Diogenes, 44*(176): 189–201. doi:10.1177/039219219604417621

Saketopoulou, A., & Pellegrini, A. (2023). *Gender Without Identity*. The Unconscious in Translation.

Young-Breuhl, E. (1996). *The Anatomy of Prejudices*. Harvard Press.

5 The many colours of the rainbow

Depathologising sexual diversity

Sergio Lewkowicz

Ailton Krenak, (2019), an Indigenous writer, in "Ideas to postpone the end of the world" wrote:

> We are definitely not identical, and it is wonderful to know that each of us here is different from one another, like constellations. The fact that we can share this space, that we are traveling together, does not mean that we are identical; it means precisely that we are able to attract each other through our differences, which should guide our life script. Diversity, not this thing of a humanity following the same protocol. Because, so far, this has just been a way to homogenize us and take away our joy to be alive.

This contemporary and complex matter is a real challenge for our theories and psychoanalytical techniques. About two years ago, I was invited to participate in a debate in Porto Alegre about the play, "The Gospel According to Jesus, Queen of Heaven", by the Scottish playwright, Jo Clifford, who is a transgender person. On the panel with me were the Brazilian actress in the play, Renata Carvalho, a trans woman, and the director, Natália Mallo, a cisgender woman. The play had already caused much controversy throughout Brazil, having been banned several times and sparked a wave of protests. There in Porto Alegre, too, it stood a risk of being banned, yet a court decision meant that the play could be presented, and so the debate also took place. The play rereads various fables of the life of Jesus, always offering a message of love, forgiveness, acceptance, and tolerance. However, the same play also triggered a chain of intense hatred, oppression, and intolerance. I do not believe it was a matter of having a feminine Jesus, because in the history of art, it is not uncommon to find characters and figures of a female Jesus, even breastfeeding. The issue seems to be precisely that of a transgender Jesus. Perhaps the use of religion might have been one aspect that triggered the reactions of hatred towards the play. Intolerance reached such levels of violence that the actress and the director were physically assaulted in the São Paulo countryside.

DOI: 10.4324/9781003531333-10

Yet the intolerance goes far beyond the realm of religion. A few months before the dramatic events regarding the play took place, there was an exhibition called "Queer Museum", also in Porto Alegre. This museum brought together works of art by different people in general – not necessarily by artists of the LGBTQI+ collective – and was also banned from opening and has been shut down since. A few months later, in São Paulo, philosopher Judith Butler was met with cries of outrage. She was called a witch, and a doll with her image was burned at the location where she had been invited to give a seminar on "The End of Democracy". Which, to say the least, is quite ironic, isn't it?

At present, there are at least 86 countries around the world that criminalise sexual practices, and gender and sexual identities. This makes being gay, performing in drag, or accessing gender care when trans a crime punishable by imprisonment or even the death penalty. A survey by the International Lesbian, Gay, Bisexual and Transgender Association (ILGA) shows that in at least 13 countries (or in parts of some of them) same-sex relationships can result in the death penalty. This group includes countries such as Mauritania, Sudan, Saudi Arabia, Yemen, Iraq, Iran, Afghanistan, and Pakistan. Then there are 73 places where homosexuality is criminalised, and people can be imprisoned. In some cases, high penalties of at least 14 years in prison or even life imprisonment can be imposed. This group includes countries such as India, Bangladesh, Malaysia, Ethiopia, Guyana, Tanzania, Uganda, and Zambia. On the other hand, we must also consider that there are countries where gender identities and sexual orientation are made illegal, yet not officially or on the record. Brazil, for instance, has the highest murder rates of trans people in the world. This data shows that homophobia and transphobia are still widespread worldwide. The important question to ask is why such violent resistance to manifestations of gender diversity and sexual orientation exists. The most radical descriptions go so far as to say that there will be a general contamination of young people and that this will represent the end of civilisation, or even the end of the world.

I define pathologising here as what happens in psychoanalysis when we consider the many non-binary sexual presentations as abnormal, and as the main cause of the conflicts that patients experience – for instance, by viewing their functioning as perverse. From a psychoanalytic perspective, we know that the development of psychosexuality is always complex, filled with ambivalence and, therefore, feelings of guilt. In fact, we all have some internal resistances to dealing with our sexuality and with the sexuality of others.

Attempting to understand this resistance within institutions, as well as within ourselves, has been a key challenge. Sexuality destabilises us and our theories may be deemed insufficient for the phenomena of sexuality that impact us today. We risk trying to apply our familiar ideas to account for these diverse presentations, which are actually different from what we have been able to articulate theoretically so far, and we, therefore, risk functioning as a Procrustean bed, considering that anything that does not fit within this theoretical model is pathological.

Attempting to depathologise gender diversity

In 2018, during the launch of the International Statistical Classification of Diseases and Related Health Problems (ICD 11), the World Health Organization (WHO) announced the removal of gender identity disorders from the Mental and Behavioral Disorders chapter. With this change, the term is now *gender incongruity* and has been inserted into the chapter on sexual health. This new classification comes 28 years after the decision that removed the term *homosexuality* from the list of diseases on 17 May, 1990. The WHO states there is clear evidence that gender incongruity is not a mental disorder and emphasises that this is an important step towards reducing stigma and discrimination against this population, and towards ensuring their access to health. Therefore, from a biomedical and mental health standpoint, gender identity is no longer treated as a mental illness, and gender identity and sexual orientation are, in fact, depathologised in the classification of diseases. Some progress, albeit small, has therefore been made.

Furthermore, if we look at certain historical myths, we will see that the difference between genders and bisexuality is not as pronounced as has been defended by the Western heteronormative culture of recent centuries. The biblical narrative of Eve being made from Adam's rib is in itself a mixture of bodies, albeit hierarchically ordered. According to Aristophanes, in one of Plato's speeches, humankind had three genders: male, female, and androgynous, the latter being a specific gender. We see it again in Greek mythology with Hermaphroditus, who was the son of Aphrodite and Hermes, and bore the name of both parents. Hermaphroditus represents the fusion of the two sexes and has no defined gender. The story goes that he was born an extremely beautiful boy, who later became an androgynous being after becoming entwined with the nymph, Salmacis. In medicine, the term then came to name intersex people. Also, in Greek mythology, we find the prophet Tiresias, who lived as a woman for seven years and was blinded by the wrath of Hera for saying that women had much more sexual pleasure than men. These myths reveal an openness to the complexity of sexuality that was later lost. In ancient Greece, except for the explicit prohibition on incest, sexual activities were not prohibited for male citizens. Sexuality only came to be condemned and prohibited with the advent of monotheistic religions (Lemma, 2015) and these prohibitions persist nowadays and have intensified with the rise of religious fundamentalism.

Generational differences

One aspect I see as important in helping us have a less pathologising view of sexual diversity relates to generational differences. A 60-year-old female patient of mine, a dentist, decided to retire. As she now had time to spare, she went to a poetry and literature workshop. On the first day of class, there were about ten students, of which she was the oldest. They were asked to introduce themselves, and one of the students introduced herself as a bisexual mother of a five-year-old. My patient felt significant discomfort, a feeling that became even more intense as she noticed how naturally the other younger students handled the situation. Apparently, no one had been shaken like her – and she does not consider herself a conservative or even a prejudiced person, yet she was uncomfortable. I believe this everyday example demonstrates one of the constant tendencies of our temporality, which is this discomfort towards new generations. Another example is the so-called sexual revolution of the 1960s and 1970s with the feminist movement, the hippie movement, and the birth control pill. Many young people were considered "abnormal" by psychoanalysts at that time, and some women were scorned as sexually active as "promiscuous" and diagnosed with mental problems.

However, it seems to me that this typical generation gap has become even more pronounced today due to the emergence of the internet and other new technologies. There are striking differences between those who are native to the virtual world and those who are immigrants to it. The media also plays a relevant role in showing several existing gender identities, and we are increasingly given opportunities to see new configurations in literature, film and in the arts in general. We should also heed the importance of the development of assisted fertilisation and the possibilities regarding body modification surgeries, which have created a true revolution as to procreation and gender change, all of which are significantly affected by generational gaps – whether we like it or not.

The diverse presentations of sexuality and gender identity have become more visible and more of a puzzle to be understood, which also triggers uneasiness and anxiety, often leading to resistance and further attempts at pathologising. We always have difficulty assimilating what is new, what is unknown. A study commissioned by L'Obs (2019) (Philippe, 2019), a French magazine, showed that 14% of the population between 18 and 44 years of age consider themselves non-binary and in the population over 45, the rate is 8%. Among the gender identity types that are endorsed by the French Academy are transgender, bigender, intergender, fluid gender, agender, neutral gender, pangender, androgynous, and others. It is these different nuances of gender identity that form the many colours of the rainbow.

Generalisations

I think everyone tends to think through generalisations. Matte Blanco (1975; Mondrzak, 2007) emphasised this notion by bringing a bi-logical theory for our psychic functioning, a view of the mind as a classifier, a mind that is eternally ordering both internal and external data that needs to be organised so that we can acknowledge it. He reformulated the Freudian unconscious from the perspective of mathematical set theory and logic-mathematical concepts, thereby introducing set theory and generalisations into psychoanalysis. He argued that the human mind tends to think in terms of sets rather than categories, which can lead to a broader and more comprehensive understanding of the individual and his or her internal conflicts. According to the author, the unconscious mind works symmetrically through generalisations. This approach has been applied in clinical practice and has expanded the scope of psychoanalysis, allowing for a deeper and more flexible understanding of psychic functioning, and helping us better comprehend why analysts tend to equate and generalise different manifestations of sexuality, and view them as pathological (Mondrzak, 2007).

Psychoanalytic theories since Freud have always shown duality. On the one hand, they rely on binarism and heteronormativity; on the other, they have a more complex understanding of psychosexuality, but they still tend to generalise and classify different sexualities. And yet, these diverse presentations simply do not lend themselves to this and are always slipping through the stiffness of these definitions. As Julia Kristeva pointed out at the 2019 IPA congress in London, we cannot generalise the feminine, we must consider each woman in her uniqueness. It seems to me that the same goes for sexualities. We ought to consider them in their uniqueness as well as in their specificity, while always recognising that they are plural.

As an illustration of such uniqueness, allow me to bring three examples of very distinct homosexual women whom I have seen in my practice. One of them demonstrated her gender identity through characteristics commonly associated with masculinity. She described having a strong identification with her father, a police officer whom she considered aggressive, and experiencing a great distance from her mother, whom she described as "very insecure" and "a weak drug addict".

Another patient conveyed a sense of ambiguity with her body and her sexual desire. This patient had an athletic body and said that she had "wanted to be a man ever since she was a child", when she imitated her male classmates wearing shorts and T-shirts. She eventually married a man. She described her father as very weak and her mother as an army officer. Her tattoos on her hands and legs, and her feminine jewelry such as rings and necklaces, which she seemed to wear to ensure that her body was perceived as feminine, drew attention to her. She eventually broke up with her husband and started a relationship with a woman.

The third example is a woman presenting with feminine characteristics, who says that she has always been attracted to women and never to men. She reports that her mother was only able to take care of her in the first six months of her life. After that, the mother began to suspect that her husband, the patient's father, was cheating on her and started blaming her daughter for her husband's cheating. She remembers that her mother used to drink and beat her up when she was a child. At the age of 15, she ran away and moved in with a female high school teacher who became her partner and initiated her into her sex life.

I think that even with an object choice for same-sex partners, these three women are unalike: they have families with very different configurations, they have distinct gender manifestations, and their experiences of suffering that brought them in search for psychoanalytic understanding were different. Each of them is unique and needs to be heard in her uniqueness. Please note that, even in reporting these cases, I realise that my descriptions demonstrate both my position as a cisgender heterosexual man and my implicit theories about the conflicts underlying their sexuality.

Countertransference

Heinrich Racker (1953, 1957, 1958) was the most original author on countertransference and probably offered the most comprehensive and profound contribution on the subject. Although he only began publishing his findings in 1953, he seems to have been one of the first to be concerned with countertransference, as he had been studying it since 1948 in Argentina. He held a totalistic view of countertransference, including its conscious and unconscious aspects. He considered that countertransference operated in three ways: a) as an obstacle, as in the classical model; b) as an important tool to understand the basics of a patient's object relations; and c) as an experience which the patient may draw on that is unlike what he or she originally experienced. Racker also described direct countertransference – with the patient, and indirect countertransference – with the patient's family, or even colleagues. Moreover, he also considered there are two types of countertransference identification: a) concordant, when the analyst's ego identifies with the patient's ego and there is a feeling of harmony between them and b) complementary, when the analyst identifies with an internal object or an undesired part of the patient's, such as the patient's superego, and there is a corresponding sense of disharmony. In addition, he warned that even experienced therapists cannot avoid complementary identifications, which he defines as the neurotic side of countertransference, and named this pathological expression as "countertransference neurosis", thus correlating it with Freud's "transference neurosis".

A recent and significant discussion looks at the notion that countertransference is not merely a creation stemming from the patient alone. The therapist's role must also be considered, that is, his transference in relation to the patient and to his own neuroses. This perspective triggers a review of the work of Heimann and Racker, given that the analyst is not an empty continent that will only be filled with the patient's projections. By the same token, the importance of self-analysis and analysis on the therapist's end becomes increasingly important (Manfredi, 1994). As a result of this shift, a new challenge arises, that of recognising how difficult it can be to separate which part of countertransference is a response to the patient, and which part relates to the therapist's neurosis or his/her personality, as highlighted earlier. Pick's contribution (1985) becomes fundamental in this context, as she explored the need for the psychoanalyst to do her own internal psychic work, and to consider how the patient's projections interact with the analyst's internal world. It is only after analysts have elaborated on and understood countertransference within themselves that they will be able to understand the role that the patient played in mobilising their own reactions. Manfredi (1994) states that we can experience countertransference through emotional discomfort, and that the first step should be to try to understand what role the patient has played in the origin of this uneasiness within ourselves. She also warns us to be careful in such moments to ensure we do not react by creating an interpretation that aims merely at getting rid of such discomfort.

Some contemporary authors consider that the greatest difficulty in therapeutic work lies precisely in the therapist's difficulty in tolerating countertransference. When the therapist is able to handle it, this may help the patient and even produce psychic change. It is about being able to better tolerate countertransference reactions, as Manfredi (1994) said, "Having a different, friendlier relationship with your internal countertransference responses" (137), not considering them as undesirable, but rather as part of the process of understanding the patient through empathy and intuition and doing the work of elaborating on one's own countertransference.

It is important to bear in mind that patients carefully observe how their analysts deal with their own internal reactions. If the analysts manage to contain countertransference, acting on it as little as possible, this could lead to patients improving through the re-introjection of aspects of themselves, which results more from non-verbal interactions than from interpretations (Pick, 1985; Manfredi, 1994; Manfredi, 1994). Similar to the descriptions by Bion and other Kleinian authors about the function of containing and the use of the analyst's mind in the therapeutic process, treating countertransference carefully is viewed as particularly significant when working with patients who have problems with symbolisation and, consequently, difficulties with verbalisation.

Another trend seeks to understand countertransference in the patient's reactions, rather than in the therapist's. Schwaber, Gill and Hoffman are authors following this trend, and the central idea is to try to observe an analyst's countertransference in the patient, that is, how a patient is reacting to their analyst and to what they say. This would be like looking for ourselves in the patient, allowing us to correct our interventions and even learn more about ourselves in the process (Manfredi, 1994). These ideas are close to Bion's statements that the patient is our best colleague, ideas which were profoundly expanded by the work of Ferro (1995) in Italy.

Other aspects regarding countertransference recently explored relate to gender and the life cycle of both the patient and the therapist. Different moments in life cycles as well as the gender of the patient-therapist pair, constitute different dyads and allow different transference-countertransference configurations to occur. Thus, it is important to consider not only the characteristics of the therapist's personality, but also those specific to the present stage of his or her life cycle, and how this entanglement of unconscious and conscious expressions is intertwined with the respective expression of what is happening to the patient (Eizirik, 1996). That said, and returning to the topic of diversity, it is my opinion that the greatest challenge that we face and must address when assisting diverse patients is precisely our countertransference. As I wrote previously, psychoanalysis has pathologised these individuals and the entire spectrum of the LGBTQUIA+ group. They went from being deemed psychotic to perverse and now to immature. This tendency to attempt to fit them into norms has been highly prejudicial and is very harmful for patients and for psychoanalysis itself.

As Kristeva (2019) points out, when psychoanalysis does not follow the sociopolitical changes of its time it loses its social authority. Or, as Cecarelli (2013) says, using Lacan, being in tune with the subjectivity of your time requires constant work in self-analysis/personal analysis. Yes, analysts can experience discomfort with patients who evoke a certain oddity, an unsettling strangeness as described by Freud, or perhaps due to the lack of aesthetic reciprocity, as described by Meltzer. However, it is essential that we understand that when we pathologise these patients, we retraumatise them, as they generally come from families that never truly accepted them.

Attempting to conclude

How can we understand resistance to sexual diversity? The first aspect that seems pertinent is that our mind tends to think in binaries. Binarism ends up repeating itself directly or even indirectly in our thinking. We have a simplifying reductionist tendency to classify everything in binaries, thus achieving more complex integrative thinking takes constant effort. When we are in binary mode, we tend to pathologise that which does not fit into either category. When our thinking works in a more elaborate way, we can integrate several elements, even when they are in conflict. In fact, we are always oscillating between binary thinking and more complex thinking. I think that Bion (1970) can help us understand this resistance when he describes the establishment's reactions of rejection towards new ideas and towards the people who bear those ideas. The new and the unknown mobilise intense reactions from our minds and from institutions - which also include psychoanalytic institutions and theories. One of Bion's examples (1970) is that of resistance to Jesus, as he brought new ideas that soon became very popular and thus threatened the establishment; he was eventually crucified for that reason. This brings me back to the play I mentioned earlier on, which was also about Jesus, and we can see clearly that, about 2000 years later, that same behaviour is still at play today.

Many of today's sexual configurations are not new and have always been present in the history of humankind. They are also common in the plant and animal kingdoms (Lemma, 2015). And yet, I think they are new as to their visibility and their demands for respect, understanding and acceptance. In addition, it may be that they are only now able to seek out health services and our consulting rooms for assistance, which ends up bringing them into sight and perhaps submitting them to even more scrutiny.

We could also consider this "new" as Freud's "uncanny" (1919): our own sexuality, which has been strongly repressed and even denied, and which reintroduces itself before our eyes. We know that psychoanalytic theory is forged in the culture of its time, as Freud's *Three Essays on Sexuality* reveal (1905). A striking example of this is reported in Rudinesco's (2016) biography of Freud, in which she describes how homosexuality was relatively well tolerated in Vienna and Berlin until after World War I. However, with England's victory, Ernest Jones suggested that homosexuality was to be considered pathological - which is indeed what happened. English culture, following Victorian morality and a more medical model, and using more pathologising criteria, started becoming an important reference in psychoanalytic theory. It is also worth mentioning the economic issues of the time, given that the death of millions of people in the two Great Wars, reproduction was greatly encouraged as a criterion of sexual maturity, even in psychoanalytic theory itself.

When I began my analytical training in the 1980s, homosexuality was considered a perversion, and the purpose of treatment was to convert the patient to heterosexuality. Trans people were considered psychotic. Though this situation has changed in the psychoanalytic environment, we know that even with the "acceptance" of gay colleagues in psychoanalytic institutions, there is still much to learn about sexualities. I feel that through this coexistence and exchanges such as take place currently, over the next few years, we will be able to better understand these diversities that have been left outside our institutions for so long.

I would like to finish with Freud's well-known letter to the mother of a young homosexual, as it demonstrates that, as early as 1935, there was already an attempt to depathologise homosexuality:

> I gather from your letter that your son is a homosexual. I am most impressed by the fact that you do not mention this term yourself in your information about him. May I question you why you avoid it? Homosexuality is assuredly no advantage, but it is nothing to be ashamed of, no vice, no degradation, it cannot be classified as an illness; we consider it to be a variation of the sexual function produced by a certain arrest of sexual development. Many highly respectable individuals of ancient and modern times have been homosexuals, several of the greatest men among them (Plato, Michelangelo, Leonardo da Vinci, etc.). It is a great injustice to persecute homosexuality as a crime and cruelty too. If you do not believe me, read the books of Havelock Ellis.

By asking me if I can help, you mean, I suppose, if I can abolish homosexuality and make normal heterosexuality take its place. The answer is, in a general way, we cannot promise to achieve this. In a certain number of cases, we succeed in developing the blighted germs of heterosexual tendencies, which are present in every homosexual; in the majority of cases it is no more possible. It is a question of the quality and the age of the individual. The result of treatment cannot be predicted.

What analysis can do for your son runs in a different line. If he is unhappy, neurotic, torn by conflicts, inhibited in his social life, analysis may bring him harmony, peace of mind, full efficiency, whether he remains a homosexual or gets changed.

Freud's letter shows an opening and does not criminalise homosexuality, yet it still pathologises, it still considers heterosexuality to be the normal standard. I wonder if 100 years later, we, as psychoanalysts, still believe it to be so. I wonder how the world and psychoanalytic theory will see this issue of diversity 100 years from now? I hope we can create a field that is sufficiently analytical to listen to this otherness that feels so radical to many of us. We must be able to try to listen and modify our theories based on the experience of people who live and express their sexuality and gender identity outside the binary standards and outside heterosexuality. We already have important productions along that path such as Foucault's, Butler's, and Preciado's, among others. In the field of psychoanalysis, I would like to highlight Jean Laplanche's ideas and the work being done in Latin America by Leticia Glocer Fiorini with her contributions to the feminine, the sexual difference and the Oedipus complex.

I firmly believe that the best compass to guide us must always be people's psychological distress, regardless of their gender identity and sexual orientation. For such, we must stop being guided by our resistances and our tendency to pathologise. Most importantly, we have to allow ourselves to be touched by the many colours of the rainbow to be able to effectively treat the specific and unique human being who sought our assistance, for that should be the essence of our profession.

References

Bion, W. R. (1970). *Atenção e interpretação*. Rio de Janeiro: Imago, 2006.

Cecarelli, P. R. (2013). *Transexualidade* (2a ed. revisada e ampliada). São Paulo: Casa do Psicólogo.

Eizirik, C. L. (1996). Masculinidad, Feminidad y Relación Analítica. In: *Psicoanálisis en America Latina – Teoría y Técnica, FEPAL*, pp. 119–138, Monterrey, México: Federação Psicanalítica da América-Latina.

Ferro, A. (1995). *A Técnica na Psicanálise Infantil*. Rio de Janeiro. Imago.

Freud, S. (1951 [1935]). A letter from Freud. *American Journal of Psychiatry*, 107(10), 786–787.

Freud, S. (1976a). Três ensaios sobre a teoria da sexualidade. In *Edição standard brasileira das obras psicológicas completas de Sigmund Freud 7*, pp. 117–231. Rio de Janeiro: Imago. (Trabalho original publicado em 1905).

Freud, S. (1976b). O estranho. In *Edição standard brasileira das obras psicológicas completas de Sigmund Freud 12*, pp. 227–270. Rio de Janeiro: Imago. (Trabalho original publicado em 1919).

Gilligan, C. & Snider, N. (2018). *Why does patriarchy persist?* Cambridge: Polity Press.

Justo, G. (2020, 19 de novembro). Pelo 12° ano consecutivo, Brasil é país que mais mata transexuais no mundo. Exame [Website] https://exame.com/brasil/pelo-12o-anoconsecutivo-brasil-e-pais-que-mais-mata-transexuais-no-mundo/

Krenak, A. (2019). *Ideias para adiar o fim do mundo*. São Paulo: Companhia das Letras.

Kristeva, J. (2019). *Prelude to an ethics of the feminine*. Paper presented at the 51th IPA Congress 'The Feminine', London, 2019, 24th to 27th July, 2019. Retrieved from: https://www.kristeva.fr/prelude-to-an-ethics-of-the-feminine.html

Lemma, A. (2015). *Sexualities: contemporary psychoanalytic perspectives*. London: Routledge.

L'Obs (2019, 27 mars). Ni fille, ni garçon: la révolution du genre. *L'Obs*, 2490 (Société). Retrieved from https://www.nouvelobs.com/societe/20190327.OBS2490/ni-fille-nigarcon-la-revolution-du-genre.html

Manfredi, S. T. (1994). *As Certezas Perdidas da Psicanálise Clínica*. Rio de Janeiro: Imago Editora, 1998.

Mambelli, F. (2020, Abril). Dossier Barthes: poétique de l'engagement. *Le Nouveau Magazine Littéraire*, pp. 22–39.

Matte-Blanco, I. (1975). *The unconscious as infinite sets*. Londres: Duckworth.

Mondrzak, V. (2007). Processo psicanalítico e pensamento: Aproximando Bion e Matte-Blanco. *Revista Brasileira de Psicanálise*, 41(3), pp. 118–134.

Organização Mundial de Saúde (OMS) (2018). *Classificação Estatística Internacional de Doenças e Problemas Relacionados à Saúde (CID 11)*. In press.

Philippe, E. (2019, 27 mars). Ni fille, ni garçon: la révolution du genre. L'Obs, 2490 (Société). Retrieved from Https://www.nouvelobs.com/societe/20190327.OBS2490/ni-fiile-ni-garcon-la-revolutión-du-gente.html

Pick, I. B. (1985). A elaboração na contratransferência. Tradução do. *International Journal of Psychoanalysis*, 66, p. 157.

Racker, H. (1953). A neurose da contratransferência. In: *Estudos sobre Técnica Psicanalítica. Estudo* 5, pp. 100–119. Porto Alegre: Editora Artes Médicas, 1982.

Racker, H. (1957). Os significados e usos da contratransferência. In: *Estudos sobre Técnica Psicanalítica*. Estudo 6, pp. –157. Porto Alegre: Editora Artes Médicas, 1982.

Racker, H. (1958). Sobre técnica clássica e técnicas atuais da Psicanálise. In: *Estudos sobre Técnica Psicanalítica*. Estudo 2, pp. 55–63. Porto Alegre: Editora Artes Médicas, 1982.

Roudinesco, E. (2016). *Sigmund Freud na sua época e em seu tempo*. Rio de Janeiro: Zahar.

Tort, M. (2005). *Fin del dogma paterno*. Buenos Aires: Paidós, 2008.

6 Towards a psychoanalytic ethics-based practice with transgender individuals

Alessandra Lemma

For many years, I have been preoccupied with the place of the body in psychic life. Body modification, the impact of technological developments on our experience of embodiment, and transgender have been areas of clinical, conceptual, and ethical enquiry. In this chapter, I want to share some personal reflections borne of my work with transgender adults and adolescents and argue for the importance of integrating psychoanalytic thinking and ethical principles to help us to navigate the heated debates that divide this field.

The exponential rise in transgender self-identification, especially in young people but not only, invites consideration of what constitutes an ethical response to transgender individuals' claims that medical interventions promote their well-being. In considering the relevance of ethics to clinical work, I restrict myself to a focus on medical transitioning because this is where we encounter the most divergent views within our own discipline. I only focus on binary and non-binary individuals who wish to undergo medical transitioning in order to minimise their distress due to the felt incongruence between the natal body (and assigned gender at birth) and the body they believe will be congruent with their gender of (self) identification. For present purposes, I am not concerned with the group more accurately described as "gender non-conforming" who often only seek partial or no medical transitioning.[1] However, the group who present for medical transitioning will inevitably comprise some gender non-conforming people who see themselves as needing full transitioning.

"Careless thought costs lives"

Thinking about transgender mobilises resistance on all sides of the debate sometimes making it very hard to listen to each other with an open mind and respectfully. Whichever position we take, it is impossible to accommodate everyone's idiosyncratic experience or viewpoint: siding with caution in affirming a transgender identification may be interpreted by one faction as transphobic whilst openness to medical transitioning as a viable option for some individuals may be judged by others to be unethical practice.

DOI: 10.4324/9781003531333-11

Moral panic can unhelpfully interfere with thinking, just as the commitment to being open-minded and liberal can gloss over the complexity of the issues.

In my attempts to "think" about transgender, I have relied on the wise caution issued by the moral philosopher Janet Radcliffe-Richards (2012) in her book about the ethics of organ transplants. The controversial subject she tackled is irrelevant to the subject matter of this chapter. However, what is relevant is how Radcliffe-Richards demonstrated systematically through analysing the debates on organ transplants how, as she put it, "careless thought costs lives". She demonstrated that how we think about an issue has practical far-reaching implications for those affected by the issue, whatever that may be. As we know, it is hard to think clearly about anything when we are in the grip of strong emotions. The question of transgender unquestionably evokes powerful emotions.

Identity politics set the contemporary stage for the epistemological privileging of individual personal identity narratives. An individual's self-proclaimed truth is the final arbiter in many debates, not least around the question of transgender. Although subjective or so-called "lived" experience is self-evidently important, if it is isolated from the perspectives that, say, research or psychoanalytic understanding can also bring, we limit our understanding of the place that transgender as a "movement" has taken up in contemporary culture. In turn, this limits the questions that we feel we can legitimately ask without incurring the risk of being labelled transphobic. The importance of triangulating different perspectives therefore underlies my approach to this area of work. I suggest that this kind of triangulation is an essential cornerstone of ethical practice (Lemma 2023c).

The heterogeneity of transgender identities and experience

We are hardwired to discriminate and frame everything in binary terms (Dutton, 2020), but this human characteristic is especially ill-suited for exploring transgender identities. I stress the plural here because this is central to my position: many of the problems that impede a considered debate in this area arise from how we use terms loosely. Transgender is a broad term, covering so many different types of experiences and developmental histories, that it can only lead to conceptual difficulties unless we take care to be qualified and specific in relation to claims and conclusions.

There can be no single theory about transgender. At best, we can talk about "patterns" or "subgroups", but the moment we pronounce ourselves without qualification on "transgender" as a homogeneous group we are on dangerous ground. Irrespective of the possible aetiologies of a transgender identification, the use made of the body and its modification to give expression to "identity" is shared by many individuals in this heterogenous group. This should not surprise us: for us all, the body is central to the construction and disruption of identity coherence (Lemma,

2015). Through the staggering advances in technology, we can now manipulate our bodies in actuality and virtually and hence our so-called identity. This opens possibilities for figurating the body in ways that enhance well-being, but we should not ignore how the customisation of the body can also signal problems that will not be resolved by changing the body or by *only* changing the body (Lemma, 2010). This is a general point addressing different types of body modification and will be applicable to only *some* individuals who identify as transgender and who medically transition. It is not an argument against the merits of medical transitioning in any absolute sense.

Heterogeneity at the level of presentation and phenomenology has been accompanied by a steep rise in referrals, specifically of young people, to gender identity services. Surveys aiming to measure prevalence have found that about 2% of high school-aged teens identify as "transgender" (Johns et al., 2017). These young people are also more likely than their cisgender peers to have concurrent mental health and neurodiverse conditions including depression, anxiety, attention deficit disorders, and autism (Becerra-Culqui et al., 2018). To date, we do not have a satisfactory account for this increase. It is unclear as to whether these trends reflect an actual increase in gender dysphoria, lowered thresholds for seeking help or whether more people are coming forwards because "being trans" is more out in the open. The widespread information available on the Internet may also facilitate quicker identification of the source of the felt distress, which spares people years of lonely agonising before they feel able to "come out" and seek help. The changing statistics and demographics could point to processes of social contagion especially amongst the young, but we have limited and poor data on this.

There are nevertheless four important trends that prompt careful consideration of whether self-certification as transgender may, at times, reflect other root psychological and/or societal problems that will not be helpfully addressed by medical transitioning. Taken together, the four strands of data I will briefly outline suggest that we have a *moral* duty to consider whether there may be psychological, social and/or cultural pressures that influence individual choice about transitioning so as to ensure that if this path is pursued, that the choice is an autonomous one in so far as we can speak about autonomy if we subscribe to a belief in unconscious mentation – a point I will return to shortly.

First, there is consistent evidence that cross-sex identity in childhood strongly predicts homosexual orientation in adulthood. Some people feel it is more acceptable, even "safer", to identify as transgender than homosexual. A risk is that in being "liberal" about transgender, we neglect the impact of internalised homophobia. We must safeguard against conversion therapy by another name through encouraging transitioning when, instead, we should be supporting the individual in being open about the direction of their sexual desire (Bartosch, 2018).

Second, children with Autistic Spectrum Disorders (ASD) are over-represented in gender identity services. Given that individuals with ASD are also more likely to struggle with uncertainty, their preference for unequivocal answers might not be best suited to the complex issues surrounding gender identity and this might be unwittingly reinforced by so-called acceptance.

Third, natal girls are now disproportionally referred to gender identity services (Kaltiala et al., 2015). We have no explanation yet for this overrepresentation, which deserves very careful consideration and urges us to investigate the role that social processes may play in the increase in referrals of natal girls.

Fourth, the number of medically transitioned people coming forward who now regret transitioning is rising (Entwistle, 2020; Jorgensen, 2023; Littman, 2021[2]). Their narratives indicate that some transgender young people felt they had not been encouraged to sufficiently explore their reasons for wanting to transition leading to later regret. Such accounts are compelling. Regret, of course, is a complicated psychological and philosophical concept that I cannot expand on here. Let me say just a few words about this. Accounts by de-transitioners that they have regretted the decision to transition provide pause for thought, but they cannot be assumed to be evidence that transitioning was, therefore, the wrong decision. This is because people regret their decisions all the time, and for reasons that are not necessarily related to the decision they took to transition as such, but its consequences (e.g., the impact on family relationships and stigma). The possibility of potential future regret, in isolation, does not provide, therefore, a strong argument for withholding treatment. The desire to prevent patient regret, for example, can be countered by appealing to the patient's autonomy, which includes the right to make decisions that they might later regret. Not transitioning, we might argue, could also lead to regret. Even so, experiences of regret invite us *at the very least* to consider what we can learn from them about how to best support individuals who face difficult decisions that carry risks and have uncertain outcomes. Moreover, as the accounts of de-transitioners accumulate, we are duty-bound to share this information with anyone considering medical transitioning because it constitutes important data about risks as much as any positive outcomes.

Keeping the body in mind

As a clinical psychologist and psychoanalyst, I have accompanied several individuals in psychoanalytic therapy and psychoanalysis from the moment of "coming out" through to their decision to undertake varying degrees of body modification, including full Sex Reassignment Surgery in some cases. I have worked with some of them for many years post-surgery. Throughout these experiences, I have witnessed some positive outcomes: these are young people who go on to socially and/or medically transition and, all things considered, this leads to an outcome that is felt by the individual to enhance their overall well-being, and I have observed their flourishing in many aspects of their lives. I cannot ignore that without long-term follow-up, it is not possible to know how these young people will fare, but it is important to stress the particular features of this small sample of patients who appeared to do well post-transition: in all these cases, the young people had been in individual therapy for *a minimum* of two and half years before they started medical transitioning, none had taken puberty suppressants, they had all struggled with body dysphoria well before the onset of puberty, they commenced transitioning when they were aged over 18 and they had relatively stable family backgrounds and support. Needless to say, turning 18 is a psychically meaningless threshold. A psychoanalytic understanding of adolescent development continues to be highly relevant during the transition between being a "minor" in the legal and healthcare systems and then entering the so-called "adult" world in terms of various rights and the decisions commensurate with those rights. It is essential to keep this *developmental frame* in mind when trying to understand the function of a transgender identification in an adolescent patient.

In my clinical practice, I have also witnessed painful disappointments and breakdowns following social and medical transitioning. I have worked with young people who fervently embraced a transgender identification and who were desperate for medical interventions. Over time the therapeutic work exposed that this was a "trans-itory" identification (Lemma, 2018). In the therapy, it was the adolescent's experience of puberty and of sexuality that emerged as "traumatic". I use the word "traumatic" advisedly because, for these young people, the re-presentation (i.e., the return) of the body to the mind at puberty was experienced as catastrophic and/or profoundly disorienting. This sub-group of young people, I suggest, turn to the modification of the body to create an illusion of bodily omnipotence. Here the trauma seems to be managed through a precarious "trans" identification, an unshakeable omnipotent belief that "I can control this body and do what I want with it".

In some of my patients, I have been struck by the recurring images in dreams and associative linkages of something "lost", "misplaced", or "missing". In these cases, transitioning (social and/or medical) represented a movement away from something in themselves that felt wrong or painful or traumatic and that had not yet been consciously recognised as such but was mistakenly attributed to gender dysphoria (i.e., a specific incongruence between the natal body and gender identity). Instead, it became a "missing" part of the self's experience. I have suggested elsewhere that the image of the "missing person" captures a core feature of analytic work with this group: it involves a search for what part of the self's experience is missing to consciousness, locked into the body, perhaps because it is not yet representable in the mind (Lemma, 2023b). Something that is "missing" not only refers to something that is lost, but also to something that we fail to note, perceive, or observe. In some cases, this reflects the developmental experience with a "missing" external object who could see and take into their mind the child's experiences.

The location of the "missing" part is not in the service of ensuring the young person "avoids" transitioning. The latter may indeed be what the individual opts for and what is best for them. However, it is important to safeguard therapeutic spaces in which it is possible to reflect on what "gender dysphoria" and transitioning mean for a given young person to support them in understanding and evaluating what is best for them. This exploration ensures that the original diagnosis of "gender dysphoria" can be deconstructed to reveal its meaning and function in the individual's psychic economy.

Just as with any diagnosis that brings the patient into therapy or analysis, it is only the starting point of a process of elaboration of the unconscious. Based on the young people I have seen to date, I am of the view that "gender dysphoria" as a diagnosis tells us very little about what is troubling a young person or what may help them. It does not elucidate what is unconsciously located as "wrong" at the level of the embodied self. Neither does it tell us much about what a more hospitable embodied form for the self could be.

The body in adolescence presents itself to the attention of the mind. In normal development the advent of puberty necessitates the integration of the sexual and aggressive urges of the post-pubertal body into the representation of the body in the mind, and so of the self. I have found that a core feature of analytic work with transgender adolescents concerns their relationship to the sexual body. The body is the primary site of inscription and meaning arising from external forces as well as internal, unconscious ones. It is also the site for the expression or silencing of sexuality. In the heated debates about transgender, all too often, we neglect the complex role of the sexual body and of desire in how we experience our gender. For some of the young people I have worked with, just as they enter a key developmental phase when sexuality is characteristically explored, the transgender identification shuts this down. This group of young people dismisses sex as something of relevance to them, as if the transitioned body they fantasise about represents a haven away from the turmoil of a live sexual body. We should be open to the possibility that the difficulty in exploring sexuality may result from the alienation felt at the level of the natal body such that it is only after medical transitioning that the person has the space to explore sexuality. This has been borne out in some of the patients I have worked with and needs to be distinguished from the other cases where the transgender identity functions as a defence against sexuality. In other words, understanding one's gender identity requires the integration of the pubertal, sexual, desirous body into the self's experience – it is *this* integration that matters, not that there is one "healthy" destination endpoint for gender identity and its figuration.

A vector that informs my work with transgender individuals thus concerns the *experience of embodiment* and the challenge this exposes: how to find a hospitable home in our bodies. As I have argued elsewhere, unless we consider this to be a central question relevant to us all, we risk engaging with the issues presented by the transgender individual from a position of observers to a challenge that we do not share. Rather, I suggest that we are helped in this work if we remind ourselves of Winnicott's caution that we cannot "take for granted the lodgement of the psyche in the body" (Winnicott, 1988, 122). Instead, we need to regard it as "an achievement" (Winnicott, 1988, 122). This focus provides a more productive, generative starting point for thinking about a transgender identification than any individual psychoanalytic developmental theory because it accommodates the heterogeneity subsumed under the umbrella term "transgender".

More specifically, I suggest that there is merit in recognising that the natal body is important psychically irrespective of what someone may choose to change in the appearance of the material body. Roger Money-Kyrle (1971) coined the important triad of the so-called basic "facts of life", which refer to undeniable features of being human, namely the universal initial dependence on the mother's breast, the exclusion from the primal scene, and the inevitability of death. Each of these facts is experienced by us as narcissistic injuries. I propose a fourth "fact of life", namely the inescapable fact of our embodied nature (Lemma, 2023b). This amounts to more than acknowledging the inevitability of death, which Money-Kyrle helpfully singled out. Rather, it is a sobering reminder that notwithstanding the significant advances in surgery that nowadays make it easier to modify the body, no amount of surgery or body-altering drugs can erase developmental history as it is recorded in the body, and no one is spared the challenge of accepting this fact. The way our bodies receive and incorporate the projections of others close to us and of society more broadly, the way our relational experiences weave their way into the nooks and crannies of our idiosyncratic form of embodiment (e.g., our posture), serve as a reminder that the earliest experiences are mediated by our bodies interacting with the bodies and minds of others, and are a constituent part of who we become. The prevailing norms in any given social milieu of how bodies *should* look inevitably inform our subjective experience of our body. The appearance of the body (e.g., its size, colour of the skin, a visible disability) in turn may leave an individual feeling that they "fit" and are valued in the wider social body or, conversely, the body's appearance is felt to "mark" the self not only as different but also as less worthy, attracting negative projections and social exclusion.

To avoid misunderstanding, my presumption requires some qualification. Suggesting that the natal body is important psychically amounts to the presumption that the natal body is, *for us all,* an unavoidable part of our narrative and identity no matter how we might later choose to modify it. In this sense, it reflects an acknowledgement of a basic "fact of life" and serves as a reminder that our personal history includes our embodied history. This does not mean that I either privilege acceptance of the natal body over its modification as the sign, par excellence, of mental health or that I consider continuity in the representation of the body over time as intrinsically more "normal" or "better" than an experience of fluidity and even discontinuity. However, the natal body and biological sex are core givens out of which our sexual and gender identities emerge, whatever changes the young person may opt for in terms of their name, pronouns, or medical interventions. Being open to, and respectful of, the varied ways in which an individual feels it is best, *for them,* to figurate their identity need not conflict with recognition of the importance of the reality of the natal body as a "fact of life" that has meaning and relevance for the articulation of *all* identity (Lemma, 2023a).

Exploring this "fact" is not in the service of imposing conformity to an analytic ideal of what is "normal" gender identity development. Rather, it is in the service of expanding autonomous choice and protecting the young person's right to an "open future" (Feinberg, 1992). This requires us to keep in mind the impact of the transgender individual's experience of "bodily disunity" on decision making. Lewis and Holm define "bodily disunity" as "…a feeling of alienation from one's body that coincides with one's inability to practically engage with one's environment in the ways one is disposed to" (Lewis & Holm, 2023, 3). They propose that this feeling of "disunity" may undermine the patient's capacity for autonomy at the point of decision making. I further suggest that a clinical focus on exploring the patient's experience of embodiment stretching back to the natal body and projected into the (modified) body-to-be is an *ethical* requirement precisely because this more integrated perspective is central to enhancing the patient's autonomy:

> …the experience of bodily disunity is normatively significant in the sense that, firstly, one can find the alienation from one's body "profoundly disorienting" … Secondly, it can…temporarily inhibit the patient from cognitively reflecting on treatment options or cognitively accessing their underlying values, desires, and motivations.
>
> (Lewis & Holm, 2023, 8)

As analysts, we have an ethical duty to respect and protect the patient's right to bodily autonomy and bodily integrity[3] and to manage responsibly the preferences and values that guide our work, often all too implicitly. However, striving to be aware of our values and respecting that our patients' preferences may differ to our own, does not mean that we therefore should simply affirm what the patient thinks is best for them without sharing our own perspective borne of cumulative clinical experience.[4] When confronted with a clinical presentation where the patient seeks relief from mental pain through changing the body, we cannot avoid engaging with the ethical challenges this poses. This is most urgent when working with children and adolescents.

Ethical considerations

In the ongoing debates, we find a recurring confounding of two independent questions. The first concerns the specific ethical issues raised by children and young people requesting medical transitioning. The second relates to how, as psychoanalysts, we understand a transgender identification in adults and whether we can approach this openly or only pathologise it. In the first instance, as I will argue shortly, questioning whether a child can meaningfully consent to uncertain and irreversible medical interventions (in terms of their potential impact on physical and psychological health), is a legitimate and important challenge to a "gender affirming" approach, by which I mean when the child's self-certified gender identity is affirmed by the clinician without exploration about the possible factors leading to a change in gender identification and a range of social and medical interventions are then recommended to affirm the child's new gender identity. I suggest that it is not *intrinsically* transphobic to invite a child or adolescent to explore what may be shaping their experience of gender or to question their capacity to consent to medical interventions; rather, such explorations are an instantiation of responsible care.

The second question is thornier for psychoanalysis. Listening to many discussions about this subject, I observe how genuine concerns about young people – which I share – nevertheless usher in through the back door, as it were, normative, homogenising assumptions about what is "normal" or "healthy" at any stage of development, and which I do not share. There is, in my view, a legitimate concern about one way of thinking within the profession that leans towards non-discriminate Pathologising of transgender identities, irrespective of age and irrespective of the question of medical transitioning. Such unexamined assumptions potentially harm people when they are held by members of a profession entrusted with helping another person to understand their own mind. The devastating impact of such normative violence can be found in our discipline's recent, painful history in relation to homosexuality (Hertzmann & Newbigin, 2023). However, in what follows, I will not concentrate on this important question; instead, I restrict myself to sharing some reflections on the ethics of gender affirmative care.

In many parts of the world, there has been considerable activism to lower the age at which young people can access services that support medical transitioning. At the time of writing this chapter, in the UK, after several court cases and service reviews, the national provider of Gender Identity Services located within the Tavistock and Portman NHS Trust, has now been closed. The Cass Review,[5] which led to this outcome, identified that once gender issues had been raised, children and young people were placed on a long waiting list for this national gender service. Once gender issues had been raised, children and young people's wider holistic needs were being neglected, with a narrow focus on *their gender-related distress*. The review has now proposed the establishment of new services spread across the country to ensure children and young people receive support much earlier in the pathway and has recommended that they should receive more extensive psychological support that addresses a broader range of problems to reduce the risk of diagnostic overshadowing. The option of any kind of medical transitioning under 18 years of age will be much more closely scrutinised and the review suggests "extreme caution" in initiating medical interventions before age 18. The UK position, whilst not an isolated instance, has not been adopted worldwide. It has been both praised and criticised. The debates about the merits and risks of a gender-affirming approach continue, and I now turn to this.

The question about whether we should "accept" or affirm, transgender individuals' claims about what will enhance their well-being can be approached from two angles: one more obvious, generalisable, but no less important and the other, more variegated, and hence not allowing any generalisations. I will first address the more obvious reading before exploring a more complex reading of "acceptance".

The etymology of "to accept" is the Latin *accipere* meaning "to receive, to let in, admit, hear, learn" (Lewis & Short, 1879). This underscores that "accepting" a person's account of their experience requires a willingness to take on board that account and give it legitimacy. However, giving an account legitimacy – be it the patient's or the analyst's – does not mean that we should necessarily accept it as true or superior to an alternative account. It simply means that it deserves to be heard and respected.

Productive engagement in a therapeutic process with someone who wants to transition medically relies partly on the therapist's willingness to "accept", as a starting point, that the transgender individual's beliefs about what will help have validity, not least because they reflect their current best understanding of their predicament, particularly their belief that it is the body that needs to change in order to find a more hospitable embodied home for the self. This point may seem self-evident. However, historically, transgender individuals have felt that their claims have been discounted and that they have been the object of "epistemic injustice" (i.e., when an individual's communications are undervalued in communicative practices) (Fricker, 2007). The patient's account of what troubles him or her and/or what is going to help, is not always regarded as having the same status as the clinician's account. This is because, for example, the patient may be considered to be mistaken about the nature of their distress and what will enhance their well-being. Current activism by the transgender community has been articulated in response to this legitimate "risk", along with a concern about the risk of suicide,[6] and has resulted in the adoption of a "gender affirmative" approach within healthcare.

In the first restricted sense of "to accept", this change in practice can only be considered to be a positive development that protects individuals from the harms of epistemic injustice. In the context of psychotherapy or analysis, an ethical approach to a patient's exploration of whether to pursue medical transitioning or not begins, in my view, with "acceptance" that the transgender individual has a unique perspective on what can make a positive difference to their predicament – this is true of any person, transgender or not. However, this acknowledgement does not mean that the decision to medically transition should, therefore, not be explored in terms of its potential unconscious meaning and function in the psychic economy. On the contrary, I suggest, exploration is clinically and ethically necessary in order to support the individual in making an informed choice about medical interventions. Yet, "gender affirmative" care has been interpreted by influential sections of the transgender community (including some professionals working in this field) as proscribing "questioning" of any kind of the person's self-certified gender and what they believe will help them. This type of "acceptance" is thus an altogether different proposition that makes assumptions deserving scrutiny, to which I now turn.

Well-being and medical transitioning

A fundamental principle of bioethics is that patients should be offered interventions that are in their best interests and support the patient's well-being. This turn in healthcare generally emphasised the importance of engaging in normative and value dialogue with patients, as well as in the exchange of facts, to identify what would best promote *this* patient's well-being in *this* particular context. Because it is the patient who is privy to their own values and to their particular life circumstances, relationships and position in society, understanding the patient's values thus becomes core to identifying the best option.

Well-being has become an important conceptual currency in ethical debates even though there is no general agreement about what constitutes well-being. One philosophical view of well-being that has gained traction over the last ten years is the "welfarist view" (Savulescu & Kahane, 2011). I draw on this approach to well-being for two reasons. First, it challenges us to consider that well-being depends on the values and interests of the individual. The emphasis on values distinguishes the welfarist model from other accounts of well-being such as "objective list" theories that identify particular "goods" (e.g., friendship) that are deemed essential to well-being. Second, and consequent to the first point, the welfarist model teases out considerations of what is best for a person from other disputed and poorly defined concepts such as "normality" or "health". This allows us to consider requests for medical transitioning in relation to the likely well-being of the individual who undergoes a change to their body instead of focusing on how the requested body modification relates to so-called normal functioning or health. In so doing, the welfarist model most clearly exposes the tension between the authority invested in medical and psychological "expertise" about what makes a life go well and the individual's right to choose what they consider to be in their best interests because of their individual values. It gives considerable weight to the individual's own desires and evaluations of their own interests. This is constructively challenging to psychoanalysis, where there are very clear positions taken about what is "healthy" and what is "pathological" development even if such positions are not always explicitly acknowledged. It is important to recognise this and the part such "positions" play in how we listen to the patient.

Values are idiosyncratic and subjective, hence, decisions about what is best can only be considered on a case-by-case basis. For some people, the risks associated with medical transitioning are deemed acceptable because the intervention is considered to enhance the psychological and/or social well-being of the person (Savulescu et al., 2011). However, even if we take the individual's claims about their well-being, in the welfarist sense, as an essential starting point, and even if we accept that a condition called gender dysphoria has validity, we still need to establish that the self-diagnosis ("I suffer from gender dysphoria") is accurate such that the medical interventions are more likely to yield the anticipated benefits. Just as it would not be permissible to perform a mastectomy, say, on someone who self-diagnosed as having breast cancer but, in fact, had bowel cancer, recommending Sex Reassignment Surgery on someone who self-identifies as transgender but may be suffering instead from an inability to accept that they are homosexual would not be morally permissible.

What matters to patient autonomy, I suggest, is the integrity of the reflective process that assists our decision-making, which might include psychotherapy/analysis, so that the patient's decisions reflect their core values, desires, and preferences. This requires a broadened view of how we conceptualise autonomy that includes the role played by unconscious factors in self-understanding and hence in decision-making.

"Acceptance", autonomy, and the unconscious

Earlier, I stated that an important principle of bioethics is that the intervention should be in the patient's best interests. An equally important ethical principle is that patients should make their own *autonomous* decisions about any interventions they are offered. Autonomy has been variously defined within ethics and moral philosophy and it is beyond the scope of this chapter to review this vast literature. Nevertheless, several definitions emphasise two features of autonomy that are particularly relevant to this discussion: "understanding" and the "absence of controlling influences" (e.g., Beauchamp & Childress, 2013).

Autonomy requires a concept and understanding of the self, that is, the being whom choice will affect. Understanding, as I use the term here, is not restricted to cognitive understanding of medical facts such as risks, but also involves self-understanding. We can only make rational, informed choices if we have at our disposal knowledge of all the facts relevant to the decision and the possible consequences for us of the potential decision. In applied ethics, the condition of "being in possession of all available relevant facts" (Savulescu, 1994, 191) refers typically to conscious facts and information. Approached psychoanalytically, however, we would want to specify that these "facts" should also involve consideration of possible *unconscious* drivers (e.g., wishes or unprocessed traumas) (Lemma & Savulescu, 2021). Even so, it is never possible to be beyond our own unconscious and to be fully appraised of its contents, but we can yet strive to know that little bit more, and broaden our awareness, which is one of the benefits of psychoanalytic work.

The autonomous agent needs to be somewhat independent of both external environmental forces and of inner forces. Our conscious choices may be limited by powerful *a priori* motivations that can only assist us in decision-making through second-order reflection and evaluation. When it comes to a decision about medical transitioning, this requires understanding not just of conscious facts about who we are or of medical information, but also understanding about what may be happening unconsciously in the mind that may be driving the decision to modify the body, sometimes extensively and irreversibly. All identities merit exploration of their "how" and of their "why". The "why" is not about Pathologising or preventing people from living the life that is most meaningful to them. It is one cornerstone of self-understanding that supports autonomy. At the best of times, adolescence is a turbulent phase. It is a time when we try on different identities and ways of presenting ourselves to the world, and our sexuality is developing. To understand the full scope and impact of a medical transition, we need to understand the full external and internal psychological context of that individual's changing body and the development of their sexuality – in this sense the "why" matters.

Affirmation or acceptance of that which is not, in fact, the truth is undermining of autonomy. If a patient holds a false belief about their distress, their decision about treatment is compromised (Beauchamp & Childress, 2013). A decision to medically transition cannot be an instantiation of autonomy if it is based on a false narrative that prevents the person from accessing the help and resources appropriate to the state that actually undermines their well-being. The individual's *current* wishes, no matter how strongly felt, are not always a reliable indicator of what will enhance well-being. By contrast, engagement *over time* in a process of psychotherapy may open new possibilities for greater well-being than that potentially afforded by (premature) transitioning. The reflective space that psychoanalytic psychotherapy or psychoanalysis provides is a good example of the kind of constructive dialogue that can support autonomy in decision-making because it is about helping the patient to understand more fully their own complex motivations and sometimes conflicting wishes. At its best, it is not about the patient submitting to the analyst's viewpoint of what they "really" feel, and it is not a covert type of conversion therapy (D'Angelo, 2023).

There is an uncomfortable tension between the current emphasis world-wide on gender affirmative care and psychoanalysis' concern with the exploration of the unconscious drivers for our consciously stated desires. Even though I have observed how medical transitioning has enhanced *some* of my young (and adult) patients' well-being, this fact does not lead me to adopt a gender-affirmative approach because I have also observed how for others it has been "catastrophic". I have carefully thought about my choice of the word "catastrophic" because it could be construed as whipping up moral panic or outrage, but clinically, this is what I have observed in more than one case. If we return to the original meaning of a "catastrophe" up until the mid-eighteenth century, it referred to a "reversal of what is expected", an "overturning".[7] This captures well the experience of some of my young patients for whom the anticipation of transitioning heralded the promise of a rescue from an inhospitable home in the body, but the subsequent medical transition was catastrophic in so far as it "overturned" the conscious fantasy, leading to a psychic collapse. If medical transitioning can potentially enhance a transgender individual's well-being, we must distinguish the laudable aims of avoiding prejudice and protecting the right of the transgender individual to self-determination from the unintended consequences of "gender affirming care", which depending on how "affirmation" is defined, may ignore exploration of the meaning and function of a transgender identification.

My work with transgender patients has prompted me to reflect more broadly about the internal position that is most helpful (to me) when working in this highly complex and emotional area for both patient and therapist. No doubt, other analysts would reach difficult conclusions or positions, but for me the therapeutic journey with my patients has focalised that the primary aim of psychoanalytic work lies not in any predetermined outcome congruent with the therapist's or analyst's explicit or implicit definition of psychic health, but in the provision and protection of the analytic space – one that privileges providing a safe space for the elaboration of the unconscious. This creates the conditions for the patient to discover the unconscious determinants of their choice(s) and so enhance autonomy. Understanding these individual meanings, which cannot be neatly separated out from the systemic cultural forces that inform our experience of embodiment, is not about pathologising or depriving people of their bodily autonomy. Rather, it is about understanding the unconscious such that any decisions about modifying the body are taken from a position of expanded autonomy (Lemma & Savulescu, 2021).

Psychoanalysis has an invidious history in relation to the prejudiced stance it took with respect to homosexuality (Lemma & Lynch, 2015). We must be careful not to repeat the mistakes of the past when we approach transgender. Psychoanalysis should never be used as a tool of coercion or conversion – however subtle – when it comes to individual choices about how to live one's life. That is not the role of any therapist. Psychoanalysis has much to offer transgender studies and practice. Like any theory, psychoanalysis has its blind spots. Much psychoanalytic theorising is principally grounded in the merits of renunciation (i.e., it is about accepting limits and loss). This orients the therapist/analyst in a very particular way to requests for modifying the so-called given body. From this vantage point, the modification of the body, in whatever form, can only be viewed suspiciously. Whilst a patient may well be deluded or in the grip of an omnipotent organisation when they seek to modify the body, we need to remain open to the possibility that this is not invariably so. Even where we can identify a history of trauma, this should not bias us to viewing trauma suspiciously as a necessary "contraindication", and instead be open to the way that trauma plays a part in acquired gender (Saketopoulou & Pellegrini, 2023). It is an all too easy sleight of mind to slip into working from the implicit presumption that acting on the body is always an unhelpful enactment such that the aim of the therapeutic work (even if not explicitly articulated as such by the analyst) is in the service of "rescuing" the patient from pursuing medical transitioning.

When psychoanalytic work is focussed on the aim of expanding the patient's autonomy through examining internal and external pressures, it becomes easier to avoid taking up implicitly paternalistic positions. Between the two poles of a so-called "affirmative" position and a "transphobic" position, lies what I have come to think of as a "trans-receptive" position: this requires an uncommitted position to what a transgender identification means so that we can be truly receptive to the idiosyncratic meanings and functions it has for a given person (Lemma, 2023b). This analytic stance applies to the examination of gender with all patients, transgender or not. We must not forget that much as we strive to be "neutral" or "uncommitted", as I advocate here, our own unconscious investments and anxieties may yet be operative and inevitably filter how we listen to our patients. No analyst is exempt from this ever-present risk in our work: we all have our own blind spots, shaped by our lived experience and irrespective of our stated gender and sexual identifications.

Of course, it is impossible to ever know with absolute certainty whether a decision is autonomous, and we must avoid infinite regression as choices clearly need to be made. However, if we accept that a decision needs to be at least substantially autonomous and substantially independent from controlling forces, then a decision about whether to medically transition should only be taken after a period of exploration given the potential controlling influences (internal and external) bearing on this decision. How long this period should be, whether exploration should only be "recommended" rather than being imposed by services, whether this should be the case irrespective of the age of the patient - these are all important ethical questions that require careful consideration and, importantly, they require active consultation with transgender individuals and the clinicians who have experience with this group.

Conclusion

The contemporary recognition of transgender experience has made it possible for people to feel less ashamed and isolated where before they may have been grappling alone with questions of identity and sexuality. However, greater access to online information and support and the affirmative approach can lead some young people to retreat into the short-term comforts of certainty about the nature of their mental pain without a broader context for understanding it. This may bring temporary relief, but it does not make the self-diagnosis correct in all cases. If "affirmation" can be said to have increased the visibility of the transgender individual's struggles and has reduced shame, it does not guarantee recognition of the idiosyncratic ways in which transgender are subjectively experienced in specific bodies with specific histories. Being visible is not the same as being seen (i.e., being taken into the mind of an "other" in all our complexity), but nowadays, these processes have become unhelpfully conflated.

Recognition is key to supporting transgender individuals because it is key to identity development for all of us (see also Honneth, 2007). However, recognition is not at all the same as "affirmation". It is about recognising the complexity of internal reality and how it shapes the experience of external reality. It is about recognising the pain that, in some cases, may lie behind the embrace of a transgender identification as much as it may be about recognising that a different form of embodiment enables some people to lead a better life. Recognition is about giving words to the unconscious. Trying to understand the origins, meaning and function of any behaviour, thought or feeling is not inherently an act of violence or oppression; at its best, it is the everyday work of psychoanalysis.

Notes

1 In the UK the most recent census data shows that 0.06% of the population identifies as "non-binary". https://www.ons.gov.uk/peoplepopulationandcommunity/culturalidentity/genderidentity/bulletins/genderidentityenglandandwales/census2021
2 The data is very recent, and we cannot draw firm conclusions, but to give a sense of numbers, a retrospective case-note review of 175 patients who medically transitioned at an adult gender clinic in the UK reported that 6.9% of patients detransitioned within 16 months of starting medical transition (Hall et al., 2021). Another study from a UK primary care practice found that 12% of those who had started hormonal treatments either detransitioned or documented regret after an average of five years (Boyd et al., 2022).

3 See Wicks (2016) for a discussion on the ethical importance of bodily autonomy and how this relates to questions of consent in minors. For an interesting counterbalance, see Chambers (2022) who articulates an argument in defence of the unmodified body.
4 See Kloppenberg (2022) for an interesting discussion of the challenges of maintaining analytic neutrality in this area of work.
5 https://cass.independent-review.uk/home/publications/final-report/
6 This remains a controversial issue in the field that I do not have space to elaborate here. In the UK, the latest 2024 government instigated investigation into the claims of increased suicide risk amongst transgender youth led by Louis Appleby concluded that: "The evidence on suicide risk in children and young people with gender dysphoria is generally poor. Most studies are methodologically weak, being based on online surveys and self-selected samples and coming from biased sources". (https://www.gov.uk/government/publications/ review-of-suicides-and-gender-dysphoria-at-the-tavistock-and-portman-nhs-foundation-trust/review-of-suicides-and-gender-dysphoria-at-the-tavistock-and-portman-nhs-foundation-trust-independent-report)
7 Online Etymology Dictionary.

References

Bartosch J. (2018). *Trans Kids: LGB Adults Come Out*. In: Brunskell-Evans, Heather & Moore, Michelle. (eds.). *Transgender Children and Young People*. Cambridge: Cambridge Scholars Publishing.

Beauchamp T., & Childress J. (2013). *Principles of Biomedical Ethics*. 7th ed., New York, Oxford: Oxford University Press.

Becerra-Culqui T. A., Liu Y., & Nash R. et al. (2018). "Mental Health of Transgender and Gender Nonconforming Youth Compared With Their Peers." *Pediatrics* 141: e20173845.

Boyd I., Hackett T., & Bewley S. (2022). "Care of Transgender Patients: A General Practice Quality Improvement Approach." *Healthcare* 10.1. https://doi-org. libproxy.ucl.ac.uk/10.3390/healthcare10010121

Chambers C. (2022). *Intact: A Defence of the Unmodified Body*. London: Penguin.

D'Angelo R. (2023). "Supporting Autonomy in Young People With Gender Dysphoria: Psychotherapy Is Not Conversion Therapy." *Journal of Medical Ethics*. 10.1136/ jme-2023-109282

Dutton K. (2020). *Black-and-White Thinking: The Burden of a Binary Brain in a Complex World*. London: Farrar, Straus and Giroux.

Entwistle K. (2020). "Debate: Reality Check - Detransitioner's Testimonies Require Us to Rethink Gender Dysphoria." *Child and Adolescent Mental Health: Child and Adolescent Mental Health*, 2020-05-14.

Feinberg J. (1992). *The Child's Right to an Open Future*. Princeton: Princeton University Press.

Fricker M. (2007). *Epistemic Injustice: Power and the Ethics of Knowing*. *Oxford Scholarship Online*. Oxford: Oxford University Press.

Hall R., Mitchell L., & Sachdeva J. (2021). "Access to Care and Frequency of Detransition Among a Cohort Discharged by a UK National Adult Gender Identity Clinic: Retrospective Case-Note Review." *BJPsych Open* 7.6: e184. https:// doi-org.libproxy.ucl.ac.uk/10.1192/bjo.2021.1022

Hertzmann L., & Newbigin J. (2023). *Psychoanalysis and Homosexuality*. London: Routledge.

Honneth A. (2007). *Disrespect: The Normative Foundations of Critical Theory*. Cambridge: Polity Press.

Johns M. M., Lowry R., & Andrzejewski J. et al. (2017). "Transgender Identity and Experiences of Violence Victimization, Substance Use, Suicide Risk, and Sexual Risk Behaviors Among High School Students—19 States and Large Urban School Districts, 2017." *Morbidity and Mortality Weekly Report* 68: 67–71.

Jorgensen S. (2023). "Transition Regret and Detransition: Meanings and Uncertainties." *Archives of Sexual Behavior* 52.5: 2173–2184.

Kaltiala-Heino R., Sumia M., Työläjärvi M., & Lindberg N. (2015). Two Years of Gender Identity Service for Minors: Overrepresentation of Natal Girls With Severe Problems in Adolescent Development." *Child and Adolescent Psychiatry and Mental Health* 9.1: 9.

Kloppenberg B. (2022). "What Happens When a Trans Patient Happens." *Journal of the American Psychoanalytic Association* 70.3: 525–546.

Lemma A. (2018). "Trans-itory Identities: Some Psychoanalytic Reflections on Transgender Identities. *The International Journal of Psychoanalysis* 99.5: 1089–1106.

Lemma A. (2022). *Transgender Identities*. London: Routledge.

Lemma A. (2023a). "The Seductions of Identity: Thinking About Identity and Transgender." *Psychoanalytic Quarterly* 92: 407–434.

Lemma A. (2023b). "The Missing: Exploring the Use of Photographs in 'Working through' the Natal Body With Transgender Youth." *International Journal of Psychoanalysis* 104.5: 809–828.

Lemma A., & Lynch P. E. (2015). *Sexualities*. 1st ed. London: Routledge.

Lemma A., & Savulescu J. (2021). "To Be, Or Not to Be? The Role of the Unconscious in Transgender Transitioning: Identity, Autonomy and Well-Being." *British Journal Medical Ethics* 49.1: 65–72.

Lewis J., & Holm S. (2023). "Towards a Concept of Embodied Autonomy: In What Ways Can a Patient's Body Contribute to the Autonomy of Medical Decisions?" *Medicine, Health Care and Philosophy*. https://doi-org.libproxy.ucl.ac.uk/10.1007/s11019-023-10159-7

Littman L. (2021). "Individuals Treated for Gender Dysphoria With Medical and/or Surgical Transition Who Subsequently De-Transitioned: a Survey of 100 De-Transitioners." *Archives of Sexual Behavior* 50: 3353–3369.

Mill J. S. (1910). *On Liberty*. London: J. M. Dent and Sons.

Radcliffe-Richards J. (2012). *The Ethics of Transplants: Why Careless Thought Costs Lives*. Oxford: OUP.

Saketopoulou A., & Pellegrini A. (2023). *Gender Without Identity First Edition*. New York, NY: Unconscious in Translation.

Savulescu J. (1994). "Rational Desires and the Limitation of Life-Sustaining Treatment." *Bioethics* 8: 191–222.

Savulescu J., & Kahane G. (2011). "Disability: A Welfarist Approach." *Clinical Ethics* 6.1: 45–51.

Savulescu J., Sandberg A., & Kahane G. (2011). Well-Being and Enhancement. In: Savulescu J, Meulen R, Kahane G. (eds). *Enhancing Human Capacities*. Oxford: Blackwell Publishing Ltd.

Wicks E. (2016). *The State and the Body: Legal Regulation of Bodily Autonomy*. Portland, Oregon: Hart Publishing Ltd.

Winnicott D. W. (1988). *Human Nature*. London: Karnac.

7 A history of reception

Falling apart as the ground for learning[1]

Oren Gozlan

With the emergence of new forms of gender variance, developing forms of community accompaniment provide gender non-conforming children with emancipatory possibilities. The changing landscape of gender and the greater insistence on and wider social recognition of the right of transgender individuals to decide how they want to live and how they want to be cared for by the "mental health" establishment push against the analyst's theories of gender. Entering gender as an experience we do not know, however, requires us to contend with our deep anxieties about re-learning everything we thought we knew, and this emotional situation is "catastrophic" (Bion, 1965). In this chapter, I turn to Stoller's famous case of Agnes, a case related to his change of mind about gender, to consider the question of transference embedded in the ways in which evidence is thought and presented. The question of transference is key to understanding current psychoanalytic responses to the question of trans as questions about gender become permanently entangled in current debates about age, nature, authority, objectivity, and the relation between biology and gender. Such debates are also places of resistance and where responses to transgender youth are already steeped in the cultural claustrum of ideality that confuses scientific "evidence" with psychological "facts". Revisiting Stoller's *nachtraiglich* thoughts on his case, I suggest, allows the reader to begin to consider their emotional susceptibility to the learning received about gender and its falling apart. At the same time, I present falling apart as the ground for learning.

Thoughts without a thinker

It is very difficult to enter discussions about gender, particularly about the figure of the child, without strong emotional attitudes and reactions, particularly at a time in which our theories have superseded the naturalisation of gender.[2] Phantasies of disruption, amputation, loss and contagion – all associated with transitioning – dominate current debates and fuel those who have not gone through gender alteration, allowing them to imagine transitioning as closer to death. These images also reflect the analyst's

DOI: 10.4324/9781003531333-12

attitude towards their own helplessness, when, in trying to think about phenomenon they may not understand they mistake their viewpoint on what constitutes naturality for a psychoanalytic viewpoint about development. Embedded in the fantasy of "contagion" is also a particular theory of learning: trans children are passive puppets of culture and, therefore, highly susceptible to corruption.[3] Such fantasies, I believe, cannot be addressed by any kind of social facts or experience. As evidenced by the use of these signifiers, clinical discussions on children are not outside of the imaginary, and the imaginary is a persecutory place, riddled with symbolic equations. What these images provide is a simplified view – and therefore a reassuring view – of a phenomenon that is far more complex and manifold, one that involves questions of desire, affect, and identifications as well as the human capacity for change; the right to be "someone else [we] were not in the beginning" (Foucault, 1982, 10).

When it comes to the trans child the question of regret takes centre stage. The dilemma of the child's autonomy and their capacity for agency structures this concern (see Bell, 2020, Lemma, 2021; Evans & Evans, 2021): what if the child changes their mind? What if a decision to transition leads to changes that cannot be reversed? These questions form a piece of anxiety: "Which emergency are we going to prevent? The emergency of despair or suicide or the emergency of regret?" A temporal dilemma bears on the question of regret in situation of gender; the fact that like many other decisions we make, gender is oriented by an agency one cannot possibly know in advance (Castoriadis, 1991). There is, after all, nothing permanent about our decisions and nothing permanent about gender. How can we possibly predict gender's fate? Like many decisions we make, we cannot project ourselves into the future and this paradox, which lies in the nachträglichkeit structure of gender also gives it its ethical dimension. It makes any notion of autonomy something that is assumed before it is known (Castoriadis, 1991). Decisions are something one has to assume in order to bring gender to existence.

The urgent question we are grappling with is this: how we are going to begin to think about children and adolescents beyond a hypothetical universal? What does that mean in terms of the specific kinds of demands that they are bringing to us? This question becomes much more complicated because we are also *in loco parentis*. We have a legal obligation then to make sure that the child is safe, physically, and also not harassed mentally when they come to work with us. At the same time, thinking with Winnicott, we may also recall that there is also no such thing as "the child". Like the Winnicottian baby, the child cannot be thought of outside the social apparatus on which the child depends. The "loco parentis" of the analyst may involve wish to delay or prevent the child or adolescent's transitioning may also reveal a certain moral dilemma which nonetheless remains unspoken: Can the analyst tolerate the adolescent's regret? Or to be more precise, can we pre-emptively eliminate all sources of regret in the future? And can psychoanalysis be prophylactic?

Questions about trans identities, particularly when concerning the child, are permanently entangled in debates about nature, problematising received conceptualisations of the relation between gender and biology. This is particularly striking in the current psychoanalytic engagements with the question of the transsexual child and the underlying premises concerning the process of coming into gender. Deep debates regarding approaches of medical and psychological care for an adolescent presenting as non-binary or transgender are vastly split. The debates[4] give rise to scientific research in search for evidence for and against gender-affirming care, and in particular the usage of hormone blockers in adolescent trans. I will not enter the plethora of debates structuring current approaches to transitioning, which I discuss in length elsewhere (Gozlan, 2018, 2022), or to the evidence presented. My focus instead is the question of transference embedded in the ways in which evidence is presented. Here, the question of authority and objectivity are entangled in particular ways as obstacles for learning something new. When anxieties arise over the impact of hormone blockers or surgery on the child's "natural development", transitioning can become equated with castration, particularly in assertions that the use of hormone blockers introduces a "disruption to the temporal link" with past generations (Lemma, 2015, 96), or as "coverup" for underlying conditions like anorexia. The naturalness of gender is a powerful construct, and the alignment of gender with biology confers on it a comforting timelessness and stability.

I want to pause for a moment to wonder, why are we so susceptible to this way of thinking? In part, this I believe has to do with our helplessness, but also with its defence – the omnipotence of "this incredible need to believe" (Kristeva, 2007). A helplessness in the face of one's own vulnerability is for Freud a primary position for the human, which Freud equates with passivity and femininity (1933). This position is also a condition of not knowing, of being unable to predict or prevent something from happening. Kristeva's (2007) notion of an "incredible need to believe" describes an omnipotent response to the helplessness of not knowing through a libidinal attachment to the dominant ideology. Our incredible need to believe is also a function of hopelessness and wanting something to believe in. This is where Stengers (2018) situates the allure to facts and the formation of a group psychology ("agree-ers") that in itself becomes a contagion of hysterical symptoms in the face of the fact that we cannot theorise a hypothetical, since it is a theory on theory. The agreement that stands in for certainty in group psychology defends against this enigmatic nature of transference and forecloses thinking.

Learning about situations we do not know or understand is always the effect of a practice of "learning to respond" (Stengers, 2018, 57). The capacity to respond, as Stengers suggests, leans upon the ability to know *how* you have come to know something. Otherwise, situations seem natural, where scientific evidence comes to be equated with a community of "agree-ers", as a matter of consent. There is a kind of fraudulence that is at stake, or at least a kind of blindness that "has become synonymous with objectivity" that works to quiet opinions down in the service of presenting a "united front" (32). Scientists, in other words, become "sleepwalkers".

I am thinking about Stengers' conceptualisation of science and her call for "slower" science - the capacity to pause and ask questions about *how* we have come to know something. Her ideas of an approach that is not hurried, certain or closed off to unknowability bring relief from the split ensconced in what is presented as evidence. The ideality of science within psychoanalysis plays out, in my view, in recent responses to developments in gender, and particularly, in current psychoanalytic discourses about the transgender child. The question then becomes, how can we have a conversation about how we are thinking about trans as opposed to what it is? This jump is difficult to make. It is a situation to where no one has any basis to respond well too because it is already in the cultural claustrum of ideality that confuses scientific "evidence" with psychological "facts".

The immediacy of "evidence" precludes agency, because it evades the undeniable fact about being human – the way we create stories about whatever it is that we confront and that means that our self-theorising is also self-authorising. That the self is both theoretical and is subject to theory, and therefore the stories we create will also be susceptible to the other's stories – to social dynamics, to family mythology, to childhood experiences – all aspects that permit a cohesive story. The binary of scientific evidence – opinion versus facts – as Stengers suggests, is also gendered. The subjective is devalued and becomes equated with femininity because it is "moosh" and formless, not so-called "hard". It is associated with small and is equated phantastically with the factual weakness of women compared to men. They are based on physical strength and capacity to dominate through power. The binaries are brutish.

Historicity

The *how* we have come to know gender is tied to the problem of what is transferred and how we *receive* ideas of gender. The question of reception and transmission of psychoanalytic theories is evidently bound up with the problem of intersubjectivity because ideas about gender are also places of unconscious psychical and libidinal investments. Reception of ideas refers to the history of our inheritance: our education, the enigmatic nature of communication, its inherent compromise, the impossibility of translation and subject to erotic traces of dependency that constitute transference. The question of psychoanalysis's post-war history is central in this sense to its dilemma of gender normativity and the medicalisation of psychoanalysis. Its post-Holocaust dispersal and in particular, psychoanalysis' arrival in the United States, created a move to the medical professions with its emphasis on biology, stabilisation of origin, classification, identification, a linear

notion of illness and health and a purpose of cure. Psychoanalysis' historical investment in normativity is seen in its treatment of homosexuality as
a pathology in the not-so-distant past. Among conservative psychoanalytic
conceptualisations, homosexuality was interpreted as perversion, and as
a narcissistic pathology (Drescher, 2008). It was also unthinkable that homosexuals could become analysts given the assumption that they have not
resolved their Oedipus complex, at the same time that the ideal of conversion to heterosexuality was thought as reparative. In this sense, psychoanalysis is not a neutral or ahistorical discourse (Gozlan, 2022; Magallanes,
2018).

In reviewing psychoanalytic theory in the context of history, I suggest,
we are also responsible for articulating how, and from which place, we –
analysts, students and teachers of psychoanalysis – are reading. Different
conceptualisation of gender reminds us that every time we think we have
arrived at a stable theory of origin, a touchstone of gender, we find out
that the touchstone is just a pebble along the way. Both affected by and
affecting its history of learning, psychoanalysis faces its own notion of
nachträglichkeit. Here, I am imagining pedagogy as transmission model and
hence about a mismatch, where meaning is deferred in two places, from the
sender and from the receiver. I suggest that the psychoanalytic pedagogy of
gender must consider the clefts between what is given to us (through cultural inheritance, education, parental unconscious etc.), what we receive,
and what we make of it. Another term for learning is, therefore, transference (Britzman, 2022), because our theories are also libidinal spaces, and
we are faced with the impossibility of articulating gender without being
caught in places of attachment, longings, identifications and idealisations.

In clinical work and in our institutes, these defences are animated
through a desire for a stable object that is known, one which can be either
be discarded or helped, attacked or rescued. The move away from the complex discourses on trans experience to its treatment, whose framing leans
on commerce and a known subject, raises the question "what do we think
knowing is about"? These are the tensions we face when we are caught
up with the possibility of opening our minds to something that cannot be
known in advance, to move into a position from which to ask: what makes
something intelligible? In asking this question, we face the challenge of
thinking about a new relation to an experience. The question is decentring
because it has not been thought before but also liberating because new
ideas can come into being. Our attempt at reparation of the dismantling
of old ideas will also suffer from the conditions of coming to know, as we
must risk destruction of something we thought we knew.

To consider our unknowability as matters of desire, as meanings that
return from the future and as passionate enigmas, also means that we
need to treat our theories as transitional spaces, as places of seduction.
Thinking of learning as a site of resistance and seduction also allows us to
consider the precariousness of the analytic situation and its susceptibility

for breakdown. The paradox we face is that the seductive nature of enigmatic messages between the analyst and analysand are repeated in the erotic qualities of teaching and learning, because learning is also an emotional situation. These enigmatic messages are untranslatable. Nonetheless, they may, at times, totally become directive in how we engage with each other. There is a fragility to psychoanalysis that also creates a paradox in psychoanalytic approaches to gender and non-normative sexuality. On the one hand, non-binary and trans undermine the dichotomous understanding of gender that sustains the institution's very structure and disrupts the fantasy of gender complementarity as an ideal with the proposition of an ethical encounter with intersubjectivity. On the other hand, institutes are themselves libidinal spaces and hence entangled in myriad anxieties, defences' ideality.

One facet of ideality posits that psychoanalytic education within the privacy of the institute – its classes, supervision, and private practice – translates to the way it functions in public spaces, in publication, presentation, and official positions. That is, that the changes of mind that occur in the privacy of the analytic space reflect or affect change in public discourse. The question of transference, movement, and consistency between private and public, and between the analyst's clinical attitude and their capacity to influence the sociopolitical situations outside the clinic touches two related problems: the idea that situations in the clinic are representation of the world as such, and the notion of analytic objectivity that does not consider intersubjectivity. These two problems are emblematic of something bigger – the future of the psychoanalytic profession that cannot get rid of its past. The question of psychoanalysis' future hinges on the condition for changing minds because the histories of psychoanalytic institutes reveal an unbridgeable gap between changes in approaches to gender within and outside the institute. Official positions made in the name of openness to different formations of gender do not necessarily reflect what is occurring within therapeutic practice, training analysis, supervision, and didactic classes.

Agnes, a story of adolescent agency and seduction

What, we may wonder, are the conditions that allow previous psychoanalytic understanding of gender to be disrupted? There are different ways to study transformation, both in the conceptualisation of gender and the resistance to change within our field. Psychoanalysis is a very intimate practice, and if we want to study the ways in which analysts change their minds to explore what constitutes openness, we must study not only the resistance to movement or shift in concepts but also the person experiencing the shift in discourse, identifications, and transference. In reading analysts' accounts of change, all we have access to are stories people wrote about their experiences. My intervention is an attempt to interpret their work while they are reflecting on their own change. One example is a change in the way I have come to understand Stoller's (1968) contribution to gender as well as his own transformation through the case of Agnes, an adolescent patient who presents herself as intersexed and who develops feminine secondary characteristics and high levels of estrogen despite having male genitalia and male chromosomes. The tension in the case involves Stoller's usage of the patient's story to confirm his theory of "core gender", an internal stable sense of identity, which he associated with a hidden "biological force," only to discover later that his patient was secretly taking effeminising hormones which she stole from her mother, since the age of 12.

While Stoller is often criticised for the biological theory of "core gender" (see Gherovici & Steinkoler, 2022; Saketopoulou & Pelligrini, 2023), the case of Agnes, in my view is, nonetheless, generalisable in the way that knowledge emerges through errors and interruptions. Gender in this regard is not an exception. The case brings into view the idea that a discipline such as psychoanalysis – which engages with unstable constructs, whose data is accessible only to the analyst, and whose conclusions cannot be subject to confirmation – cannot possibly be scientific. The case challenges the conceptualisations that render science intelligible (rather than the subject of science as such), because Agnes is an adolescent who has engaged in an *activity that determines gender* (taking hormones, stealing, lying, being seductive and getting her way). It moves us in this way to the question of agency in creating gender because Agnes is an adolescent subject who made a choice by taking hormones and by lying about it in order to get the care she wants. Reading Agnes as a subject of agency turns biology into an "always already" interpreted biology rather than a bedrock. It is a testimony to science's failure to capture the singularity of experience and the inability for scientific observations to be teased apart from its structuring phantasies. Stoller's famous case of Agnes can stand as an exemplar of what people do to create "who they were not before" (Foucault, 1982). Her actions move the reader's notion of gender from the dilemma of identity to the question of construction. Through a series of actions, an adolescent engages in an activity that determines gender.

Like Stoller, we do not know what it is that we are observing when we encounter our patient's narratives of gender, and the way we proceed is error by error. The case is an exemplar of how something may appear comprehensible, until it is no longer intelligible. This is also the condition of paradigm crisis, where errors form the basic way that scientific knowledge is created and then, theory supplants it. Agnes' revelation created a paradigm crisis that exposed the limits of theory, but her case is also a threshold to the idea that biology is useless in determining gender because gender is not transparent. It, too, is subject to interpretation. Her revelation crashed the system on which Stoller's views on gender were built, because if there is no essential biological core that expresses gender, then the "force" that brings Agnes to express her gender in a particular way is not biology but desire. Biology no longer explained what Agnes was doing; it rather became a matter of the pliable object of her desire.

The problem with the paradigm crisis is that there is an Oedipal structure to knowledge (a misrecognition that disrupts the sense of knowability) that produces a tension between science and its object of study. In Stoller's case, Agnes' revelation acted as this third. Stoller (1968) is aware of the psychical qualities to scientific knowledge when he responds to criticism of scientific observation and quips:

> Granted all observation is theory driven, nonetheless, certain observations lead to bridges that do not collapse, atom bombs, larger chickens, and shoelaces that take longer to wear out…. Of course, there is no such thing as reality, and of course there is no such thing as free will. But of course, I consciously choose to believe that I exist and that I can choose to choose… We are doomed not only to be chasing our own tail but to have forever caught it and never have known to let it go.
>
> (Stoller, 1968, p. 63)

Stoller's comment brings into view a notion of analytic objectivity that does not take into account intersubjectivity. Such notion is a situation of failure in a sense that it is grounded in ideality and what remains obscured is the transference whose *leitmotif* is presence-absence, a relation that is also incommensurable because it is made from the stickiness of libidinal investments and the passion to eschew anything that one is unprepared to receive.

Stoller's responses also threw into relief his capacity for uncertainty along with the ability to play. Stoller, after all, is a psychoanalyst, not a biologist. He is a very creative physician and theorist who listens to speech acts, rather than looking at cells. Though he had one foot in a normative way of thinking about gender, we can read him today very differently, in ways other than being the enemy of transgender. That is how Forrester (2017) reads him, and that is how I am reading his theories in this book. While great discussion exists on Stoller not changing his mind, I am struck by his experimentation and the disciplinary approach he has taken in his attempt to figure out the nature of gender. The question of whether he fails is secondary, because, like the reader, Stoller is also a creature of history. Nonetheless, through being affected by Agnes, Stoller's frame of understanding is also changing.

Changing minds

I have turned to Stoller's case not as a commentary about his patient but about the work of the analyst and how they may think through the analytic content the patient brings. The case touches on the broader question of the conditions for changing one's mind. How do our minds change through our encounter with a new subject? How are we, who may be in a position of gatekeeping, to decide what it is we see? Stoller lets himself be swayed by Agnes' presentation until he is struck by what he did not know. What I sense as I read Stoller's cases is a willingness to be affected by his patients and to change his views. His article is retrospective, and it is only in retrospect that he, and the reader of his case, come to know Agnes as a transwoman. Retrospect is a nachtraiglich engagement, and in this is why a film, "Framing Agnes", made by Chase Joynt (2019), a Canadian filmmaker who identifies as trans, is interesting in recreating a nachtaigliche fantasy about the case. At this point, Agnes is presented as seductress and very cynical. She plays with and flirts with the doctor figure. Joynt's film, in a way, is a revengeful fantasy where Agnes gets to push back against Stoller and Garfinkle, who presented as absolutely persecutory in the intrusive questions they pose to Agnes. Joynt is bringing these dreamy figures of the archive as he is dreaming the unrepresented history of pain in the attempt to work through it. The tension of taking it through revenge – reversing the hierarchy – involves the affect of a need to destroy, because of the consequence of the experience.

The case of Agnes dislodges any sense of stable origin once Stoller recognises his patient's active production of gender through hormones, attitudes, clothes, and lies. Reading the case of Agnes, we see in Stoller's re-writing of his case a kind of receptivity to change that hinges upon recognition of his patient's subjectivity and on the idea that his understanding of his patient cannot be separate from the transference. While his transference to Agnes can only be hypothesised, his description of Agnes' complexion – "peaches and cream" – gives us a sense of how the scientist's perception has to do with desire; a question that returns us to the dilemma of subjectivity in science that is a basic Freudian insistence. Agnes case, in fact, does not succeed in elaborating a distinction between sex and gender (Garfinkel, 1967). Rather, it reveals their slippery qualities. But it also brings to light the inseparability of theory and transference. Theories, Forrester (2017, 65) suggests, "[obey] the same laws of transference and countertransference as the analytic situation itself". In reading case material or theories, we enter a place of irreconcilable tension between sameness and difference because our observations are never outside of the transference. The analyst's transference to gender is played out in the tacit ideality of a coherent life history. The incapacity of the analyst to take their transference into account also suffers from this ideality, or what Kristeva terms "the adolescent crisis of belief" (2007). "Adolescent", because it characterises a zeal tinged with omnipotence in the analyst who is "in the know".

One gets the sense that Stoller cannot see Agnes in ways other than a little girl: "pretty young girl with a fine figure" and a "peaches and cream complexion" (Stoller, 1964, 224). Stoller's description attests to how he was affected by his patient to the point where he was able to submit to her lies. Presenting herself as intersex, Agnes gave Stoller a phantasy. Her motivation was Stoller's capacity, as a medical doctor, to provide access to medical transitioning. A paradoxical structure lies at the heart of this turn: in this scene, an unsaid expectation associates truth-telling with a certain narrative of self to make trans experience legible; so, Agnes delivered a "deceitful" phantasy on such terms in order to get what she wanted and to arrive at the truth of her gender. Stoller's discovery that his patient lied about being intersex and that she had been taking hormones moved him to see his theory of "core gender identity" as flawed. Another tension arises through this paradox: while Stoller used his theory of "core gender" on his patient's phantasy, he also realises through Agnes's "deceptive truth" that his theory of core gender was also a phantasy.

There is a dimensionality to the case that is very interesting and easily bypassed, and that is the fact that Stoller was not only seduced by his attractive patient but also by his own theory. This dimensionality brings us to Kristeva's (2009) incredible need to believe. It has to do with the very basic fact of humans as self-theorising creatures, which means that we are also susceptible to the other's theories. Our theories are significant webs that we have spun and are caught in. Stoller is able to change his mind because he can, retrospectively, analyse his desire. Through being affected by Agnes, Stoller's frame of understanding also changes because he must ask himself how he had come to know. His process marks a slowing down that occurs through what Stengers describes as "the presence of something that provokes hesitation and brings about another way of thinking, feeling, and imagining" (2023, 10). This hesitation suspends determined ways of thinking and creates an aperture that makes us susceptible to the assertions of possibilities we have not considered.

While a change of frame does not necessarily translate to a change of view (in changing his frame, Stoller's social explanations for transsexuality are still in search of origin story such as a dominant mother, absent father, etc.), new framing allows for retrospective possibilities. From a contemporary vantage point, Stoller's move allows us to consider social explanations not as points of origin or causes but as involuntary situations that are subject to interpretation and that push for creative solutions in gender. Stoller's writing of the Agnes case allows for a different interpretation of gender. With the realisation of Agnes' agency, questions of desire and libidinal investment arise. Once we enter, the topic is Eros, and we inevitably turn from questions of deficit or origin to phantasy. The question of agency offers a way to think about the patient's actions in ways that privilege breadth, understood as the dispersal of affect over depth – what lies behind. This mode of thinking is of interest when distilling the temporality of the analytic situation and the interplay between internal and external conflict. Unconscious temporality involves the dilemma of unpreparedness: In learning, experience precedes understanding. It is within the gap between receiving and learning that also allows for new translation.

Changing times

The case of Agnes touches on the conundrum of how concerns over the child's future, autonomy, and nature flatten the capacity to speak of gender as a question of desire - of livability, erotic pleasure and agency. Sexuality is important to psychoanalytic understandings of gender. Arriving at one's singular interpretation of gender is an affective process, and hence, it depends upon desire and libidinal investments. It is a universal challenge, not a problem for a few individuals. As a psychological experience, the biology of sex difference is laden with phantasy and requires interpretation. If we turn for a moment to Laplanche, traces of enigmatic messages, including femininity and masculinity, are implanted in the child. But their traces may migrate to gender, and also to sexuality and love relations, complicating the meaning of gender difference and the inevitability of castration, well beyond genitalia. Indeed, what is unavoidable for the human is being born, being met by the other and hence, the experience of separation and loss. It is also the case that the capacity for interpretation of "enigmatic messages" (Laplanche, 1995) is also narrowed by the nature of the symbolic codes. And yet, wouldn't we say that what is also unavoidable is the idea that we can make something beyond what we inherit? This idea is tied to a notion of freedom, because we have the internal capacity to imagine ourselves, as Other to what we receive. And in the late 20th and early 21st centuries, it is a freedom that we can elaborate through gender. Exploring the meaning of gender for a particular individual may be part of the analytic endeavour. Gender as such, however, remains mute: we can never say what gender is, aside from a screen of projections.

Agnes' boldness and deception emphasises that at a certain point, the social is so oppressive that something has to break and the only way to break into its defensive shield is to be outrageous, to shock, to perform the horror of what is experienced. An intermediate space between the self and culture elaborates psychic phenomena as a susceptibility for humans to create themselves from within a particular zeitgeist. Today's zeitgeist involves adolescent protest that is deeply tied to larger cultural discussions involving the capacity to perform gender in the way one chooses.

These intermediate situations between the individual and culture resemble the intersubjective space in clinical work, where we increasingly encounter adolescents who show a capacity to take risks and a desire for something beyond what is found. This capacity, in my view, is also tied to demands to be seen on one's own terms and thus involves ruthlessness (Gozlan, 2022).[5] As notions of gender shifted culturally, the proliferation of representation, technological advancements, and options for gender "allow for announcement and pronouncement and are an incitement for changes not only for the adolescent but, via adolescent demands, in the social world" (Gozlan, 2022, 471). The cultural scene of gender emphatically shifts psychoanalytic curiosity away from how we change our patient toward how our encounter with our new subject changes us and our interpretive capacities.

The radical change of gender, both internally and externally, poses a challenge to psychoanalysis, as it too is situated in a conceptual hybrid between its relation to the unconscious, and the more concrete ways in which gender has been thought about for decades, in and outside psychoanalytic education. The analyst's learning is itself a liminal experience because one is affected before one can grasp or understand. In this emotional scene, we are in a borderline world, between estrangement, the desire for stability, the desire to help, and the frustration of not understanding. The analytic relationship is at stake in the changing terrain of gender, because analysis is a *relationship* in which the analyst is also always in transition. What prevents relationality in the analytic situation with new gender formations? Several competing experiences in analytic relationships – curiosity, wanting to know, the wish to help, have the capacity to cancel each other out, and this takes the form of an "attack on linking" (Bion, 1965). One competing experience is the analyst's theoretical loyalties and the reasons for them. The aporia of gender might also create the conditions for an aesthetic conflict that is hard to bear.

The psychosocial dilemma of changing minds and the obstacles to it is an urgent question because we are now in a cultural war over sex education, sexual orientation, and gender identity. The odd thing about this war is that it is not specific to a particular area such as the military or sports. It also pertains to the police, the law, and the government. In other words, it is atmospheric. One of the dilemmas we face is that it is very difficult to talk only about gender now because gender is also raced, aged, sexed, and cultured. We can talk about the current condition of gender as *Umwelt*, and as soon as we look at the atmosphere of gender, we no longer talk about attributes or identities. We are talking about gender as a *situation*.

The analyst must consider, I suggest, the dissociative way in which transsexuality and transitioning are often taught – mainly as phenomena that concern only a few well-defined populations – despite the psychoanalytic insight that the conflict between identity and unconscious is a universal dilemma for the subject. This universal dilemma is not one that can be settled, implicating struggles with embodiment, recognition, and the tension between sexuality and identity. In positioning itself as an outsider looking in (e.g., in questioning the transgender's transgression of the "laws" of gender), psychoanalytic discourse obscures its own instrumentality in the articulation of these very laws of gender. As a science concerned with questions of subjectivity and the complex exchange between the external and internal worlds, however, psychoanalysis cannot stand outside the very scene of culture from which it has emerged. Looking at the apparatus of psychoanalysis from within the field requires us to examine its ever-evolving nature as well as the vicissitudes of its own resistance.

In the current zeitgeist, the analyst too might be compelled to transition their conceptualisation of gender in order to be relevant to their patient's demands for care. And while the analyst may not agree or understand these demands, he or she cannot stop or prevent them from occurring, partly because the analyst cannot fully grasp their own resistance to it. The possibility that some change of mind will occur depends on the challenge to the analyst's authority of knowing something before the patient does. The capacity for change leans upon admission of blind spots, and a study of the emotional susceptibility to the ideas received from one's education and the history of its reception. The ability for change is also subject to resistance. Here, the transference presents a dilemma for our capacity to recognise that our theories are not omnipotent or believable, only places of seduction.

A scene of seduction in institutional education relates to group psychology and to the vulnerability of dependency in education. This problem prioritises an analytic objectivity that does not consider intersubjectivity – the transferences to theory and to the institute. The seductive quality of theory also evokes the theoretical situation as what Laplanche (1995) calls "the anthropological situation," inviting an emotional fantasy constituted by the miscommunication of it. As long as we are in this situation of reception, we will be unable to know the nature of reception or the fact that something has been received. A nachträiglich understanding of things in one's training and in the clinic allows our previous understanding to be disrupted. Partly, this disruption happens through the capacity to be affected by our patients before we "know". But change of mind also occurs within a historical zeitgeist. The zeitgeist today includes larger cultural discussions involving the capacity to perform gender in the way one chooses, drawing from proliferations of signifiers that were not available before.

We see a psychosocial dilemma of changing minds about gender that potentiates the acceptance that one's discourse is an effect of one's history. We cannot study the reception of history, including the history in which the concept of gender has been transferred to us through our institutional education. We can only observe the effort of receiving it. This conundrum creates a paradox that applies to the relationship between theory and practice. Theory can only tag along to the situation but must not lead. Therefore, it is always out of step with experience. Freud is masterful in this regard, where he speculates about what he observes without being certain about the permanency of his observations. The privileged domain of psychoanalysis, Freud suggested, is the psychic world. Its uncertain and fleeting qualities can only be explained in the clinic, and this means that we must tolerate the uncertainties that structure it.

The analyst's mind is a "wondering mind" (Gozlan, 2022), but we are subject to our socialisation and education, and it takes a while to feel that we can comment on what is happening to us and what our impressions are. Still, this understanding does not protect us from having a break-down in meaning during the session, which is a kind of falling apart, in our own minds. Our transferences will bring current emotional situations into the consulting room, and that also means that thinkability will lean upon our capacity as analysts to create the conditions for both us and our patients to see what it is that we are confronting before we feel we must be confrontative in our approach, There are only a few places where the waiting mechanism, the capacity to take time, to contain the hyperactivity of wanting to know, to think beyond either or, is operative. One of these situations is education and another is psychotherapy or psychoanalysis.

The analytic notion of taking time does not necessarily mean, in my view, deferring action about transitioning. Waiting in this regard is not equated with not acting. It is, rather, an experimental form of action: creating in your mind what you might do, rather than doing something in the hope of having a mind. The child or adolescent might make choices that they will later regret. Like with any choice, they might survive their choices, or they may change their life in such a way that the fate of these choices will haunt them. That is true of any choice our patients make, and we have no control over the fate of their choices. Taking time in the context of analysis means, in my view, being curious about the ways in which time is being created *in* an urgency. That is, an uncanny time between knowing and unknowing. There is nothing the analyst can do in either situation other than face the question of how we are thinking about these matters of concern and where we see their importance. Freud gives us a very interesting model for thinking and that is dreamwork: the capacity to tolerate contradictions and the condition of timelessness. All those processes are essentially what some call "metabolisation" the way in which the force of experience constitutes the structures of trying to take it in. This is also a space of agency and autonomy. No matter what, no matter when, the reality of our body is always a problem of interpretation and theorisation. That is what we do with the world, and that means that communication is not a direct experience. If we treat it as if it is, then all we have is brute force.

Notes

1 Parts of this chapter are reworked from the article, Gozlan (2022), has psychoanalysis reached its limit in the question of the trans child and adolescent? *Psychoanalytic Review,* 109 (3): 309–333.
2 For detailed discussions of these difficulties see Ehrensaft (2015); Gozlan (2018, 2022); Saketopoulou (2020); Gill-Peterson (2022).
3 Discussions of the uses of the figure of the child can be seen in Young-Bruehl's work on "Childism" as well as in Gill-Peterson's chapter in Gill-Peterson's chapter: *The Cultivation of Queer and Trans Childhood: Eugenic Logics of Genetics and Endocrine Science,* in *The Queerness of Childhood* (2022).

4 See: Lemma (2015, 201); Gozlan (2018); Bell (2022); Saketopoulou (2022); Evans
   & Evans (2021).
5 As I suggest in previous work (Gozlan, 2022), features of ruthlessness (Winnicott, 1971) may come into play in the encounter between adolescents, who
   may demand recognition and rebuke insight, and the analyst, who may become
   preoccupied with questions about the adolescent's future: a worry over later
   regret, or search for an underlying causality.

References

Bell, D. (2020). First do no harm. *International Journal of Psychoanalysis, 101,*
   1031–1038.
Bion, W. R. (1965). *Transformations: Change from Learning to Growth.* Butterworth-
   Heinemann.
Britzman, D. P. (2022). *Anticipating Education: Concepts for Imaginary Work.* State
   University of New York Press.
Castoriadis, C. (1991). Power, politics, autonomy. In *Philosophy, Politics, Autonomy:
   Essays in Political Philosophy (Odéon),* D.A. Curtis (ed.), Oxford University Press,
   UK, pp. 143–174.
Drescher, J. (2008). A history of homosexuality and organized psychoanalysis. *Jour-
   nal of the American Academy of Psychoanalysis and Dynamic Psychiatry* 36(3): 443–
   460. https://doi.org/10.1521/jaap.2008.36.3.443
Ehrensaft, D. (2015). Listening and learning from gender nonconforming children.
   Psychoanalytic Study of the Child 68: 28–56.
Evans, S., & Evans, M. (2021). *Gender Dysphoria: A Therapeutic Model for Working With
   Children, Adolescents and Young Adults.* Bicester, UK: Phoenix Publishing House.
Forrester, J. (2017). *Thinking in Cases.* Cambridge: Polity Press.
Foucault, M. (1982). Truth, power, self: Interview by R. Martin. In *Technologies of the
   Self: A Seminar With Michel Foucault,* L.H. Martin, H. Gutman, & P.H. Hutton (eds.)
   Amherst: University of Massachusetts Press, 1988, pp. 9–15.
Freud S. (1933). *Femininity*: New Introductory Lectures on Psychoanalysis. Stand-
   ard Edition, 22, 112–135
Garfinkel, H. (1967). *Studies in Ethnomethodology.* Englewood Cliffs, NJ: Prentice
   Hall.
Gherovici, P., & Steinkoler, M. (Eds.). (2022). Psychoanalysis, Gender, and Sexu-
   alities: From Feminism to Trans* (1st ed.). Routledge. https://doi.org/10.4324/
   9781003284888
Gozlan, O. (2018). From continuity to contiguity: A response to the fraught tempo-
   rality of gender. *Psychoanalytic Review* 105(1): 1–29.
Gozlan, O. (2022). Has psychoanalysis reached its limits in the question of the trans
   child and adolescent? *Psychoanalytic Review* 109: 309–332.
Gozlan, O. (2022). Adolescent ruthlessness and the transitioning of the analyst's
   mind. *Journal of the American Psychoanalytic Association* 70(3): 459–484. https://
   doi.org/10.1177/00030651221104483
Joynt, C. (Director). (2022). *Framing Agnes* [Documentary feature]. Canada: Fae Pic-
   tures and Level Film.
Kristeva, J. (2007). Adolescence, a syndrome of ideality. *Psychoanalytic Review* 94:
   715–725.
Kristeva, J. (2009). *This Incredible Need to Believe,* transl. B. Brahic. New York: Columbia
   University Press.
Laplanche, J. (1995). Seduction, persecution, revelation. *The International Journal of
   Psychoanalysis* 76: 663–682.

Lemma, A. (2015). *Minding the Body: The Body in Psychoanalysis and Beyond*. London, UK: Routledge.

Lemma, A. (2018). Trans-itory identities: Some psychoanalytic reflections on transgender identities. *The International Journal of Psychoanalysis* 99(5): 1089–1106.

Lemma, A. (2021). *Transgender Identities: A Contemporary Introduction*. UK: Routledge.

Magallanes, F. (2018). The oedipal complex and the oedipal myth. In *Psychoanalysis, the Body, and the Oedipal Plot* (1st ed.). UK: Routledge.

Saketopoulou, A. (2020). Thinking psychoanalytically, thinking better: Reflections on transgender. *International Journal of Psychoanalysis* 101: 1019–1030.

Saketopoulou, A., & Pelegrini, A. (2023). *Gender Without Identity*. New York: The Unconscious in Translation.

Stengers, I. (2018). *Another Science Is Possible: A Manifesto for Slow Science*. Cambridge: Polity Press.

Stoller, R.J. (1964). A contribution to the study of gender identity. *International Journal of Psychoanalysis* 45: 220–226.

Stoller, R.J. (1968). A further contribution to the study of gender identity. *International Journal of Psychoanalysis* 49: 364–368.

Winnicott, D.W. (1971). *Playing In Reality*. London: Routledge.

Part III
In search of complexity

Introduction

Nicolas Evzonas

Gender is a matter of complexity rather than controversy. By complexity, I mean the epistemological paradigm used in physics (Prigogine, 1980), philosophy (Morin, 2007) and, more recently, psychoanalysis (Glocer Fiorini, 2017). Contrary to the exclusive dualism stemming from the logical reasoning of Aristotle, complex thinking accepts heterogeneity, even if it does not always put forward a dialectical synthesis. Rather than limiting itself to binary polarities, it relies on an inclusive logic in which a third element is inserted into the dual opposition. The underlying thread of the three chapters presented here is indeed complexity, which shares affinities with deconstruction as originally conceptualised by Derrida (1967/1976). In the field of psychoanalysis, the paradigm of complexity can contribute to the de-essentialisation of theory and the de-normatisation of clinical practice.

One of the most prominent manifestations of decomplexified thinking is the obsession with the etiopathogenesis of sexual and gender diversity – and transness in particular – as typified in the book of Evans and Evans (2021), critiqued by Avgi Saketopoulou in her chapter. Family conflicts, identification with a dead sibling, unresolved grief, internalised homophobia or misogyny are evoked as the "causes" of socially nonconforming identities. The radical banishment of the "why" question in favour of the "how" homosexual or "how" transgender, as promoted by some queer analysts (Corbett, 2009; Hansbury, 2017), can likewise be problematic. Physicist Markus Reiner (1932) pointed out the confusion arising early in the history of psychoanalysis between determinism and causality. Dominique Scarfone (2019, 42) has the merit of distinguishing between these two notions:

> [Determinism] is undeniable, but unlike the idea of causality, it leaves a margin of indeterminacy in which contingent, even random factors also come into play, factors that can only be discussed in the après-coup. The force of the earth's gravity may determine

DOI: 10.4324/9781003531333-14

the collapse of a bridge, but it does not cause it in the same way as the contingent explosion of dynamite that shatters its pillars. This is good news for humans. It means that as the receiver of the gender message, he or she can, in most cases, enjoy the relative freedom of translation or repression, a freedom that is nonetheless not consciously experienced. Let us call this phenomenon, in the manner of the statisticians, "objective degrees of freedom," which appear in a process involving both unconscious and social determinisms

(My translation)

Unconscious determinism or rather overdetermination, to borrow the Freudian term, plunges us into the heart of the complexity paradigm. In contrast to a linear, causal and normative approach according to which a particular factor or event leads to gender dysphoria or a deviant identity, exploring the multiple and complex determinants of subjectivisation can prove to be a genuine therapeutic lever. When therapists do not show excessive curiosity about their analysands' gender and welcome all enunciated signifiers with equal interest, patients spontaneously establish connections between their gender identity and childhood experiences, thus complexifying both the "why" and the "how" of their gendered subjectivity. As Adrienne Harris argues in a Laplanchian vein in this edited book, suffering diminishes when we are able to attribute new meanings to our life trajectory and create new narratives about our past.

Given the complex overdetermination of gender, how can we apprehend the standardised and oversimplified wrong-body narrative? It is first important to grasp the impact of the setting that encompasses a discourse. This biologically driven tale is most often deployed within public gender clinics seeking "evidence" of transness, or it is put forward by activists for political purposes. Asserting that homosexuality or trans identities are innate is a way of protesting against normative approaches and conversion therapies. "We were born this way, and we have no choice." Whether or not this theory is accurate, the militant approach is underpinned by a clear goal: putting an end to discrimination, exclusion, and persecution.

Although this logic is perfectly understandable, it is essential to preserve the freedom to think without being hindered by ideological prohibitions extrinsic to the clinic, which tend to conflate problematisation with pathologisation. Let us not forget that the patients who enter our offices, whatever their gender identifications, ultimately express their suffering caused by pathogenic mechanisms, which we need to identify and elaborate on. Hence, a totally depathologising approach as advocated by the proponents of an overly trans-affirmative model, conceals certain therapeutic risks. For instance, excessive empathy shown towards systemic violence and the denial of all pathogenesis in atypically gendered patients may prevent us from hearing their primary anxieties or even some unrepresented psychotic elements that need to be symbolised and historicised.

In her chapter, Dana Amir tackles the issue of psychosis, the most emblematic and traumatic "diagnostic insult" (Ayouch, 2015) in the history of trans. The unfortunate association between trans subjects and this overloaded signifier has its origins in the Lacanian rereading of the Freudian Schreber case, a magistrate who, in his delirium, imagined himself as a woman penetrated by God. The "transsexual jouissance" described by Lacan (1958) in the context of Schreber's psychotic breakdown prepared the breeding ground for an efflorescence of theories concerning "transsexual madness": the confusion between the signifier (phallus) and the organ (penis), the failure of representational capacities, and the collapse of symbolic castration into surgical emasculation. In an attempt to depathologise transness, Patricia Gherovici (2017) presents the Lacanian notion of the "sinthome," which provides a creative solution for trans subjects to exist as well as for any individual dealing with their symptom. However, Gherovici involuntarily reconnects with the notorious notion of psychosis, since Lacan (1975–1976) theorised the sinthome in the context of Joyce's foreclosure of the Name-of-the-Father, or in other words, the failure to integrate the paternal function.

What may be problematic is the pathognomonic approach to trans identities, that is, the promise of transness as a psychotic, sinthomatic, hysterical, perverse, or any other solution. How can we reduce the colourful mosaic of patients with hybrid becomings to a homogeneous group bound together by ontological suffering? Asserting that all trans people are psychotic is just as perilous from an analytical point of view as claiming that they are all devoid of psychosis, which would deprive those concerned of adequate care. The psychoanalytic method is defined by the uniqueness of each and every case as well as the singularity of the subject. Consequently, any generalisation, whether positive or negative, should be avoided.

Dana Amir's courageous contribution in this chapter suggests that a transgender person, like any individual, can present psychotic traits with symbolising deficiencies or, on the contrary, they can have a psychic structure with flourishing abilities of symbolisation. In short, she abolishes the discrimination between trans, cis, or otherwise identified analysands. Does gender dysphoria or gender euphoria not affect everyone to a certain degree? It is worth recalling here the plethora of cis patients who suffer due to their image of masculinity or femininity. What about some cis-male perpetrators of sexual crimes, whose hypermasculine identification often conceals the visceral fear of the feminine and an unprecedented gender malaise (Corbett et al., 2014)? By way of contrast, let me mention the excitement born from certain states of transitioning tantamount to "gender euphoria." In short, the authors in this Part de-exceptionalise transness, regardless of whether it relates to healthy or pathological states of mind. Ultimately, gender diverse and gender creative people are no different from other analysands.

That said, we should not overlook the fact that certain transitions, detransitions, or retransitions are influenced by our overly medicalised culture. While access to contemporary somatic health care is a great privilege in Western societies, medical imperialism often threatens to bypass psychic work or even to freeze the thinking process. In some cases, body transformations are promised as magical solutions to suffering, even though a working-through of psychic material might have proved more beneficial.

Attention, however, as the aforementioned cases cannot be transposed to other patients for whom hormonal and surgical gender procedures are a matter of life and death, as argued by Avgi Saketopoulou here. Preventing such patients from moving in this direction, for the sake of normativity, only increases the risk of suicide. Lending an attentive ear to these subjects, we can understand that medically assisted gender transition primarily refers to a transition from unviability to livability. Accordingly, medical treatments should not be hastily equated with pathological acting out. Just as Emily Kurilof (2005) reminds us that there are words equivalent to actions and that actions can lead to the flourishing of thinking, Dana Amir here differentiates acting out from meaningful actions, which opens into symbolisation. Acting through the body can sometimes be the only way to cope with psychic conflicts. As analysts, our duty is to help patients transform every type of action into a signifying narrative and livable experience, hence, the opposition of the authors here to the dualistic argument according to which analysis and body modifications (including trans surgery) are mutually exclusive.

Let us underscore that binary logic is exclusive insofar as it excludes the third element, resulting in a straightforward choice between two opposing and contradictory assertions. As the three authors illustrate in their contributions, the logic of complexity, which fights against polarisation and taking sides, can prove fruitful in the understanding of gender, since it adopts a polyphonic and holistic view that is less prone to extremist positions intrinsically hindered by blind spots. Given the psychic diversity and social situatedness of typical or atypical gender identifications, complex epistemological paradigms that draw on metapsychology, interdisciplinary thinking, and intersectional approaches are necessary.

Such paradigms can be associated with the "negative capability" or, in other words, the ability to bear uncertainty, doubt, and non-knowledge, which, according to Bion (1970), is the paramount quality of the analyst. In fact, strong opinions about transness, such as the certainty of catastrophe if patients transition or, conversely, the certainty of overwhelming euphoria if they alter their gender expression, constitute a failure of the negative capability, a capability characterised by hollowness that requires, as Claudio Neri writes, "not giving form to what is still evolving and is likely to take shape in the analytic field" (Neri, 2009, 51; my translation). That said, unsaturated listening that is receptive to the not-yet-shaped and not-yet-formulated experience represents in itself a complex challenge, since it demands the constant working-through of our countertransference and potential of transitioning, namely the potential of theoretical, clinical, and subjective transformations.

References

Ayouch, T. (2015). L'injure diagnostique. Pour une anthropologie de la psychanalyse [The diagnostic insult. For an anthropology of psychoanalysis] [on line]. *Cultures-Kairos* http://revues.mshparisnord.org/cultureskairos/indeux.php? id= 1055

Bion, W.R. (1970). *Attention and Interpretation*. London: Routledge.

Corbett, K. (2009). *Boyhoods: Rethinking Masculinity*. New Haven: Yale University Press.

Corbett, K., Dimen, M., Goldner, V., & Harris, A. (2014). Talking Sex, Talking Gender, *Studies in Gender and Sexuality* 15(4): 295–317.

Derrida, J. (1967/1976). *Of Grammatology*. Baltimore; London: Johns Hopkins University Press.

Evans, S., & Evans, M. (2021). *Gender Dysphoria: A Therapeutic Model for Working With Children, Adolescents and Young Adults*. London: Karnac Books.

Gherovici, P. (2017). *Transgender Psychoanalysis: A Lacanian Perspective on Sexual Difference*. New York: Routledge.

Glocer Fiorini, L. (2017). *Sexual Difference in Debate: Bodies, Desires, and Fictions*. London: Karnac Books.

Hansbury, G. (2017). Unthinkable Anxieties: Reading Transphobic Countertransferences in a Century of Psychoanalytic Writing, *Transgender Studies Quarterly* 4(3–4): 384–404.

Kuriloff, E. (2005). What's Going on With Dora? An Interpersonal Perspective, *Psychoanalytic Inquiry*, 1(25): 71–83.

Lacan (1958/2007). The signification of the phallus. In *Ecrits: The First Complete Edition in English*. New York: W.W. Norton.

Lacan, J. (1975–1976). *Seminar XXIII*, 1976 in Ornicar? (1976): 6–11, ed. Jacques-Alain Miller, trans. Luke Thurston. Paris.

Morin, E. (2007). *Introduction to Complex Thinking*. Porto Alegre: Sulina.

Neri, C. (2009). La capacité négative du psychothérapeute de groupe [The negative capability of the group psychotherapist]. In *Le Processus thérapeutique dans les groupes* [The Therapeutic Process in Groups] (p. 51–66). Edited by René Kaës et Paul Laurent. Paris: Dunod.

Prigogine, I. (1980). *From Being to Becoming. Time and Complexity in the Physical Sciences*. San Francisco, USA: W.H. Freeman and Company.

Reiner, M. (1932). Causality and Psychoanalysis – A Letter to the Editor of the Psychoanalytic Quarterly, *Psychoanalytic Quarterly* 1: 701–714.

Scarfone, D. (2019). L'assignation de genre et le sexuel infantile [Gender assignment and infantile sexuality], *Filigrane* 28(1): 33–42.

8 Gender fixed and fluid

Gender and suffering, gender and transformation[1]

Adrienne Harris

In a day-long conversation with Jacqueline Rose in 2018, she and I and a very engaged audience, struggled with the still-potent gravitational force of heteronormativity and gender/sex difference and, at the same time, the need to remain accountable to the many lived experiences of complex creative forms of subjectivity: gay, straight, gender fluid, gender queer, trans (CMPS Conference, November 2018). I flag the word "accountable" and want to assert this as a Levinasian principle: our responsibility to the "other", a responsibility which, he argued, we cannot, must not refuse. It is our ethical charge. How might we invoke that charge in regard to the process and collective experience of racial, class, gender and sexual difference?

This chapter is indebted to that discussion in all its demands. Gender/sex differences are forms of potent interpellation and continue to impose a demanding grip on all of us. We resist and comply. As I will argue, however, we organise these "polyvalent" forms, we suffer AND we resist (Saketopoulou, 2014a, 2014b). In 2017, a book on misogyny, *Down Girl: The Logic of Misogyny* (Manne, 2017) made the case for a political and not a psychological reading of the hatred of women. Much of my book is organised around the necessity of a joined perspective, both political and psychoanalytic, for a full understanding of subjectivity and subjectivisation (Harris, 2008).

I was reacting to Rose's very moving essay in the London Review of Books in 2017, which had made a powerful case for the interpellative force and crushing force of gender/sex difference within cultures and within psyches. For all the talk about gender fluidity and the widening scope of forms of identity and embodiment and desire, the iron law of gender difference exerts its power. This system drives the engine of Male Privilege though, of course, men are coerced within its projects as well as women. This is not unlike White Privilege. This makes me want to hold on to a term used in regard to racism: White Fragility, and thus to notice the presence and place of Male Fragility in thinking of how gender/sex differences operate. Gender fluidity and gender prison interweave.

In a kind of homage to my dear friend, Muriel Dimen, I write this chapter as a series of notes. It was a form she used to wondrous effect, and

DOI: 10.4324/9781003531333-15

I am missing her voice in these conversations (Dimen, 2003). I explore the contemporary question of gender fluidity and gender fixity, the power and danger of gender masquerades in men and women and then the scale and reach of misogyny, between genders and within them.

Gender fluidity but gender as suffering

Thinking about gender and its vicissitudes, I realise, I wear at least two hats, thinking as a developmental psychologist and as a psychoanalyst. I do this from a relational, intersubjective perspective, imagining gender as an unpredictable outcome of communications, messages, interactive processes in which the developing child is engaged and constituted. Earlier, my inspiration was chaos theory, a system of nonlinear emergent development which allows a potent two-person (multi-person) process to evolve. Currently, a very similar kind of model is available in the work of Laplanche, now much more widely translated and available in English. The core of Laplanche's teaching (represented in the work of Stein, Saketopoulou, Scarfone and others) centres on 4 crucial features: the asymmetry in early developmental dyads, the enigma of messages, the sexuality in such messages as constitutive of unconscious in the receptive child, the process of translation, culminating in the particular renarratisation of *après coup*. Drawing on Laplanche and others, we can appreciate and understand the volatility, the mixture of fluidity and flexibility in which gender and sexuality emerge. At the same time, we must continue to attend to the psychic (and actual).

The binaries and divides of gender, of sexual difference, sexuality, of race, class, and of the generations, dissolve, and reform. We hold them. They hold us. We see how obsolete and also how dangerous these binaries can be. We can remain in thrall, and we rebel. Jacqueline Rose (2016) reviewing a series of books, articles, and memoirs on trans experience, spoke of the "suffering" in managing or failing at gender performance. She was speaking, with great empathy and identification, about the ordeal of meeting or challenging or missing the conventions of gender even as we know and assume their social construction. This is where I find Erving Goffman so helpful. In 1963, in his book *Stigma: The Management of Spoiled Identity* (128), he put it this way: In an important sense there is only one completely unblushing male in America: a young, married, white, urban, northern, heterosexual Protestant, father, college educated, fully employed, of good complexion, weight, and height, and a recent record in sports. In the more than a half-century since Goffman's work in what he termed symbolic interactionism and which certainly influenced several generations of social science and anthropology, matters both in scholarly disciplines and in the social and intrapsychic world have changed and they have not.

I will argue, indeed I will insist, that *interpellation,* a term migrating from political science (Althusser, 1971) is a crucial concept to integrate into our psychoanalytic understanding of unconscious transmissions or, as Apprey (2014) terms them, unconscious trans hauntings. This project of attending to interpellation is central to many relational theorists, Rozmarin and Guralnik in particular. Althusser's project was to attend to the imposition of external state-driven forces and meanings on the individual. Here is the model scene so often conjured up to represent acts of interpellation. You are on the street. A policeman catches sight of you and shouts, "Hey, you". You startle and in that anxious reaction, affects like shame and guilt, and surely also fear work their spells. In this scene, surely it is also important that it is the police who call and that the you who are called are on the street. The address must carry with it some evocation of violence, capture and apprehension. In the "Hey, you", there is an intention and an effect to capture and to mark body, mind, and soul.

We might see that this emblematic, signature moment, which will in some form happen to all of us, is a moment/time/experience in which we can see the social and the intrapsychic, the collective and the individual entrained and intertwined. It is also a moment/experience, which in Laplanchian terms is potent because of the asymmetry of big/little, empowered/vulnerable, authorised/helpless. These conditions Laplanche understood to be primary moments of unconscious and conscious transmission, the origin point of messages, in which sexuality, identity and relationality are being installed. There are many things to say about this moment/concept. First, it is not just a "moment" but ongoing praxis. This concept has often been critiqued for ignoring class differences and other social/psychic constructs. It will surely matter if you are a man or woman, your conscious, preconscious and unconscious identity may trigger these messages or affect the outcome. But more than gender and sexuality are involved. Class, and most obviously, race will factor into the style, demand, address, and emergent meanings of these encounters.

As others have and are arguing, the phenomenon of interpellation in its multiple incarnations does have a natural affinity to and from psychoanalysis. From within psychoanalysis, there is increasingly the conviction that this encounter with the state in its various incarnations engages conscious and unconscious forms of experience (Dimen, Guralnik, Rozmarin, Stein and others). The spell of history, state and culture is constitutive of so much of psychic life. Here, I want to notice how much affect these communicative forces, from actual police, potent cultural or personal forces, parental figures, and emissaries from the world of intergenerational haunting. It is, I feel, a crucial element in understanding the emergence and character and meaning of gendered and sexual life.

An adult gay man remembers a terrible moment when his father says to him in a voice and with a face filled with contempt: "We have to teach you to walk like a boy". How deeply is that face and that voice etched into earlier communications? Is it a screen memory? Do screen memories carry some of the history of enigmatic messages? And as the patient and I unpacked a lot of history with this father, how much of the father's contempt was disavowed terror about his own sexuality. To invoke Moss' (2003) ideas about phobic hatred, how much of the homophobia in that comment is disavowed desire?

In clinical examples, there are many moments when we feel that we know a lot about the conscious and unconscious aspects of the adult's relational and sexual experiences. At other moments, sometimes over the same material, sometimes not, we come to realise that the richness of the contribution of the adult's "others" remains speculative and "enigmatic", now as they were at the time of first transmissions. This is one of the most useful and complicating aspects of Laplanche's model of enigmatic transmissions. Laplanche and Abraham and Torok (1994) are committed to the enigmatic aspects of transmission. Meanings and intentions may remain opaque and off radar for adult sender and child receiver. Translations may be accurate and insightful or misattuned or inaccurate or lost. Reconstruction, building a developmental narrative, the work of treatment or of any developmental process is filled with a wide array of experiences, rendered, understood, mystified or missing. There are gaps, misconstructions, potent understandings and deep readings in all developmental transactions, in and out of treatment. In giving up the certainty of "the analyst who knows" and even the patient that knows, we accept a much more difficult unstable, generative set of conditions in which to work and in which to understand ourselves and our patients. This is, I believe, an inevitable aspect of the legacy of the "enigmatic".

Binaries as forms of interpellation

Gender, race, sexuality, generation. There are a number of binaries which saddle/logjam our theories, our practices, and certainly our perceptions and judgment. Many of these experiences occur at high speed and outside awareness. Drawing on the work of Kahneman (2011) and Kahneman and Tversky (2000), we understand that much judgement and decision and ascription of meaning and value is conducted at very high speeds and much below the level of conscious awareness.

From queer theory and from cultural studies, we can grasp that binaries are among the important and primary tools of interpellation, and of control. And, on the ground, far from wherever we think the State is located, we, through much unconscious intersubjective transactions, in our lives and in our psychoanalytic lives continue to do and to resist doing the policing. These messages also participate in and are aspects of what constitutes the communications – micro-aggressions – around race that operate way below our radar for the rules and conduct and meaning of interaction across racial and cultural divides (Leary et al., 2000). I want to link Erving Goffman (see the earlier quote) and Frantz Fanon to develop this argument. Goffman's work examined the complexity of social transactions in everyday life. His model, symbolic interactionism, influenced a generation of social scientists interested in how groups often carrying lethal sites of difference (race, gender, and sexual identity) code and judge and manage social and interpersonal life. Goffman's 1963 book, *Stigma: Notes on the Management of Spoiled Identity,* opened up a close and deep examination of the way individuals track the elements of self and other that carry such powerful forces of otherness/danger/excitement while remaining very resolutely under the radar of consciousness. Now, of course, we are open to variation and difference and many complex social categories. We understand more and more deeply that imagining identity must take on the question of desire, of sexuality, of race and culture. Several articles published recently on the death of Toni Morrison noted that she insists on the dimension of colour, linked to but also distinct from race. Many of the most crucial judgments and experiences of self and others draw on these intensely loaded experiences and states of mind and body. Yet often, these judgments are the outcome of less conscious high-speed judgments we make minute by minute. Hence the term from Leary et al. (2000) and others: "micro-aggressions".

Althusser's well-known elaboration of interpellation interestingly focuses on guilt at the point of contact of state and person. The policeman shouts, "Hey, you" and the person (in whatever state of innocence or compromise) startles guiltily. This is the site where the State makes its claim on the subject. Yet, I want to add the dimension of shame here as well. The coherence of identity is structured to manage shame and the puncturing voice of "Hey, you" carries a hot searing experience of shame. This is the suffering in gender performance that Rose (2016) is speaking of. Two of the most forceful writers about shame, coming in different generations, are Sylvan Tompkins and Alan Schore. Neither is exactly native to psychoanalysis, but their ideas are central to a dynamic and unconscious-focused reading of shame. McLaughlin (1988), writing about impasse in treatment, noted that it had always something to do with an impasse in the analyst, a pre-relational relational idea. In his case, his own woodshedding – a term he gave his own self-analysis – led him to recognise a core, intense, dynamic of "shame", which he linked in his own history to maternal abandonment, an abandonment in the form of a bereavement. McLaughlin believed he carried with him always the ghost of an idealised doctor father, dying through selfless heroism in caring for patients in the 1919 influenza epidemic. He was aware also that he lived always in an intense internal relation to a mother, overworked and mournful, who was caught up in a bereavement that turned her gaze away from her children. And he makes an important connection between abandonment and shame, a link we might find explanations for in the work of Alan Schore (1994), who describes shame as an outcome of the exuberance of the young child met with silent mismatch by the parent, a mismatch that leads to a wildly dysregulated affective crash in the child (Harris, 2008).

The binary of big/little: Laplanche, helplessness, and the other

The one binary that I/we cannot do without is the generational binary: Big/little. Laplanche terms this the "fundamental anthropological situation". That asymmetry of mature and immature, though susceptible to many transformations over time and development, combined with the presence of unconscious communication, leads him to the inevitable conclusion that even under non-pathological situations the experience of encounter in, and exposure to, these messages is inherently excessive, more than manageable (Stein, Laplanche). At the same time, for Laplanche, the difference between the normativity of implantation and the pathology and excessive trauma of intromission is a central matter. So, he sets us up in a conundrum. When is excess expected and when it is abusive or criminal? Laplanche's work addresses very powerfully the concept of intersectionality, particularly the sensitivity and susceptibility of the child to sexualisation from "others". This work is a definitive move from the notion of innate drive and endogenous forms of sexuality, without reducing the power and presence of the reactivity and sensory activity of the child. What makes Laplanche such an important theoretical partner for Crenshaw (1989) is his commitment to the power of the other, a parent or sibling, someone other than the child as a transmitter of messages (conscious and unconscious) to the child. These messages and the process of translation, mistranslation and failure to process slowly and inexorably constitute the child's sexuality and infantile unconscious sexuality.

This is a theory of sexuality, one of the crucial elements also in Crenshaw's model, that is socially and interpersonally constituted. Laplanche offers a model of development in which the forces of history, social experience and desire will inevitably arrive in, to, and for the child. It is a model of intrapsychically and interpersonally derived forms of identity; as in Crenshaw's model, the relational mechanism involves conflicting identity experiences that are instantiated in the individual child, at a stage of early helplessness and vulnerability.

Intersectionality and the incomprehensibility of perpetration

Kimberle Crenshaw employs the term *mutual elision* to describe the negating force that, as an outcome of intersectionality, at once conceals and, as a consequence, simultaneously reinforces the subordination of multiply marginalised groups. This section will elaborate on this concept to reveal and explicate how *perpetration*, as an incomprehensible identification, is nonetheless another critical aspect of the "mutual elision" that Crenshaw describes. For Crenshaw, "intersectionality" occurs where two or more potentially powerful axes of identity are "inertly juxtaposed," whereby, for example, in her thesis on gender and race:

> … to the extent that they can forward the interest of 'people of color' and 'women,' respectively, one analysis often implicitly denies the validity of the other. … These mutual elisions present a particularly difficult political dilemma for women of color. Adopting either analysis constitutes a denial of a fundamental dimension of [her] subordination.

Mutual elision is therefore an unconscious societal/collective process, through which people who straddle two or more subordinated categories in the social field fall through an implicit, socially established hole in the floor of political allegiance, where the denial of a fundamental dimension of their subordination in enacted. It is around this elisive hole in the floor that I examine the questions: *who is doing the denying* and *what is being denied?* I will use the lens of psychoanalysis, while also critiquing that lens to explore how intersectionality not only reveals the subordination of certain people, but uncovers an active, if unconscious, *perpetration* by others through that denial. As an incomprehensible identification, *perpetration* in these complex power matrices is thus, and likewise, psychically, and socially elided at the intersectional nidus.

A crucial dichotomy developed by Laplanche is that between *implantation* (the inevitably excessive experience of the sexual messages from the other) and *intromission* (a process that was inherently traumatic and constituted abuse). These distinctions are inevitably hard to absolutely and inevitably distinguish. Yet much hangs on the question of transmission. However, we may parse intromission; the inevitability and potency of transmission of messages is the constitutive force of sexuality. Within French psychoanalysis, Chetrit-Vatine (2004), Aulagnier (2015) and the Botellas (2013) would be important examples of work addressing this theoretical space. Chetrit-Vitane has a particularly felicitous way of interweaving the attunements of attachment processes and the excess of sexuality. She weaves together Levinas' theory that the child is faced with the unrefusable task of being responsible to the other with Laplanche's idea of the parent's equally demanding task of attending to the helplessness of the infant. Levinas makes no space for the unconscious in his model. For Laplanche, it is crucial and ubiquitous on both sides of the dyad. Interestingly, in his work on seduction and revelation, he asks us to consider the helplessness that is our condition over the life span, helplessness against death, against the power of the world in its political and natural conditions.

The enigma Laplanche is attending to is not solely in the transmission phase but continues its unpredictable effects in the longer process of translation, which may include or happen during or consist of solitary reflection, unconscious transformation or dialogic interaction in which conscious and unconscious forms persist. It is a lot of negative capability to have to live with. But this model of transmission and translation allows us to craft developmental models less harnessed to or highjacked by genetic and biologically driven approaches.

Yet the binary of generational difference, Big/little, is susceptible to change and transformation. Disorganised attachment research looks at role reversal in parent-infant pairs. In an important and influential book, *The Mind as an Object* (Gordon & Corrigan, 1995), an international group of analysts looked at the costs and gains of ego precocity, the experiences whereby the child takes up adult functioning often significantly early in life. Whether as small terrorist or precocious caretaker, the child in a disturbed family system can seize or be given power in a way that has great long-term costs.

Ego precocity might be one way of describing a child's capacity to undertake translation and even the work of *après coup*, earlier in development than one might expect. Lyons-Ruth's (2003) work on the possible outcome of experiences of disorganised attachment may be illuminating. She describes, in longitudinal work, the presence of role reversal in disorganised attachment and the capacity for *some* children to "tend/befriend "and become precociously adult and parental figures with systems of disorganisation and tumultuous affects. This is an interesting variation on Laplanche's ideas about helplessness and asymmetry. The degree and character of such differences will be different in different family systems and with different constitutional resiliencies in particular children. Forms of identity, gender and sexual formations may arise in a variety of family systems, where translation and the construction of message's meanings will have many different developmental outcomes.

Others have worked to engage this model with the asymmetries of attachment (Chetrit-Vatine, 2004; 2014; Scarfone, 2014) and currently in the asymmetries and enigmas of the analytic encounter. In these developments, speech is treated as a layered series of experiences differing in structure, in representational complexity, in symbolic and nonsymbolic experiences. There are different ways of naming these distinctions. The Botellas (2013) speak of the *regredient*, the dissolution of structure that nonetheless remains an aspect of presentation and registrations of experience. The complex building blocks of representation take us further away from the organisation and focus of Lacan and closer both to Laplanchian theory and to Bion.

Within the interpersonal tradition, Levenson and Bromberg would locate these deep attunements to unsymbolisable experience in Sullivan and his theorising of dissociation and "not-me" experience. All these models of the structure of speech and the layering of representation and consciousness contribute to the elaboration of gender complexity and its interface and encounter with sexuality and other aspects of subjectivity.

Laplanche's model of enigmatic maternal seduction is a version of the Bionian "alpha work", though much more erotic and embedded and somatic than a Bionian focus on the grid might envision. I am mindful of a patient, who long after her children were grown, as she contemplated the difference that the child's gender had made in her mothering, remembered with great shame and sadness how different her experiences of breastfeeding had been. A first child, a boy, was nursed with great pleasure and commitment. The erotic charge in the experience was part of its meaning and pleasure to her. Several years later, nursing her newborn daughter was much different. Whatever the temperamental or constitutional differences in the infant, what the mother remembered was her anxiety about her erotic engagement with nursing her girl baby. The homoerotic elements of this experience were intolerable. Without being able to make a very full account of the trajectory of translations and *après coup* in this dyad's interactions, we can imagine the complexities of the messages this mother was unconsciously sending, messages in which excitement and anxiety had unique and unpredictable effects.

In this way, we can imagine that amidst the enigmatic message of desire is the message as to its moral, its unconscious but critical, and perhaps even legal character. Laplanche himself engages a discussion of the function of taboo in translation but perhaps misses an opportunity to notice how much the impossibility or pathologising of desires and identifications may be embedded in the transmission and thus eligible in unimaginably complex ways for translation. What renovations or reworking of binaries in identity formation might be visible if we understand that the excessive, what is beyond easy registration of unconscious transmission whereby binaries are projected and introjected, includes both the phenomena of desire implanted from the other to the emerging self, along with instructions about what is enjoined and what is forbidden, what is sick and what is healthy.

The enigmatic message will likely come with instructions regarding what we now call heteronormativity, and like all enigmatic messages, these instructions may be replete with conflict and contradiction. I use the term "instructions" not to stress conscious awareness, rather to make contact with the writers thinking of unconscious messages transmitted in regard to life agendas, trauma, etc. (Faimberg, Apprey, Davoine and Gaudilliere, Salberg and Grand, and others).

Perhaps we might see that psychoanalysis, as one of the interpellating police forces, may through the discourse around perversion, have added a particularly disruptive and shaming aspect to certain "enigmatic" messages. Unconscious transmission must include the social field's input as well as the intrapsychic projects and forms of relatedness in the adult "other". Dimen (2003) and Corbett (2009) placed these ideas at the corner-stone of their understanding of gender experience as productive of, and responsive to, regulatory anxiety.

Gender: Strange attractors, chaos theory, fractals, and caesura

I could not have imagined the powerful social shifts to come in the decade since that book. There is a huge, brilliant expansion of psychoanalytic and cultural writing in which gender and sexuality are being considered that I am thrilled to be part of. Much of the current construction of layers of rep-resentation, both material and imaginary; the concept of intersectionality as it makes gender move and transform in classed and culturally significant formations, was not yet as tangible or accessible.

Now one sees the presence of nonlinear dynamic systems aka complex-ity theory or chaos theory in a very wide range of theoretical approaches (Galatzer-Levy, 2016). I turn now to new concepts in the creative hands of Galatzer-Levy. In a recent lecture (2018) on fractals, he made a strong case for considering the presence and function of boundaries in psycho-analytic technique and theory as following a fractal organisation. The pres-ence of fractals as the site of boundaries creates conditions of emergence and ambiguity. He argues that fractals, products of post-1970 mathematical theorising, allow for complexity by allowing for and creating space for a range of surfaces in which complexity is played out. One point that Galatzer-Levy (2018) stresses is that phenomena are at their most complex and most ambiguous right at the boundary's edge. An interesting focus on gender boundaries and gender ambiguities opens up.

The mathematician Benoit Mandelbrot in search of a theory of such sur-faces developed the concept of fractals. Fractals are mathematical objects that have the quality that they are infinitely complex in the sense that no matter how much they are magnified, they reveal layers of structure that are themselves complex, i.e. not simple, smooth curves. One astounding feature of fractals is that they may be/are easily defined but produce arbi-trarily complicated forms and structures.

Fractals, which are often of extraordinary beauty, occur in many natural situations. Fractal structures are evident in speech and the structure of psy-choanalytic sessions. The structure of a fractal has two important features particularly relevant to a discussion of psychoanalytic boundaries. First, as boundaries one grows closer to the fractal itself it is less and less predict-able on which side of the boundary one will find one's self. The boundary becomes literally infinitely complex. The difference between being inside or outside becomes a matter of tiny differences in the positions of points. If being inside or outside matters, which it very often does, these tiny differ-ences still make a huge difference in what happens.

Performance AND materiality, imaginary and real, gender binaries, I would say, give way to fractals and caesura. Caesura has had a particularly rich life in post-Bionian Italian theory (Civitarese, 2008). Registering the simultaneity of continuity and discontinuity, caesura makes room for gaps and instability and fluidity and ongoingness. Imagine gender or sex binaries through the lens of caesura and the world moves and opens up. Civitarese summarises the complex way that Bion uses caesura to take us beyond binaries. After a considerable focus on the force of rupture and movement in caesura, the caesura of birth, of death, of truth and lies, of self and other.

Note

1 Paper presented at the Brussels Study Day, Belgium, 27–28 September, 2019 (unfinished).

References

Abraham, N. & Torok, M. (1994). *The Shell and the Kernel*. Chicago, IL: University of Chicago Press.

Althusser, L. (1971). Ideology and ideological state apparatuses. In L. Althusser (Ed.), *Lenin and Philosophy and Other Essays*. New York: Monthly Review Press.

Apprey, M. (2014). A Pluperfect Errand: A Turbulent Return to Beginnings in the Transgenerational Transmission of Destructive Aggression. *Free Associations: Psychoanalysis and Culture, Media, Groups, Politics*, 66: 15–28.

Aulagnier, P. (2015). Birth of a Body, Origin of a History. *International Journal of Psychoanalysis*, 96: 1371–401.

Chetrit-Vatine, V. (2004). Un espace matriciel pour Mr E [A matricial space for Mr E]. Annual Conference of French-speaking analysts 'Le processus psychanalytique: Communications préalables'. *Bull Soc Psychanal Paris*, 72.

Chetrit-Vatine, V. (2014). *The Ethical Seduction of the Analytic Situation. The Feminine-Maternal Origins of Responsibility for the Other*. London: Routledge https://doi.org/10.4324/9780429481659

Civitarese, G. (2008). Caesura in Bion's Discourse on Method. *The International Journal of Psychoanalysis*, 89: 1123–43.

Corbett, K. (2009). *Boyhoods: Rethinking Masculinity*. New Haven CN: Yale University Press.

Crenshaw, K. (1989). Demarginalizing the Intersection of Race and Sex: A Black Feminist Critique of Anti-Discrimination Doctrine, Feminist Theory and Anti-racist Politics. *University of Chicago Legal Forum*, 139. https://scholarship.law.columbia.edu/faculty_scholarship/3007

Dimen, M. (2003). *Sexuality, Intimacy, Power*. Hillsdale, NJ: The Analytic Press.

Galatzer-Levy, R. (2018). *Talk at the New York Psychoanalytic Institute*.

Galatzer-Levy, R. M. (2016). The Edge of Chaos: A Nonlinear View of Psychoanalytic Technique. *The International Journal of Psychoanalysis*, 97: 409–27.

Goffman, E. (1963). *Stigma: The Management of Spoiled Identity*.

Gordon, E. G. & Corrigan, P.-E. (Eds.) (1995). *The Mind-Object: Precocity and Pathology of Self-Sufficiency*. London: Karnac.

Harris, A. (2008). *Gender as Soft Assembly*. New York: Routledge.

Kahneman, D. (2011). *Thinking, Fast and Slow*. New York: Farrar, Straus and Giroux.

Kahneman, D., & Tversky, A. (Eds.). (2000). *Choices, Values, and Frames*. Cambridge University Press.

Leary, M. R., Patton, K. M., Orlando, A. E., & Wagoner Funk, W. (2000). The Impostor Phenomenon: Self-Perceptions, Reflected Appraisals, and Interpersonal Strategies. *Journal of Personality*, 68(4): 725–756. https://doi.org/10.1111/1467-6494.00114

Lyons-Ruth, K. (2003). Dissociation and the Parent-Infant Dialogue: A Longitudinal Perspective from Attachment Research. *Journal of the American Psychoanalytic Association*, *51*(3): 883–911. https://doi.org/10.1177/00030651030510031501

Manne, K (2017). *Down Girl: The Logic of Misogyny Get Access Arrow*. Oxford University Press. https://doi.org/10.1093/oso/9780190604981.001.0001. Online ISBN: 9780190605018

McLaughlin, J. T. (1988). The Analyst's Insights. *Psychoanalytic Quarterly*, 57: 370–89.

Moss, D. (2003). *Hating in the First-Person Plural: Psychoanalytic Essays on Racism, Homophobia, Misogyny, and Terror*. New York: Other Press.

Rose, J. (2016). *Who Do You Think You Are*. London Review of Books, 38(9), p.5. https://www.lrb.co.uk/the-paper/v38/n09/jacqueline-rose/who-do-you-think-you-are

Rose, J. (2018). *Paper given at Modern Psychoanalytic Center Conference*, November 9, 2018.

Saketopoulou, A. (2014a). Mourning the Natal Body: Developmental Considerations in Working Analytically With Transgender Patients. *Journal of the American Psychoanalytic Association*, 62(5): 773–806.

Saketopoulou, A. (2014b). To Suffer Pleasure; the Shattering of the Ego as the Psychic Lie of Perverse Sexuality. *Studies in Gender and Sexuality*, 14(3): 245–52.

Scarfone, D. (2014). The Unpast, Actuality of the Unconscious. *Revue Française De Psychanalyse*, 78(5): 1357–428.

Schore, A. N. (1994). *Affect Regulation and the Origin of the Self: The Neurobiology of Emotional Development*. London: Taylor and Francis.

9 Gender crossing as caesura versus gender crossing as cut[1]

Dana Amir

Gender dichotomy is probably the most primary dichotomy internalised in human thinking. It acts as a prototype for all the later dichotomies, in a sense inaugurating dichotomous thinking in general – first within the imaginary of the parent who holds the soon-to-be-born infant in his or her mind – and afterwards within the mind of the infant itself. This chapter focuses on the conditions which enable the establishing of a dialectic and unsaturated gender space – one that enables both a concrete and fantasised creative mobility between the two gender poles – versus the conditions which generate a polar, saturated, gender dichotomous stagnation and stasis.

Bion's (1989) notion of the "Caesura" simultaneously contains a break and a continuity. A break beyond which there is no continuity is a cut rather than a caesura. Bion himself situates the caesura between the pre-catastrophic state and the post-catastrophic state of change, treating it not as a static point in space or time but rather as a rich dynamic space in itself: "It is in course of transit, in the course of changing from one position to another that these people seem to be most vulnerable - as, for example, during adolescence or latency" (Bion, [1977] 1989, 53). However, this vulnerability is precisely why the state of caesura constitutes the richest potential for change. Bion compares the dividing of the world into polar states, which exclude one another – with the state in which two different views or perspectives function together in a dialectical, caesura-like and productive manner. Development is always related to the preserving of different views in a non-saturated state, thus avoiding the fixation of the components of consciousness in a stasis which does not allow them to absorb new meanings.

Gender crossing: Caesura or cut?

One of the most important questions that arise in the current context is whether we formulate gender crossing in terms of caesura or in terms of a cut, or even more precisely, under which conditions should gender crossing be formulated in terms of caesura, and under which in terms of a cut?

DOI: 10.4324/9781003531333-16

Gender dichotomy is probably the most primary dichotomy internalised in human thinking; as with any dichotomy, it may collapse into a saturated state, becoming fixated in a way that enables it only a miniscule degree, if any at all, of transformability – or, alternatively, it may remain unsaturated and in this sense contain movement, richness and layered meanings. When does gender dichotomy become a rich dialectic – as opposed to being constituted as a saturated excess, that is, as a dichotomy whose two poles are not only distinct but also exclude each other?

An excess of saturated gender dichotomy forms in conditions that *a priori* encourage saturated divisions. The propensity for saturated divisions may be innate or acquired, always related to an anxiety of ambiguity and the need to defend oneself through rigid thinking against the unexpected and the impermanent. In most cases, this propensity for saturated divisions is a general inclination of thinking and language, which is not solely related to gender dichotomy – but it becomes especially charged in children who do not find themselves at the "expected" end of the gender dichotomy. In such cases, the combination of the primary gender ambiguity and the acquired propensity for saturated dichotomies might evolve into a need to situate oneself on one gender pole, losing the freedom to experience (even in fantasy) dialectical movement between the two poles. Where gender categories do not serve thinking but rather block it, children whose primary "gender experience" is ambiguous might feel trapped in a saturated dichotomy in which they cannot find their place.

In "On the Lyricism of the Mind" (Amir, 2016,1989) I suggested a "lyrical dimension" of mental space, which is in charge of the integration of two experiential/perceptual modes: the continuous mode, which perceives the world as predictable, explainable and logical - and the emergent mode which perceives the world as unpredictable, unexplainable and constantly changing. The integration of these two modes of experience, which Bion (1970) originally identified as constituting the container/contained interaction, yields the capacity to presuppose constancy and continuity on the one hand, and to tolerate severe deviations from that constancy and continuity without losing one's sense of "identity" and "biography" on the other hand.

Formulating his notion of the *container-contained* interaction, Bion (1970) pointed at three possible types of this interaction, of which the one with the most powerful capacity for change is the symbiotic interaction, while the one with the most destructive power is the *parasitic* (in between Bion posited a somehow neutral interaction he entitled "commensal"). If we formulate the interaction between the emergent and the continuous principles of the self in Bion's terms, we may suppose that wherever the interaction between the emergent and the continuous is parasitic in nature or takes the form of a "malignant containment" (Britton, 1998, 28) – one of two things might happen: the continuous self may smother the emergent self, leaving the latter no space for movement or development, or alternatively, the emergent self might stretch the continuous self beyond its breaking point, crashing through its boundaries. Bion (1970) argued that the sense of catastrophe that attends such an interaction between the emergent and the continuous is related to the fact that the psychic space is unable to supply an experience of constancy beyond change, a constancy which is the primary condition for change. When the continuous principle prevails, the psychic space becomes lacking in depth and resonance, while when the emergent principle takes over – the psychic space turns into a terrifying nightmare. If, by contrast, the interaction is compatible – integration may occur, inaugurating the lyrical dimension of the psychic space. The emergent is the force that preserves things in their unsaturated condition, whereas the continuous is the saturated state. The more fertile the interaction between the two, the more likely one is to experience oneself as owning a historical and biographical continuum on the one hand – and as being a singular individual whose creativity is allowed to interrupt this continuum, on the other hand.

Gender experience can also be formulated in terms of the relationship between the continuous and the emergent. For example, an excess of a "continuous" gender experience as opposed to an "emergent" gender experience could damage the possibility of establishing a "gender space" which holds the continuous and the emergent in a fertile dialectic relation. On the other hand, an excess of "emergent" gender experience, in which every shift threatens to change the deep nucleus of identity may undermine the possibility of a cooperative relationship between the two poles of gender dialectic (the actual and the phantasmatic). Gender is constantly in the process of emerging. Yet every emergence needs a continuous container for its forcefulness and volatility. When there is a "continuous" gender that can contain the various gender emergences in a way that doesn't force the self to undergo a catastrophic identity change – "a gender space" is created.

However, where the continuous (which manifests itself, for example, in the *a priori* propensity towards saturated dichotomies) is too fragile and rigid, and its encounter with the volatile and powerful emergent threatens breakdown, parasitical relations may form between the actual and the phantasmatic gender, resulting in anxiety that further builds up fragility and rigidity. Whether these parasitical relations end in confinement within the original gender or whether they lead to a concrete sex change procedure, they share the same "parasitic" quality that refuses transformation. In this sense, even if they lead to gender crossing, this is a "saturated crossing," one with the characteristics of a "cut" rather than a caesura.

Quinodoz (1998, 99) distinguishes between gender crossing deriving from a very early experience of being "imprisoned" within the wrong actual gender, as opposed to gender crossing deriving from unprocessed hatred towards the actual gender, not because it contradicts the natural experience but because it arouses psychotic anxieties. Can we really discriminate between these two situations? Undoubtedly, we often witness a mixture of both, with the anxiety towards the actual gender being related to it being experienced as nullifying the phantasmatic gender (which is experienced as the natural one). Perhaps the distinction here should not refer only to the conscious and unconscious reasons for gender crossing – but also to the level of their symbolic organisation. Certain instances of gender crossing are indeed related, as the following case bears out, to a concrete or imagined significant object that becomes a saturated object, and the identification with this becomes malignant. When this occurs, crossing might be a psychotic-fetishistic expression of the wish to become that very other, a wish that dangerously and deceptively hides, through the possible physical transformation, a psychic transformation that could not have taken place.

From a cleft lip to a cleft tongue

Dan, a 29-year-old male, seeks psychotherapy during a sex change procedure (male to female). After approximately two years of hormonal treatment, he turns to me for consultation since he feels that the psychiatrist who has been treating him thus far is "pushing" him to complete the full transition, whereas Dan himself does not feel ready for it. He is terribly anxious and does not know how to explain why now, of all times, a moment before his planned surgery – he suddenly hesitates. Recently, he has also reverted to using his original name, presenting himself alternatively as a male (Dan) and as a female (Dania).

Dan is a twin brother to Anne. They were born to relatively old parents (both in their forties) after years of fertility treatments and painful miscarriages. From the moment they were born, Dan recounts, there was a division of roles between them. Anne was a beautiful, fragile and sickly girl who attracted a lot of attention and evoked great concern. Dan, on the other hand, was a chubby and robust baby, healthy and lively, but since he was born with a cleft lip, his face was, at least in his own opinion, "damaged" in relation to Anne's face. He remembers how for years – even after the aesthetic defect was surgically corrected by two successive plastic operations – people would avert their eyes, as if searching for a more "comfortable" place to "rest" on. That "more comfortable" place was Anne's pretty face. Although Dan was in every way a clever and talented boy, he felt that he was living in her shadow, or more accurately, in her light. He always felt that he must protect her – yet he remembers feeling completely exposed when he was not by her side. He describes the gazes of others, to which he was exposed whenever Anne was not with him, and her face could not serve as his refuge – as intolerable and persecutory. The relations between brother and sister were symbiotic in many ways, including early experiences of joint masturbation and sharing everything they were given or owned: toys, clothes, food. When Anne was diagnosed with celiac disease, Dan stopped eating the foods she was forbidden to eat. When Dan suffered insults from fellow players in his football team, Anne ripped pictures of herself in the team uniform from the walls of her room. This symbiosis was not without a price. They had very few friends who were not shared; their attachment to one another limited their areas of interest; and above all, Dan recounts, their togetherness left out their parents. They both felt that all they needed was each other. Except for their physical care, neither of them remembers their parents having a significant role in their concrete or emotional lives. Dan recently felt this loss when meeting his father in the hospital where his mother was recovering from a heart attack, realising how little they knew about each other. It seems as if, very early on, the parents gave up on any attempts to penetrate their children's symbiotic dyad. Dan describes their emotional connection to their children, as well as to one another, as distant and poor.

Dan remembers himself, already at an early age, jealous of Anne's beauty and wanting to be like her. Most of all, he was jealous of her face. While he experienced his own face as "mutilated," hers was the ideal image of the face that he could or should have had. He remembers standing next to her by the mirror, looking at her reflection instead of at his own. He also remembers the fantasy he had about his face having been mutilated during their birth (and not prior to it, as is the factual truth) and believing the cleft in his upper lip to be the result of his having sacrificed his face in order to let Anne be born whole and unharmed.

Dan recalls experiencing the words he was trying to utter as "spilling out of his mouth" in the most concrete sense: "every word was accompanied by spitting, I couldn't articulate a single word without it coming with something physical in the form of spit, or if I had been eating - chewed food that would spill out along with the words." He remembers many social occasions on which he would let Anne complete his sentences since it was more convenient for him not to "use his mouth," and since "she always knew what [he] intended to say anyway." Thus, words constituted "somatic" objects rather than symbolic ones. This bears a huge significance, as will be discussed later, when it comes to Dan's decision to undergo the physical transformation, which in many ways substituted for his incapacity to work through his feelings.

Anne seemed to have served as Dan's perfect imaginary image. He remembers feeling at a very early age that since Anne was born a girl, she had somehow appropriated what should have been his: the beauty, the delicateness, the caring she received – all these were attributed to her being a girl rather than to her being who she was. He recalls his envious passion for everything she had had: her clothes, her makeup accessories. In her wardrobe cupboard, there were several dresses and shirts she bought and kept especially for him, pretending they were her own. He detested his body, which he experienced as cumbersome and damaged, and the early signs of puberty only added to his abhorrence. He fell in love with girls but felt that he loved them as a girl and not as a boy. He wanted them to caress his hair, to touch his breasts. His sexual fantasies were never related to penetration but rather to friction, and in masturbation, he always visualised his genital as a female genital rubbing against another female genital. The few sexual experiences he had were indeed experiences in which he "masturbated against" a woman's body without penetrating her. His sexual wish was to "come on her" and not to "come inside her," and he repeatedly emphasised this. This phrasing might hint at the aggression, envy and hatred towards women (who, for him, were all extensions of Anne) concealed behind his desire to become a woman. This hatred may also explain the anxiety that arose during the process of preparing for sex-change surgery, which will be described later.

The symbiotic twinship with Anne along with the critical physical difference between them created an inner environment of splitting: her perfect face as opposed to his damaged face, the love that she aroused as opposed to the aversion and embarrassment he aroused, at least in his own experience – all these were attributed to the gender dichotomy, turning it simultaneously into a rigid and an extremely fragile dichotomy. When he reached the age of 18, he began to speak openly about his wish to undergo a sex change. His parents reacted with "shocked alienation or alienated shock," as he put it, but nevertheless supported the process. During it, however, many misgivings began to emerge. Dan felt he could not find himself in his new body (which, due to the hormone treatment, was beginning to show feminine characteristics). He did not want to return to his old body, which he detested, but then did not feel "at home" either in the new body he had developed. Even as a woman, he still felt awkward and damaged compared to Anne; he wanted to be as pretty as her but discovered that, in actuality, he was not going to become a prettier woman than the man he had previously been. Gradually, the therapy sessions revealed that his unconscious phantasy was not to be a woman – but to be Anne herself. She was the object of his admiration and passion, and the process he had begun was a process whose purpose was not to join her but to be her, perhaps even to replace her.

Another aspect, emerging from Dan's dreams, was related to mutilation. As previously mentioned, Dan's fantasy was that his face had been "mutilated" to allow Anne to be born flawlessly. Now, instead of experiencing the gender change procedures as remedial, he experienced them as "adding mutilation to mutilation." In one of his dreams, he is lying on the operating table. One of his legs is apparently longer than the other, and the purpose of the operation, so he is told by the doctor, is to shorten the longer leg, which will enable him to walk without limping. During the operation, however, it is his short leg that is mistakenly shortened, and he completely loses his ability to walk.

I understand this dream as touching upon Dan's immense anxiety around his body's change processes: the surgery that was supposed to fix what he had experienced as an *a priori* failure was revealed in the dream as likely to bring about an even bigger and irrevocable failure. The longed-for surgery reflecting his wish to undo the prenatal mutilation became the enactment of this mutilation. At this stage, it was clear that the wish to undergo a sex change was related to the excessiveness of Anne as a saturated object of identification. The splitting and projections which characterised Dan's relationship with her positioned Anne as an object of persecutory wholeness, the identification with this had a psychotic-fetishistic tone, accompanied with the phantasm of wholeness without lack (the lack, for him, was signified by his cleft lip). In effect, the only way to get rid of this persecutory object was by fusing with it – that is, by becoming it. Yet the sex change was experienced as a cut rather than a caesura: a moment in which he would murder and be murdered, losing both Anne and himself. Dan's desire to gender cross may be understood as a wish to unite with an object of *jouissance* – but no less than that, to annihilate this object by appropriating its identity. The gender dichotomy, in this case, was psychotically charged by the splitting between Anne's whole face as opposed to Dan's mutilated face, and between her "whole lip" and his "cleft lip," while the gender crossing was aimed at acting out that excess. It is thus possible to relate to Dan's psychotherapeutic treatment as a treatment intended to turn "the cleft lip" into a "cleft tongue," i.e., to transform the actual cleft into a symbolic one, which can be worked through rather than acted out.

Discussion

The difference between gender crossing procedures that are based on a psychotic organisation, as in the case described above, as opposed to transformative gender crossing, involves the degree by which the new gender is constituted as a concrete actualisation of the phantasm of wholeness. When gender crossing comes to confirm the illusion that it is possible to fill the essential, inherent lack (Lacan, 1958/2007), then, disguised as the realisation of subjectivity, it actually undermines this very subjectivity. Oren Gozlan (2015, 54) writes beautifully in this context that "surgery in itself becomes irrelevant to the question of pathology, because what distinguishes an Act from an acting out is not the activity but its ability to be enjoyed as lacking." "To be enjoyed as lacking" suggests the preserving the unsaturated quality of gender in a way that allows it to draw ever more meanings, turning from being what serves "the dictatorship of [body] parts" (Cixous, 1976, 889) to a transformative object, a source, that is, for psychic mobility.

Danger appears where gender crossing loses its symbolic quality and becomes a mere concrete act, one which constitutes a psychotic rejection of the depressive work of mourning or a magical replacement of the experience of body's incompleteness. In such cases, what is at stake is the act itself erasing the experience of lack, thus turning into an act that nullifies, through the concrete gratification it enables, the need to create meaning. Where, however, gender crossing constitutes *an act of meaning* rather than one that nullifies meaning – rather than a rejection of the experience of incompleteness it constitutes the very effort to get to know this incompleteness from all its sides, and to play, at any given moment, with its infinite manifestations both in the domains of body and mind.

Note

1 Presented at EPF panel online, March 2021, previously published in part in Amir, D. (2018). The Two Sleeps of Orlando: Transsexuality as Caesura or Cut. In O. Gozlan (ed.), *Current Critical Debates in the Field of Transsexual Studies: In Transition* (pp. 36–47). London & New York: Routledge.

References

Amir, D. (2016). *On the Lyricism of the Mind: Psychoanalysis and Literature (trans: Mirjam Hadar)*. London and New York: Routledge.
Bion, W. R. (1962b). *Learning from Experience*. London: Heinmann. [Reprinted London: Karnac books, 1984.]
Bion, W. R. (1967). Catastrophic Change. Unpublished paper.
Bion, W. R. (1970). Container and Contained Transformed. In *Attention and Interpretation*. London: Tavistock [Reprinted London: Karnac books, 1984.]
Bion, W. R. (1977). *Two Papers: The Grid and Caesura*. Rio de Janeiro: Imago Editora. [Reprinted London: Karnac Books 1989]
Britton, R. (1998). *Belief and Imagination*. New York: Routledge, 120–127.
Cixous, H. (1976). The Laugh of the Medusa (trans: Keith Cohen and Paula Cohen). *Signs*, 1(4): 875–893.
Gozlan, O. (2015). *Gender Crossing and the Art of Transitioning: A Lacanian Approach*. New York: Routledge.
Lacan, J. ([1958] 2007). *Écrits*. B. Fink, translator. London: W. W. Norton.
Quinodoz, D. (1998). A FE/Male Transsexual Patient in Psychoanalysis. *Int. J. Psycho-Anal.*, 79: 95–111.

EVA REICHELT DISCUSSION OF CHAPTER 9

Dana Amir's chapter is rich in condensed thoughts on transgender phenomena. Its merit consists in offering a space, which we need when transgender patients come to seek psychoanalytic treatment. Amir invites us to "establish a dialectic and unsaturated gender space." We need a space to be able to think freely, to allow our various emotions to come to the surface, to reflect our many countertransference reactions. One might be inclined to say that we need this space for each person who seeks treatment. With transgender persons, however, usually, different perceptions, emotions and thoughts arise in us than with persons with a cisgender identity. We need to review our psychoanalytic theories and develop conceptualisations during our treatments with every single analysand – and with transgender patients in particular.

Amir refers to Bion's notion of the Caesura and later of the continuous and emergent modes. Before looking at her use of these notions, I want to make a step back and make a brief and incomplete review of European psychoanalytic literature in the field. Many European psychoanalysts are familiar with Roger Money-Kyrle's concept of the "Facts of Life" described in 1968 and 1971. John Steiner says that "Money-Kyrle describes why 'the facts of life' are so difficult for us to accept. These facts are all to do with differences. First, the difference between generations, second, the difference between the sexes, and third, the reality of the passage of time. They are hated because they provoke envy and threaten omnipotence, and a mythology is invented to deny them and to avoid having to face our mortality, and our dependence on others."

Not to acknowledge the "difference between the sexes" therefore is tantamount to omnipotently denying a fact of life. Over decades, this clear way of thinking has been the prevailing psychoanalytic theory towards transgender persons – at least in Europe, as far as I can see. We easily acknowledge that we have to accept the first fact of life, the difference between generations, and the third one, namely that we have to face death. Why should we then put into question the second fact of life, the difference between the sexes? Our patients teach us to try to develop further thinking.

Reviewing recent psychoanalytic literature from European colleagues, we find the IPA publication in the series "Controversies in Psychoanalysis" from 2009, edited by Giovanna Ambrosio with the title "Transvestism, Transsexualism in the Psychoanalytic Dimension." This volume collects various interesting papers presented during a COWAP conference in Sicily in 2006. One of the authors, Simona Argentieri, clearly argues that "transvestism and transsexualism (…) both are to be considered, at least theoretically, as perversions" (11). She goes on: "(…) we must (…) recognize (…) the defensive mechanism of denial typical of the perversion and the consequent unequal structural splitting of the ego" (Argentieri, 2006). In her experience, "the psychopathological organization of transsexualism is substantially the same in men as in women: the delusional conviction (a typical circumscribed delusion) of belonging to the opposite sex, and the compulsive conviction of wanting to regain it, mask the unconscious fantasy of attacking the 'bad,' drive-dependent part of the body." (12)

In my opinion, this has been the predominant "doctrine" with which many of us in Europe have grown up psychoanalytically, so to say, regarding transgender phenomena. A mainly pathologising view: a typical circumscribed delusion. At the same time, Argentieri conveys her enormous clinical experience and her interest in the field. She honestly describes her observations, e.g., when she sees that a student assigned female at birth who comes for a consultation exactly moves like a boy, and Argentieri realizes that she is "quite unable to help (this person) in the only way she would like" (21). She does not express it explicitly, but her therapeutic goal is clear: to dissuade the transgender person from their subjective feeling of being of the opposite sex. The author doesn't openly recur to Money-Kyrle but clearly shares this point of view that we must accept the difference between the sexes, a binary concept.

Danielle Quinodoz, quoted by Dana Amir, has described the course of psychoanalysis with a transsexual patient (1998), stressing her counter-transference reactions, including her brief visual hallucinatory experience during the very first initial contact at the door with a male to female trans-sexual patient. Danielle Quinodoz openly discusses her countertransfer-ence difficulties: feeling uncomfortable, uneasy and not knowing if the patient is a man or a woman for her. She decides "to experience fully this discomfort of this countertransference uncertainty while continuing to hope that one day a certainty could take shape, but without prejudging that shape" (97). Put into other words, Danielle Quinodoz communicates her proceeding: "to be prepared to see (the patient) as a human being, without trying to determine that human being's sex (…). In the transference, I had the role of parents at the beginning of a pregnancy, expecting a baby whose sex they could not yet know (…)" (Quinodoz, 1998). The English text shows first a certain confusion of notions: Quinodoz speaks here about gender, not about sex. Her attitude reveals the difficulty of the analyst to acknowledge the analysand's subjective gender: feeling female even though this person was assigned male at birth. But Quinodoz at least tries to be open in her countertransference to bear the uncertainty and does not pretend to know *a priori* better.

In my view, the gender space which Dana Amir suggests can be extended to Danielle Quinodoz' idea of parents expecting a child of still unknown sex. This might serve as a helpful attitude of "no memory, no desire" (Bion, 1967): to be prepared to open a space, to share the – often unbearable – uncertainty because of the sense of gender and body incongruity and not to pretend to possess *a priori* a theoretical understanding.

In recent years, Alessandra Lemma has published various papers where she discusses transference/countertransference dynamics such as "a disturbing otherness" the analyst is confronted with when seeing a transgender individual. Lemma (2013) suggests "that in some cases of transsexuality the primary object(s) did not mirror and contain an early experience of incongruity between the given body and the subjective ex-perience of gender: it remains unmentalized and disrupts self-coherence leading to the pursuit of surgery that is anticipated to 'guarantee' relief from the incongruity." She focuses on the visual relationship between ana-lyst and patient during a face-to-face psychotherapy describing the impor-tance of the respective gazes. Her account in my view also opens a "gender space" when Lemma admits that she had difficulties to take her transsexual patient in and describes how she could work through these difficulties in her countertransference.

Amir now suggests that we can use Bion's notion of caesura juxtaposing it with a cut when we think of gender crossing. A caesura is a break when we can take breath in music, singing or playing a wind instrument, but also to increase dramatic tension when reciting a poem. Afterwards, after the caesura, the music or the text will continue. According to Bion's thoughts on catastrophic change the caesura is located between the pre-catastrophic and the post-catastrophic state of change. Just to avoid any confusion: obviously Bion does not speak about sex change, and in my view, Amir does not imply this, either. She pleads for a balance between unsaturated and saturated thinking concerning gender. In my view, many of us psychoanalysts are not yet quite used to unsaturated thinking – we still tend to give definite and unambiguous interpretations – and that is why this plea might induce some unease.

In the next part, Amir reminds us of some of Bion's thoughts from his work *Attention and Interpretation* on the two modes of experience, the continuous one and the emergent one, how they function and how they interact with each other. Dana creates the notion of "Gender Space," which "holds the continuous mode and the emergent mode in a fertile dialectic relation." She suggests two poles of gender dialectic, the actual and the phantasmatic one, and states that gender "is constantly in the process of emerging." Her use of Bion's concept of continuous and emergent modes of experience combining it with her own thoughts on gender seems playful to me. However, when Dana explains to us how a gender space is created – that is "(w)hen there is a 'continuous' gender that can contain the various gender emergences in a way that does not force the self to undergo a catastrophic identity change" – it seems to me that there is a kind of symbolic equation between the concept of catastrophic change and gender identity change.

With Amir's clinical example, we can understand easily what she means with the concept of "gender crossing as cut". We can imagine that Dan obviously must have had a quite sane part, which led him to seek a psychoanalytical consultation shortly before his planned surgical intervention. This clinical vignette is interesting in various aspects: Amir did not share much about her own countertransference reactions when encountering Dan/Dania for the initial interviews – and in how far her countertransference might have changed during treatment. We can wonder how Dana felt about Dan, if she could grasp "Dania," that is, Dan's female personality traits, at all or if this transgender idea seemed rather unfounded to her.

We can try to imagine this visible narcissistic wound – the cleft lip – and moreover not only Dan's face but also their voice and their way of speaking. The question arose how the analyst could feel connected to Dan, how well Amir could understand this person, how the analyst could connect to the analysand's suffering.

Dan came originally for consultation, and later Amir writes that "(g)radually the therapy sessions revealed that his unconscious fantasy was not to be a woman – but to be Anne (his sister) herself." We can try to imagine what kind of setting had we offered to Dan if they had entered one of our offices. We can wonder on which setting the two agreed, that is, face-to-face or on the couch, how many sessions per week and the reasons for these decisions. Such details can serve as a support when embarking in these unknown voyages of psychoanalytic treatment with transgender patients. Surely, we must develop as many individual solutions as we do for all our other patients.

Dan's case serves as an example for gender crossing as cut. In the future it would be desirable to share clinical experiences with gender crossing as caesura.

Amir's concluding remarks seem very relevant both in a theoretical and in a clinical way. If any intervention for gender crossing is meant to "undo" the basic lack, this will serve as a denial. If, however, patient and analyst are able to acknowledge a lack, which will remain, as well after any medical intervention, gender crossing can occur in a more playful way, conscious of the fact that the lack cannot be plugged, cannot be eliminated. But by acknowledging this fact, the lack can paradoxically and dialectically be remedied.

References

Argentieri, Simona (2009). Transvestism, Transsexualism, Transgender: Identification and Imitation. In Ambrosio, Giovanna (Ed.): *Transvestism, Transsexualism in the Psychoanalytic Dimension*. London: Karnac.

Bion, Wilfred R. (1967). Notes on Memory and Desire. *Psychoanalytic Forum* 2:272–3, 279–80.

Lemma, A. (2013). The Body One has and the Body One is: Understanding the Transsexual's Need to be Seen. *Indian Journal of Pediatrics* 94(2):277–292.

Lemma, A. (2018). Transitory Identities: Some Psychoanalytic Reflections on Transgender Identities. *Indian Journal of Pediatrics* 99(5):1089–1106.

Money-Kyrle, R. (1968). Cognitive Development. *Indian Journal of Pediatrics* 49:691–698.

Money-Kyrle, R. (1971). The Aim of Psychoanalysis. *Indian Journal of Pediatrics* 52:103–106.

Quinodoz, D. (1998). A FE/Male Transsexual Patient in Psychoanalysis. *Indian Journal of Pediatrics* 79:95–111

Steiner, J. (2015). *Endorsement to Roger Money-Kyrle: Man's Picture of his World* (New edition of a book of M-K's classic works); London: Karnac.

ELDA ABREVAYA DISCUSSION OF CHAPTER 9

The painful dilemma of being a male or a female

Introduction

The question of gender has nowadays become a central issue in psychoanalysis and in other aspects of cultural life. Jacques André enumerates two reasons for the necessity of a dialogue with gender studies: on one hand, the denaturalised dimension of human sexuality and on the other hand, the hierarchical position of heterosexuality, marked by male domination. For these reasons "psychoanalysis finds itself in the same ground with *gender studies*" (My translation) (André, 2017, 33). Judith Butler and others find support to their arguments against heterosexuality in Freud's interrogation on this matter. In *Three essays* (1905d), in a note added in 1915, Freud summarises:

> On the contrary, psychoanalysis considers that a choice of an object independently of its sex - freedom to range equally over male and female objects - as it is found in childhood, in primitive states of society and early periods of history, is the original basis from which, as a result of restriction in one direction or the other, both the normal and inverted develop. (p. 146)

However, as André puts it, Freud's view on this matter does not mean that the subject has the freedom to choose his/her gender, nor to make a "natural" object-choice to the extent that psychical reality is greatly determined by the unconscious. On the other hand, polymorphous perversity, one of the characteristics of infantile sexuality, does not consist in the freedom to multiply the sexes. Even if it is possible to imagine, as Jean-Michel Lévy (2019) notes, the free exercise of this polymorphy as a liberation with respect to gender and identity, it is never exempt from conflict and anxiety. Psychoanalysis has demonstrated the conflictual character of sexuality, which arises as a consequence of the necessary repression to cope with the intense excitation emanating from infantile sexuality.

Psychoanalytic practice becomes the place where the analyst experiences the complexity of the question of gender, especially when it concerns problems of sexual identity. Dana Amir presents the case of a young man who is on the verge of a sex-change. She suggests that when gender crossing is not experienced as a saturated dichotomy, Bion's (1989) idea of the caesura, which simultaneously contains a break and a continuity, can be useful in grasping this complex situation. The passage from one gender to the other puts the subject in a vulnerable position, but this vulnerability can become the occasion of a fecund analytic work. As a result, it can be possible to imagine, as Amire writes, an "unsaturated gender space - one that enables both a concrete and fantasised creative mobility between two gender poles - versus the conditions which generate a polar, saturated, gender dichotomous stagnation and stasis."

Constitution of gender identity

Amir situates the origin of a saturated dichotomic thinking in an ambiguous primary gender experience. I would like to look at how primary gender experience is constituted in the child. Jean Laplanche (2007) points to the primacy of the other in the process of assignment of gender. In this sense, he is in agreement with Robert Stoller's (1964,1989) view on gender identity. Laplanche remarks that the other corresponds to parents and relatives, but also to influential figures in the family, who "bombard" the child with their preconscious-conscious messages about assignment of gender. However, among the enigmatic messages that are communicated by the adult, those that have a major impact on the child are the adult's unconscious fantasies. In fact, the parents' unconscious fantasies convey "noises" belonging to the sphere of the *sexual*. By using a neologism such as *the sexual,* Laplanche refers to the parents' repressed infantile sexuality, reactivated by the perception of the child's body. The newborn's body triggers the parent's unconscious fantasies. Hence, under the effect of such fantasies, the parents attribute "the sex of a fantasised anatomy" to their child, independently of the anatomical sex.

We know that in "The split-off male and female elements to be found in men and women,"Winnicott's (1971) male patient had been received as a girl at his birth and the mother had taken care of him as such. This had led to a dissociation between the feminine and the masculine elements. The mother's madness that consisted in seeing a girl where there was a boy had been enacted in the session by the analyst: Winnicott had seen a girl on the couch when he knew that there was a man who was lying there. The patient had talked about his penis-envy and Winnicott had thought that only girls could experience penis-envy. The elaboration realised by the analyst in this and following sessions enabled the patient to overcome the dissociation in his psychic reality and to accept his bisexuality, which reflects a quality of a total self. For the first time, the patient could experience an authentic relation with the analyst, which gave him the feeling of a sense of identity. Very curiously, it was this male patient who had facilitated Winnicott's discovering of the feminine element at the beginning of life, from which the masculine element can emerge. It is the feminine element, in relation with the breast or the mother, that allows the establishment of the narcissistic foundation of the subject.

Psychoanalytic work with transsexual patients

Danielle Quinodoz's (1998) remarkable paper, "A fe/male transsexual patient in psychoanalysis," examines the case of a male patient who had undergone a vaginoplasty 28 years ago before his demand for analysis. The patient resorted to both psychotic and neurotic mechanisms. "On the psychotic level, the delusional neo-reality of the appearance of a woman sought to replace the unbearable reality of being a man, whereas the neurotic part was aware that s/he could never really be a woman" (79). From the first interview with Simon(e), the analyst could feel that the request for help came from a painful sense of her basic identity, which is why the analyst resorted to Winnicott's concept of the feminine element: "the intensity of the initial bond with the mother permits the construction of a sexually neutral sense of basic identity (along the lines that masculinity is a process that has to be initiated out of femininity)" (97). Thus, a sense of basic identity permits the subject to assume all the different forms from birth to death. In the transsexual:

> these changes of form might include the transition from the appearance of one sex to that of the other without affecting this basic certainty of personal identity. Conversely, is it quite impossible to imagine a sense of identity inseparable from the fact of belonging to a given gender, if not a given sex?
>
> (97)

The question that we would pose is the following: is it possible to conceive a sex-change that would not be related to conflicts in the sense of basic identity? In the case of Amir's male patient, the wish for a sex-change reflected the conflicts with respect to his sense of basic identity.

Dan was twenty-nine years old. His request for psychotherapy had coincided with the process of sex-change, from male to female. For two years, he had been receiving hormonal treatment and had reached the final stage of undergoing surgery. However, he was anxious and did not feel ready for this decision. Dan had a twin sister, Anne. From the moment they were born, Anne was perceived as the beautiful but fragile baby requiring most of the parents' attention, whereas Dan was the healthy and lively baby who had been born with a cleft lip. Hence, he felt that he could never be as attractive as Anne. In spite of having undergone two plastic surgeries, he still felt that his face was repulsive. Anne seemed to provide Dan with his perfect image, his ideal-ego with which he identified, in the absence of an affective and warm relation with the parents. His parents were relatively old, who had succeeded in having their twins after numerous fertility treatments. From very early, Dan had the feeling that Anne possessed qualities such as beauty, delicateness and charm precisely because she was a girl. He hated his own body and at the age of 18, he began to express his wish to undergo a sex-change and began hormonal treatment. However, he found himself in a very painful dichotomy, as he did not like his changing body with the feminine traits or his old one. By means of a sex-change, he wished to be like Anne but realised that it was impossible.

At this point, we find a similarity between Quinodoz's patient and Amir's patient. The sex-change in both aimed at replacing the intolerable reality of being a man. Quinodoz's patient, Simon(e), had a certain awareness that she could never really be a woman, whereas Dan knew that he could never be like Anne. In both of them, a splitting between the feminine and the masculine elements had taken place. Dan's alienating identification with Anne acquired its full meaning in the absence of a primary identification with the mother, as well as in the absence of the father as a third and as the object of the mother's desire. Dan needed Anne's face as a narcissistic support, in the absence of the mother's face serving as a mirror (Winnicott, 1971). According to Lacan (1949), the child's recognition of his/her image in the mirror around six months has as a condition the establishment of an emotional tie with the primordial object. In front of the mirror, the child is held by the mother, whose gaze sustains him/her. In Simon(e) and Dan, the need for a sex-change reflected their suffering with respect to their sense of basic identity that they perceived as faulty. Dan's identification with the twin sister had come to replace the defective bond with the mother (or the breast). As to Simon(e), as a small child, he had a strong unconscious wish to be admired by his father, whose profession involved receiving women and spending a lot of time with them. He had thought that he did not have much chance of being loved as a boy and that the parents would have preferred to have a girl.

After having, at the age of eighteen, undergone a vaginoplasty that Simon(e) had seen "as an urgent and inescapable reality" (Quinodoz, 1998, 97), her internal turmoil had not ceased. She had sought psychotherapy, which had been important for her and had helped her. However, twenty-eight years later, she needed to continue the psychic work with respect to herself and had come to request analysis. One of the difficulties that the analyst faced consisted in not knowing if she addressed the patient as a female or a male. She had decided to use the masculine form for the pre-surgery period and the feminine form after the sex-change, an aspect that was in accordance with the official civil identity. I have also used the male form to refer to the period before the vaginoplasty and the female form for the period after. During the preliminary interviews, the analyst had the impression that Simon(e) was asking for help to recover her childhood, which had been disavowed by her and that without it, she could not reconcile with a hateful part of herself. The patient had communicated to the analyst the feeling of having a painful sense of inner fragmentation that was related to her inability to represent her pre-surgery period. Let us remember that the analyst had described her patient as having both neurotic and psychotic parts. Thanks to her neurotic part, she could have great lucidity with respect to herself:

> I know that I have not become a woman even if the surgeons have given me a vaginoplasty, I shall never be able to be a woman, but only have the appearance of one; for me, that is already not so bad.
>
> (95)

At the beginning, the analyst had to take into consideration the patient's mental capacity with respect to what could happen to her once she discovered the unconscious motivations that had led to the sex-change. Could she bear this reality or end up with a breakdown or a suicide? Nevertheless, the analyst decided to accept Simon(e) for analysis, as she trusted her patient's capacity for symbolisation and her force for life. The progress of analytic work very painfully confronted the patient with her psychic reality. At one occasion, the patient, with her psychotic part, had projected her desperate feelings to the analyst, accusing her to wish to convert her to become a man again. "That's unthinkable, you can't rebuild what has been broken, and I have to come to terms with what I am" (100). Analysis effectively helped her to reconcile with whom and what she was. At the end of analysis, the self-revelation that she had attained was moving. She questioned her initial reasons for the vaginoplasty despite that she considered it as inevitable:

> When I look at myself in the mirror in the mornings and see a man, I think that the operation did not deliver what I was expecting. It was an illusion … If I had known that I would not look like a man or a woman, but a bit of both, I would not have had the operation. I wanted to have a sense of *existing* (italics added) and to go unnoticed, but it failed.
>
> (108)

In fact, since the first interview, the analyst had had the intuition with respect to the patient's experience of herself: in a preliminary interview, she had said to her: "You have the past of a boy and now you live as a woman, but you are still the same person, you are still yourself" (104). In this sense, the analyst had addressed the patient's narcissistic sense of being, which would be independent of the anatomical sex as a man or as a woman.

At this point, could we say that the experience of the self in the Winnicottian sense, which confers a primordial identity to the subject, *resists* the anatomical changes realised by the sex-change? The primordial identity allows a continuity of a sense of being and precedes the awareness of anatomical differences. However, Simon(e)'s confrontation with her truth and the acceptance of it was possible due to her analysis. At the end of analysis, the patient expressed her longing for a stable relationship with a partner, independently of the partner being male or female. The most important thing for her was to be able to establish a meaningful emotional relationship with the object. Can we also say that the awareness that she had reached at the end of analysis, the fact that she did not look like a man nor as woman but a "bit of both", is a *resistance* to the binary logic, that is, the dualism inherent in the masculine and the feminine, which is deeply anchored in our representations (Glocer Fiorini, 2019)? Simon(e) had not chosen to be either a man or a woman, but she came to accept this painful reality. At this point, it is possible to think that she did not wish to convert completely to female and that she needed to partly maintain her original male identity, and that this was what resisted the sex change on an unconscious level.

References

Andre, J. (2017). Quel genre de sexe?, *Quel Genre de Sexe?* Paris: PUF.
Freud, S. (1905d). *Three Essays on the Theory of Sexuality.* London: Hogarth Press, pp. 123–243.

Glocer Fiorini, L. (2019). Vers une déconstruction du 'féminin': discours, logiques et pouvoir. Les implications théorico-cliniques. *Revue française de psychanalyse* 83(3):825–839.

Lacan, J. (1949). *Le stade du miroir comme formateur de la fonction du Je telle qu'elle nous est révélée dans l'expérience psychanalytique, Ecrits*. Paris: Seuil, 1966.

Laplanche, J. (2007). *Sexual*. Paris: PUF.

Lévy, J.M. (2019). Ombres et lumières de la bisexualité. *Revue Française de Psychanalyse* 83:1421–1476.

Quinodoz, D. (1998). A FE/Male Transsexual patient in psychoanalysis. *International Journal of Psychoanalysis* 79:95–111.

Winnicott, D.W. (1971). The split-off male and female elements to be found in men and women. In: *Playing and Reality*. London: Tavistock.

Winnicott, D.W. (1967). Mirror-role of mother and family in child-development. In: *Playing and Reality*. London: Tavistock, 1971.

10 On trying to pass off transphobia as psychoanalysis and cruelty as "clinical logic"

Avgi Saketopoulou[1]

Gill-Peterson (2018, vii) writes:

> A libel placed on the very existence of trans children … is what passes
> for a rational object of "debate" among adults every day in the me-
> dia, online, in schools and clinics, and in the social milieu in which
> trans children must find a way, despite all the odds [against them],
> to survive, to grow, and to endure …. [Trans children are] subject …
> to being dismissed as unreal or brainwashed … as if such determina-
> tions are not procedurally genocidal in their holding open the world
> where trans life would be violently extinguished in the first place.

Ideological entanglements

*Gender Dysphoria: A Therapeutic Model for Working with Children, Adolescents
and Young Adults* presents itself as a primer for clinicians and a guidebook
for parents of atypically gendered youth. The book's attitude, David Bell
writes in the preface, is "neither affirmation nor opposition but a kind of
deeply engaged neutrality" (xv). But "deeply engaged neutrality" is not
what one encounters in its pages. Despite touting an "objective scientific
appraisal" (xix) and stating that the authors are "neither 'pro' nor 'anti'
transition" (7) and will "keep an open mind" (8), this highly political
volume gives us, instead, a remarkably stale and dangerous recycling of
anti-trans rhetoric.

I am not using the word *dangerous* lightly: its cloak of scientific neutrality aside, this book's ideological positioning and language motor
weighty clinical recommendations for treating the "problem" of children
who only mistakenly think they are trans, and whose "fixed belief system" (207) may well trick the adults surrounding them. In this book,
therapy is not an open-ended exploration, but a targeted course correc-
tion toward the predetermined end that its authors, Susan Evans and
Marcus Evans, know to be true, no matter the specific child's dynamics:
namely, that "gender dysphoria is a psychic retreat" that interferes with
"reality testing" (203).

DOI: 10.4324/9781003531333-17

For these authors, the child's or adolescent's wish to transition is uniformly about managing fears, anxieties, and vulnerabilities "by projecting unwanted aspects of the self into their natal body which is then regarded [by the patient] as the problem that needs to be changed or eradicated" (57). The Evanses thus insistently caution the clinical reader to "not fall in with the view that gender identity is something unconnected to the person's mental health" (28), sounding an alarm about "the *ideological* drive to separate all gender incongruence from mental illness" (133, emphasis added). Gender dysphoria, we are repeatedly told, is frequent in "patients with a history of serious and enduring mental illness or personality disorder" (31).

"There is a risk," write the authors, "that by writing this book, we open ourselves to accusations of 'transphobia'" (8). But how else can one read statements such as this one regarding a transfemale child: "Paul, by requesting castration, will do permanent damage to his capacity to have children, while also assaulting the sexuality his parents bestowed upon him in conception" (183). Referring to trans patients by their pretransition name - often called *deadnaming* – disrespecting their preferred pronouns, and describing surgical interventions needed by some trans individuals as "castration" is contemptuous, countertherapeutic, and reveal how uninformed the authors are about the lived realities of some trans subjects. Furthermore, the notion that fertility needs to be preserved at all costs, independently of the particular patient's needs, suggests that, for the Evanses, reproductive potential is an expectation if not a duty to be fulfilled.

Still, what is even more problematic is not just this book's transphobia – a bar this volume easily clears – but that, as I will discuss, it is glaringly uninformed about the lived possibilities and potential pleasures of trans life; it is poorly researched; it is strikingly solipsistic, engaging none of the many existing discourses on trans; and it is clinically dogmatic. More specifically, while the authors worry that it is the volume's psychoanalytic inflection per se that will invite criticism, the problem is not the psychoanalytic angle they take (good psychoanalytic thinking, as we'll see, would be a relief in this volume), but rather it is their use of psychoanalysis to launder antitransness. Instead of insights gleaned from long-term psychoanalysis of trans individuals, its data set comes from high-traffic gender clinics where patients have to guard themselves against therapists who have a say over whether they receive medical care or not.

The authors thus don't seem to be aware that trans individuals often have to do considerable psychic work to articulate *even to themselves*, let alone to their therapists, their transness; that the fiction of transition as having a final destination recedes with analytic time; that when not forced to defend their gender experience, trans patients oftentimes welcome thinking about gender as a continuously evolving process; that the ostensible unidirectionality of transitioning is but a normative fantasy, often the therapist's; that suicidality is not wielded to control parents, nor is it a political manoeuvre, as the authors intimate, but for some trans people it is an unbearable truth.

Last and most important, there is no evidence that the authors have experienced the wonderment that can accompany watching a patient awake into a body that can newly look *and feel* like it's theirs, or that transitioning can be one of the most meaningful and joyous things some patients will do in their lives.

In contrast, *Gender Dysphoria* recounts the work of therapists who enter the clinical setting armed with indisputable confidence about how gender works and with a certitude as to where the diagnostic probe should intervene. While some of the therapists supervised by the authors entertain more complex ideas about a patient's gender, the Evanses' supervisory input is to correct them, interpreting them (the therapists) as supporting "the patient's concrete thinking" or as colluding in the patient's pursuit of "magical solutions" (181). This stance creates a closed feedback loop where no new ideas about gender and its embodied possibilities can be explored, and where the authors' clinical stance is claustrophobically reinforced. By describing trans childhood as unquestioningly pathological and by insisting on clinical approaches that seek to "treat" it out of existence, the book thus advocates a clinical praxis that offers no viable path to trans adulthood. Such a framework constitutes an elimination not only of trans children themselves, but also of the possibility of future trans adults overall. This, in short, is what *Gender Dysphoria* tries to pass off as *clinical logic*, and it is also the sort of process that historian Gill-Peterson has named *genocidal* in her archivally rich book, *Histories of the Transgender Child* (2018).

Part of the difficulty of reviewing *Gender Dysphoria* is that it is, at times, so extreme in its positions and so excessive in its claims that even to point this out and document it risks this essay itself being read as partisan and extremist. But these two positions (the book's and this essay's) are not symmetrical. The differences between them, that is, do not simply require some neutral judge who will decide what's right and fair, as if between the book's extremism and my strong criticism of it, an objective third party could settle the matter. Such an attitude would miss how out of step – and how harmful – a democratic approach to opinion-making can be (Jakobsen & Pellegrini 2003). The counter, of course, is not an anti-democratic stance where people can't freely express their opinions; what we need instead is a more careful appraisal of what these opinions are and are not based on.

Clinical questions

As a psychoanalyst with extensive experience working with trans and gender nonconforming children and adolescents in long-term treatments, I am often asked if specialised training or a distinctive set of skills is necessary for this work. I think that any psychoanalyst who is also solidly trained in child/adolescent work could *potentially* work with trans children/teens. But two qualifications are in order.

First, countertransference: even well-trained and well-intentioned clinicians can lose their capacity to think or work well when confronted with a trans patient. Hansbury (2017a, 2017b) and Pula (2015) have documented and theorised how and why contact with trans subjects can arouse the analyst's fragility around her own body and gender. This can have a range of problematic effects: the analyst's thinking can become overly concrete, strangely sadistic, or fearfully controlling, thus forfeiting the attitude of open inquiry and receptive curiosity so crucial to good therapeutic work. Moreover, trans patients can be especially vulnerable *to the analyst,* which means that working with trans patients (as with other non-normative or minoritised subjects) makes issues of psychoanalytic ethics critical. The Hippocratic "do no harm" has to include stipulations about not forcing patients into normative psychic paths that can be soul-killing for them (e.g., the therapist's or parent's insistence on retaining fertility whatever the cost, which may or may not be in the child's best interest). If a special toolkit is thus needed to treat trans patients, it is not filled with new techniques, but with an attentiveness to the many levels of distortion, scotomisation, and confusion that analysts, many of whom have not encountered trans individuals in their social or personal lives, inadvertently introduced to the work.

Where can such analysts get these skills? One way is by turning to and learning from other discourses – and here queer theory, trans studies, and trans of colour critique can help analysts discern how trans subjects may be unfairly pathologised in ways the analyst was not aware of and had not intended. Also critical is an active engagement with the psychoanalytic literature on trans patients, which now spans more than two full decades, and consultation with other colleagues working analytically with this population.

Second, an up-to-date, general sense of the medical literature around transitioning can help orient analysts who are unfamiliar with – and would be surprised by – what is and is not realistically achievable. For example, many clinicians don't know that a transfemale parent can breastfeed (Reisman & Goldstein 2018; Yeginsu 2018), or what the fertility ramifications actually are for young people who take puberty blockers versus cross-sex hormones (e.g., Neely et al. 2010). Such knowledge does not answer analytic questions per se and can exert its own normative tug. But having a sense of what is and is not realistically achievable can help put patients' wishes and fantasies in some perspective, freeing the analyst to focus on the psychic meanings of medical interventions, rather than becoming inordinately alarmed about the ostensibly catastrophic consequences awaiting children who receive trans-related medical care.

This is not to say that there aren't ramifications for every choice made (whether it is a *doing* or a *not doing*); it is only to underscore that a basic familiarity with medical facts can help disentangle the analyst's realistic concerns from her countertransference-based fantasies, her own gender fears, and her own embodied anxieties. In short, we don't need special training to work with trans patients; rather, we need tools to manage the reign of normative beliefs in *ourselves.*

Offered as a manual to help clinicians work more substantively with trans youth drawing on an analytic perspective, *Gender Dysphoria* fails in both these respects. To provide some necessary context, let me note that the volume's stated goals are to "to deepen empathy" (6) for trans patients and to offer a much-needed clinical framework that does not traffic in platitudes or oversimplifications. There is indeed a pressing need for a psychoanalytically informed volume that explores soberly and with thera-peutic steadiness the layered issues involved in treating trans children and working with their families. Such a book would need to sidestep shallow and unhelpful formulations (such as "trans people are born in the wrong body"), and also to avoid overdramatising the conversation by imprecisely inflating the "dangers" of transitioning or unnecessarily inflaming parental fears. The authors of this volume are aware of these problems, and it is in that spirit, they argue, that they offer their clinical perspective.

But the book they have given us is not the book they promise. What we get instead is exaggerated panic and dangerously careless metaphors. Consider, for example, the Evanses' likening of the increasing numbers of youth coming out as trans to the opioid crisis, as though transness were an epidemic (which has been contested in the literature [Ashley 2020]) and a deadly one at that! Predicting that "the medical treatment of young people with gender dysphoria may follow a similar path" (39) betrays a gross misunderstanding of how that crisis unfolded: it was not, as the authors write, by "overprescription" (217), but by purposeful misrepresentation of medical data and strategic manipulation by pre-scribing doctors to drive up profits. The Evanses' insinuation that the rubric of addiction applies to trans children – whom they describe as "addicted to 'dressing up'" (129) – may not be evidence-based, but it is attention-grabbing. And it can panic and mislead parents who struggle vis-a-vis their child's transness, as well as therapists who are trying to learn how to work with trans children.

Moreover, the authors present a vision of gender dysphoria in which nothing is uncertain or as-yet-unknown, organising all clinical cases around the so-called pathological gender of the child discussed. Therapists are directed toward resolution-oriented goals to remove gender dysphoria in order to "return" the child to a normative life, whether that be hetero- or homonormative. Nowhere do we encounter the humility of uncertainty or of *learning from* our trans-identified patients.

Throughout this book, the Evanses don't "see" transness, but instead a defence against homosexuality. Transition, they argue, is a warped solu-tion to homophobia: by switching gender, the patient becomes "straight." But – and here is another place where the authors' inexperience comes through – not all, or even most, trans people identify as "straight." Not only are many trans people homoerotically attracted, but gendered attractions keep shifting. Nor should psychoanalysis settle for the pyrrhic victory that homosexuality is the preferred resolution of "gender dysphoria." Is an anti-homophobic psychoanalysis to be purchased at the price of pathologising gender nonconforming children?

In this context, it may not surprise the reader to learn that the authors never tackle the problem of countertransference. Not once in the book's 240 pages is there any serious inquiry into whether, for example, describing trans experience as "a fixed belief system" (28) with a "delusional intensity" dominated by "the psychotic part of the personality" (207) might belie the therapist's (or the authors') conscious prejudices or unconscious beliefs about what gender is and what it isn't? For example, the Evanses note that misgendering and deadnaming can be intentionally hurtful or, at times, a genuine slip. Their focus, however, is on the patient's "extreme responses" that "vilify" the offender (218), as if the therapist's parapraxis doesn't warrant psychoanalytic investigation. As we already saw in their description of "Paul," who is deadnamed and misgendered, they are not in the least thoughtful about the meanings of their own enactments or slips. The authors thus miss the opportunity to examine which anxieties and gender panics may inform the therapist's error – and what kind of psychoanalytic stance is that?

Throughout the volume, the authors speak with a self-confidence that is at odds with clinical humility and ethical curiosity. What's worse, this self-confidence is only possible because they admit into their argument nothing that would challenge their own position. They don't engage, let alone cite, any of the bodies of scholarship that labor to understand trans children, including *any* of the rich psychoanalytic literature in this area. Whether they are aware of this literature or not is hard to know, but what this absence does is make the volume read like a period piece. Like all period pieces, it is strangely nostalgic for a long-gone era, here a psychoanalytic one in which the analyst was seen as knowing with certainty the precise cause of the patient's ailment, reliably diagnosing the problem to prescribe the correct course of treatment and doing so with disinterested objectivity. At a time, however, when gender possibilities are proliferating with astonishing velocity (forget about the trans tipping point; new gender permutations enter our lexicons every week), the promise of a therapist who can identify with certitude what is going on with the patient's gender and has a solid theory as to why *by only the second session* – as is consistently the case in this volume's clinical accounts – should give us pause. Omnipotence, here, is not the patients' but the authors'. Of course, it is precisely this kind of all-knowing therapist who may be deeply appealing both to anxious parents and to struggling clinicians.

Nevertheless, however, pressed we may be as a field to better organise our thinking and guide clinical praxis around trans children, we need to resist the urge to cling to such imperial models. Consider, for instance, one of this book's most idiosyncratic propositions, namely, that "the family's wish to support transition" may be a case of "Munchausen by proxy" (74). *Munchausen by proxy,* the authors explain, involves "the parents pushing fears of their own illness into the child, then presenting them to medical services for treatment" (93). This shift of focus from the child's transness to diagnosing *the family's* supportive attitude as medical maltreatment is astounding. And while, I suppose, anything is possible in cases of severe parental mental illness, nowhere in the professional literature – be it research-based, clinical, quantitative, or anecdotal – have I ever encountered an association between Munchausen and trans childhood.

Nor do the authors offer any clinical or other data to support their rather bizarre association of transness with Munchausen's. Where that claim does appear, however, is in Texas Attorney General Ken Paxton's (2022) legal opinion, which argued that "gender-based procedures" are "non-medically necessary" and thus "comparable to Munchausen syndrome by proxy or criminal injury to a child" (8). (See also American Psychoanalytic Association [2022].) Is this the kind of politically motivated claim that we as psychoanalysts want to abide by or contribute to? In a volume addressed to both therapists and parents, such propositions linking transness and Munchausen are not only of uncertain value; they are frankly irresponsible.

Countering blind spots: How to do better

The book's problematic formulations could have been helped if the Evanses had engaged existing knowledge from long-term treatments of trans children, if they had looked more closely into the existing literature on trans parenting (e.g., Meadow 2018), and if they had turned to knowledge from other disciplines regarding the imbrication of the psychic and the social. For example, the idea that a wish to transition is spurred by unconscious envy of the other sex and the proposition that trans may be a way of "unconsciously withdraw[ing] from the competition" of performing normative gender successfully (25) would be contested by much feminist theorising. Trans studies would also importantly unpack and challenge the Evanses' too-simple notion that an AMAB[2] child dressing up in the mother's clothing is a "manic solution" (130) and an "erotized defense," a proposition that has already been put forward and heavily criticised (Serano 2020). Trans of colour critique would also help this volume in which, startlingly, race is not mentioned *even once,* as if social location is unimportant, as if all trans children worthy of our consideration are to be imagined as White, and as if gender can be thought of outside of race (Snorton 2017). In work with gender-variant kids, cross-disciplinary engagement is not a luxury but a necessity to help alert us to our field's normative assumptions and to put them under scrutiny.

Also problematic is the fact that, while the volume is populated with unqualified statements about the grave dangers posed to trans children by hormonal treatments, there is no reliable indication that the authors are familiar with the medical literature on this topic. While a survey of the medical literature would obviously be beyond the scope of a psychotherapeutic volume, the continuous ringing of alarms over hormone therapy requires some substantiation. For example, the claim that "evidence [shows] that 61% to 98% plus of children resolve their gender dysphoria if provided with essential psychological support and care" (203) has been heavily contested in the trans research literature on methodological grounds and is generally considered overinflated (Temple-Newhook et al. 2018). More significantly, the claim that gender variance resolves, if ignored, implies problematically that if only adults were able to contain their anxieties, and if therapists didn't support patients "in pursuing magical solutions" (181), gender-variant children would mostly outgrow their atypicality, developing into normatively gendered adults. Such claims not only overlook studies indicating that access to medical care improves trans children's mental health outcomes (e.g., Green et al. 2021; Turban et al. 2022); they also contribute to the continued dismissal of trans kids' experience and to discouraging clinicians from listening attentively to the gender complexities that trans youth bring to our consulting rooms.

Strikingly, the authors seem to understand themselves as whistleblowers who are "uncovering" what they see as a uniform, mindless, and uncritical clinical stance that carelessly facilitates transitioning for young people who only and always mistakenly think they are trans. The term *whistleblower* marks the Evanses as rebels when, in fact, what this book offers is not a radical psychoanalysis, but a very conservative one. A whistleblower is one who takes the risk of defying the status quo to say something unpalatable and to reveal the workings of systems that operate without our knowing. But gender clinics, the sites where this book unfolds, are not CIA black sites of sinister gender transformations; their operating principles are explicit, documented, and fleshed out in their published materials. What exactly is the concealed goal here that the Evanses are so bravely revealing?

Casting themselves as whistleblowers would make any criticism of the authors appear to be further evidence of their speaking truth to power. But what exactly is that power? In fact, this book emerges out of ongoing debates in the United Kingdom over puberty blockers, leading off with a discussion of a legal action that restricted trans kids' access to puberty blockers, an action that has since been reversed. So much for the book's promise of "deeply engaged neutrality" (xv).

Imagining otherwise

Gender is a more serpentine matter (Stockton 2021) than this volume admits or seems to know. What its authors most critically miss is that trans lives are not meant to be lived according to the syntax of adaptation to the existing world order. Trans seeks to *dis-order* the world, to bring new possibilities into being, to unseat the very principles by which the body, gender, and pleasure are lived. The notion that hormones are magical solutions, for example, fails to discern that something far more complex and nuanced is at work. Hormone therapy, writes Preciado, "is not an end in itself: it is an ally in the task of inventing an elsewhere" (Preciado 2019, 29).

Ultimately, one of this volume's most decisive failures is a failure of imagination. What the authors do not see, but which we should not forget, is that we are living in thrilling times. Things are happening around us that we as psychoanalysts do not fully understand and for which our theories offer inadequate guide maps. This is challenging but not catastrophic – except for those who see only danger in the unexpected. The quick, ongoing transformations of the very category of trans, the questions raised by hormone treatments, the fact that a growing number of people are asking for surgeries whose precise psychic effects they cannot anticipate but that they nevertheless sense they need – all these open up vistas that can generate new analytic thinking, and not only because they require us to revisit our epistemologies of gender and sex. "Genders are changing day by day," writes Stockton, and "we are riding the wave coming at us, which can be gleeful and cruel by turns. We can innovate and fantasize …. We can, minute by minute, *fail* norms" (2021, 170, emphasis added).

It is this failing of norms viewed not as pathology but as an emerging vista that this volume is unable to dream of. That, I would say, is why it fails trans children, their parents, and the clinicians who treat them – and it is also why it fails psychoanalytic thinking. Yes, novelty can feel scary. "You are free to decide," writes Preciado (2019), whether you believe that the psychoanalytic epistemology of gender is mutating, "but believe this at least: life is mutation and multiplicity. You need to understand that the future monsters are also your children and your grandchildren" (89).

Coda

Gender Dysphoria does not cite the scholarship of any trans-identified clinician, and the voices of trans patients are heard only in response to those of their therapists. In this essay, as a corrective, I have primarily drawn on the scholarship of trans-identified or otherwise gender-nonconforming clinicians and academics. All quantitative research cited is from peer-reviewed journals.

Notes

1 Avgi Saketopolou presented *Gender, binding, and the sexual: On the analyst's countertransferential agitation* at Contemporary Psychoanalytic Perspectives on Gender and Sexualities, Brussels 27–28 September, 2019. This chapter is reprinted from Saketopoulou, A. (2022). On Trying to Pass off Transphobia

as Psychoanalysis and Cruelty as "Clinical Logic." *The Psychoanalytic Quarterly*, *91*(1), 177–190. https://doi.org/10.1080/00332828.2022.2056378, reprinted by permission of Taylor & Francis Ltd, https://www.tandfonline.com on behalf of The Psychoanalytic Quarterly.

2 AMAB stands for *assigned-male-at birth*.

References

American Psychoanalytic Association (2022). APsaA statement condemning Texas governor's attacks on trans children and their families. https://apsa.org/content/apsaa-statement-condemning-texas-governor%E2%80%99s-attacks-trans-children-and-their-families.

Ashley, F. (2020). ROGD is scientific-sounding veneer for unsubstantiated anti-trans views: A Peer-reviewed analysis. *Sociol. Rev.*, 68(4):779–977. doi:10.1177/0038026120934693

Gill- Peterson, J. (2018). *Histories of the Transgender Child*. London: University of Minnesota Press.

Green, A. E., Dechants, J. P., Price, M. N. & Davis, C. K. (2021). Association of gender-affirming hormone therapy with depression, thoughts of suicide, and attempted suicide among transgender and nonbinary youth. *J. Adolesc. Health*, 70(4):643–649. https://www.jahonline.org/article/S1054-139X(21)00568-1/fulltext. doi:10.1016/j.jadohealth.2021.10.036

Hansbury, G. (2017a). The masculine vaginal: Working with queer men's embodiment at the transgender edge. *J. Amer. Psychoanal. Assn.*, 65:1009–1031. doi:10.1177/0003065117742409

Hansbury, G. (2017b). Unthinkable anxieties: reading Transphobic countertransferences in a century of psychoanalytic writing. *TSQ*, 4:384–404.

Jakobsen, J. & Pellegrini, A. (2003). *Love the Sin: Sexual Regulation and the Limits of Religious Tolerance*. New York: NYU Press.

Meadow, T. (2018). *Trans Kids: Being Gendered in the Twenty-First Century*. Oakland: University of California Press.

Neely, E. K., Lee, P. A., Bloch, C. A., Larsen, L., Yang, D., Matia-Goldberg, C. & Chwalisz, K. (2010). Leuprolide acetate 1-month depot for central precocious puberty: Hormonal suppression and recovery. *Int. J. Pediatr. Endocrinol.*, https://www.ncbi.nlm.nih.gov/pmc/articles/PMC3062984/.doi:10.1186/1687-9856-2010-398639

Paxton, K. (2022). https://texasattorneygeneral.gov/sites/default/files/global/KP-0401.pdf.

Preciado, P. (2019). *Can the Monster Speak? Report to an Academy of Psychoanalysts*. London: Semiotext(e).

Pula, J. (2015). Understanding gender through the lens of transgender experience. *Psychoanal. Inq.*, 35:809–822.

Reisman, T. & Goldstein, Z. (2018). Case report: Induced lactation in a transgender woman. *Transgender Health*, 3(1):24–26. doi:10.1089/trgh.2017.0044

Serano, J. (2020). Autogynephilia: A scientific review, feminist analysis, and alternative "embodiment fantasies" model. *Sociol. Rev.*, 68(4):763–778. doi:10.1177/0038026120934690

Snorton, C. R. (2017). *Black on Both Sides: A Racial History of Trans Identity*. Minneapolis, MN: University of Minnesota Press.

Stockton, K. B. (2021). *Gender(s)*. Cambridge: MIT Press.

Temple-Newhook, J., Pyne, J., Winters, K., Feder, S., Holmes, C., Tosh, J., Sinott, M. L., Jamieson, A. & Picket, S. (2018). A critical commentary on follow-up studies and "desistance" theories about transgender and gender- nonconforming children. *Int. J. Transgenderism*, 19(2):212–224. doi:10.1080/15532739.2018.1456390

Turban, J. L., King, D., Kobe, J., Reisner, S. L. & Keuroglian, A. S. (2022). Access to gender- affirming hormones during adolescence and mental health outcomes among transgender adults. *PlosOne*. doi:10.1371/journal. pone.0261039

Yeginsu, C. (2018). Transgender woman breast-feeds baby after hospital induces lactation. https://www.nytimes.com/2018/02/15/health/transgender-woman-breast-feed.html.

Index

Note: Page numbers followed by "n" refer to end notes.

abjection 10, 30, 36–38, 40, 42, 44n6
Abraham, N. 122
acceptance 10, 16, 33, 73, 79, 83, 85–86, 88, 106, 147
Acosta, S. 1–4
adolescence/adulthood/adolescent 8, 10, 24–25, 47, 49, 53–55, 76, 78, 80–81, 84, 88, 95–96, 99–102, 105, 107, 108n5, 131, 150–151
affirmative position 50, 84–86, 89–91
Agnes, case of (adolescent agency and seduction) 3, 94, 99–104
Ai Weiwei 56
Allison, L. 3, 9–10, 19–29
Althusser, L. 123
Ambrosio, G. 139
Amir, D. 4, 115–116, 131–145; *On the Lyricism of the Mind* 132
analytic listening 32, 43
analytic neutrality 42
anatomical difference 17, 147
André, J. 142–143
anxiety 3, 19, 30, 32–35, 37–41, 53–54, 62, 68, 78, 95, 127–128, 132–133, 136, 143
Apprey, M. 121
Argentieri, S. 139
Aristophanes 67
assigned-male-at birth (AMAB) 155
atypical gender identity organisation (AGIO) 52–53
Aulagnier, P. 125
autistic spectrum 44n4, 47–48
Autistic Spectrum Disorders (ASD) 79
autonomy 8, 33, 55–56, 78–79, 83, 87–90, 95, 104, 107

Bakhtin, M. 11
beliefs and fantasies and states 50
Bell, D. 149
Bergler, E. 30–32
Bergstein, A. 32
binaries/binarism *see* gender binaries/ binarism
Bion, W. R. 25–26, 55, 71–72, 117, 126, 129, 133; alpha work 127; *Attention and Interpretation* 141; container-contained interaction 132; *Emotional Turbulence* 25–26; *see also* caesura
bisexuality, psychic 9–10, 30, 32, 34–36, 40–41
bisexual movement 43
Bleger, J. 61
bodily autonomy 83, 89, 92n3
bodily disunity 83
bodily integrity 83
Boehm, F. 31–32
Bonnard, P. 47, 55
Botellas 126
Brazil 3, 65–66
Britton, R., *Belief and Imagination* 50
Butler, J. 66, 142–143

caesura 4, 128–129, 131–133, 137–138, 140–143
Cass Review 84–85
Castoriadis, C. 17–18
castration 8, 14, 16, 33–34, 96, 104, 115, 150
catastrophic change 35, 39–40, 44, 80, 89, 94, 131, 133, 141, 152, 157
Cecarelli, P. R. 72
chaos theory 120, 128
Chetrit-Vatine, V. 125

child and adolescent mental health service (CAMHS) 54
childhood 8, 20, 25, 42, 48, 53, 55, 78, 97, 114, 143, 146, 151, 155
child protection conference 54
Clifford, J. 65
contagion 78, 95–96
container-contained interaction 132
Corbett, K. 128
countertransference 13, 61–63, 70–72, 102, 117, 138, 140–141, 152, 154
Crenshaw, K. 124–125

deadnaming 150, 154
De Beauvoir, S., *The Second Sex* 12
depathologise/depathologising approach 114–115; gender diversity 67; homosexuality 73
Derrida, J. 113
desire and gender 15
determinism 113–114
diagnostic insult 115
di Ceglie, D. 3, 8, 47–56
Dimen, M. 128

ego precocity 126
emotions/emotional 9, 19–24, 26, 31, 41–42, 61, 71, 77, 89, 94, 99, 105–107, 135, 138, 146–147
ethical considerations 84–91
Evans, S. and Evans, M., *Gender Dysphoria* 113, 149–151, 153–157
Evzonas, N. 3, 113–117

facts of life 82–83, 139
Fanon, F. 123
feminine/femininity 3, 7, 9–17, 32–37, 41, 43, 53, 65, 69, 74, 96–97, 100, 104, 115–116, 136, 144–147
Ferenczi, S. 33
Ferro, A. 71
Fonagy, P. 22–24
Forrester, J. 101–102
fractals 128
Freud, S. 2, 9–10, 13, 22–28, 30, 33–37, 42–43, 44n2, 68–69, 72–74, 96, 102, 106–107, 114–115, 143; *Recommendations to Physicians Practising Psycho-Analysis* 28; *Three Essays on the Theory of Sexuality* 8, 13, 19–21, 24, 73, 143; transference neurosis 70; *see also* Oedipus complex; psychoanalysis

Galatzer-Levy, R. 128
gender: affirmative approach 84–86, 89, 96; and biology 94, 96, 100–101, 104; crossing 131–134, 137, 140–143; dichotomy 131–132, 136–137; diversity 1–4, 10, 12–13, 47, 49, 56, 66, 113, 116; dysphoria 8, 44n4, 53–56, 78, 80–81, 87, 92n6, 114–115, 149–156; experience 128, 132–133, 143, 150; fluidity 119–122; historicity 97–99; identity 8, 22, 29, 47–56, 62, 66–69, 74, 76–84, 90–91, 114, 116, 141, 143–144, 150; incongruity 67; overdetermination of 114; sex difference 104, 119; space 131, 133, 138, 140–141, 143; variance 94, 156
gender binaries/binarism 4, 11, 34, 69, 72, 97, 120, 122–124; intersectionality and incomprehensibility 124–128; Laplanche, helplessness, and the other 124; strange attractors, chaos theory, fractals, and caesura 128–129
Gender Identity Development Service (GIDS) 47, 50, 53–54
generalisations 68–70, 85, 115
generational differences 67–68, 126
Gherovici, P. 115
Gill-Peterson, J., *Histories of the Transgender Child* 149, 151
Glocer Fiorini, L. 3, 7, 10–18, 74
Goffman, E., *Stigma* 120, 123
Gordon, E. G. and Corrigan, P. -E., *The Mind as an Object* 126
Gozlan, O. 3, 94–107, 137
Green, A. 22
group psychology 96, 106
Guattari, F. 18

Hansbury, G. 152
Harris, A. 3–4, 114, 119–129
Hepworth, M. 22
Hermaphroditus 67
heterogeneity 77–79, 82, 113
heteronormativity 27, 69, 119, 127
heterosexuality 14, 16, 20–21, 27, 32, 37, 70, 73–74, 98, 120, 142–143
homophobia 32–34, 37, 66, 78, 113, 122, 153
homosexuality 10–11, 13, 15, 19–22, 27, 30–33, 35–37, 43, 66–67, 69, 73–74, 78, 84, 87, 90, 98, 113–114, 153–154
homotransphobia 61, 62, 63
hyper-complexity 16–17

implantation 124–125
infantile sexuality 3, 9, 14, 24, 33,
    143–144
International Lesbian, Gay, Bisexual
    and Transgender Association (ILGA)
    66
International Psychoanalytical
    Association (IPA) 61, 69, 139
International Statistical Classification
    of Diseases and Related Health
    Problems (ICD 11) 67
interpellation 119, 121–124
intersectionality 124–125, 128
intersex people 67, 100, 103
intolerance 26, 61–63, 65–66
intromission 124–125

Joseph case (sexualisation of abjection)
    37–42
Joynt, C. 102
Juusela, M. 30–31

Kahneman, D. 122
Keats, J. 25
Klein-Bion model 53
Krenak, A. 65
Kristeva, J. 30, 33–34, 36–37, 40, 69, 72,
    96, 102–103
Kurilof, E. 116

Lacan, J. 72, 115, 126, 145–146
Laplanche, J. 4, 42, 74, 104, 106,
    120–122, 124–127, 143–144
Lemma, A. 3, 76–91, 140
Lévy, J. -M. 143
Lewkowicz, S. 3, 65–74
LGBTQI+ people 3, 61, 66
loco parentis 95

male-female design 21
malignant containment 132
Mandelbrot, B. 128
Manfredi, S. T. 71
Manne, K., *Down Girl* 119
masculine-feminine dichotomy 15, 34
masculine/masculinity 1, 3, 7, 9, 11–17,
    28, 33–35, 39, 41, 43, 48, 55, 69, 104,
    115, 144–147
Matte-Blanco, I. 68–69
McDougall, J. 38–39, 43
McLaughlin, J. T. 123
Meltzer, D. 42, 47, 72
mental health 1, 67, 78, 83, 94, 150, 156
migrant dysphoria 50

Money-Kyrle, R. 82, 139
Morin, E. 13, 17
Morris, J., "On the sadness of living
    abroad" 50
Morrison, T. 123
Moss, D. 122
mutual elision 124–125

nachtraiglich/nachträglichkeit
    engagement 94–95, 98, 102, 106
natal girls 79
National Human Rights Commission 62
neologism 144
neosexuality 38–39, 43
Neri, C. 117
non-thinking 31–32

Oedipus complex 3, 7–8, 14–16, 74, 98
otherness 3, 9–10, 12, 17, 23, 25, 30–41,
    43–44, 74, 123, 140

paranoid-schizoid-depressive
    continuum 53
passivity 34, 96
paternal function 15–16
pathology/pathological 2–3, 21, 23, 26,
    30, 32, 35, 66–70, 72–74, 84, 88–89, 98,
    114, 116, 124, 127, 137, 139, 151–154,
    157
Paxton, K. 155
Pick, I. B. 70–71
polymorphous sexuality 8–9
Pontalis, J. -B. 42
Posadas, M. 1–4
Preciado, P. 157
primary and secondary bisexualities 44
productive engagement 85
psyche 10, 16, 30, 32–35, 37, 39, 41, 43,
    82, 119
psychic bisexuality 9–10, 30, 32, 34–36,
    40–41
psychic change 42–44, 71
psychic qualities 48
psychic space 133
psychoanalysis 2–3, 9, 11–12, 15, 19,
    21–22, 24, 26, 28, 30, 41–42, 66, 69, 72,
    74, 79, 84, 87–91, 95, 97–100, 105–107,
    113, 121, 123, 125, 140, 142–144, 150,
    154, 156
psychosexuality 19–29, 42, 66, 69
psychosis 115
psychosomatic anxiety 38–39
psychotherapeutic exploration 48, 52,
    137, 156

psychotherapy 24, 48, 50, 52, 86–88, 107, 134, 140, 145–146, 156
Pula, J. 152

Queer Museum 66
Quinodoz, D. 133, 140, 144–145

Racker, H. 70
Radcliffe-Richards, J. 77
recognition 9, 17, 49, 83, 91, 94, 102, 145–146
Reiner, M. 113
resistances 1–2
retrospect 1, 91n2, 102–103
Ricoeur, P. 62–63
Rilke, R. M., *Letters to a Young Poet* 28
Rose, J. 119–120, 123

Saketopoulou, A. 4, 113, 116, 149–157
Sandler, P. C. 43
Scarfone, D. 113–114
Schore, A. 123–124
Schumann, A. 3, 9–10, 30–44
secondary psychic bisexuality 36
serious illness 21
Sex Reassignment Surgery 79, 87
sexual/sexuality 104; aim 20; archaic languages 38; arousal 9, 24, 39; bisexual movement 43; Dan case 24, 134–137, 141–142, 145–146; desire 69, 78; destabilises 66; difference 12, 14, 17–18, 30, 74, 119–120; heterosexuality 14, 16, 20–21, 27, 32, 37, 70, 73–74, 98, 120, 142–143; homosexuality 10–11, 13, 15, 19–22, 27, 30–33, 35–37, 43, 66–67, 69, 73–74, 78, 84, 87, 90, 98, 113–114, 153–154; identity 66, 90, 143; and identity 105; infantile 3, 9, 14, 24, 33, 143–144; intersex people 67, 100, 103; neosexuality 38–39, 43; normal 20; orientation 17, 28, 66–67, 74, 105; polymorphous 8–9; psychic bisexuality 9–10, 30, 32, 34–36, 40–41; psychosexuality 19–29, 42, 66, 69; revolution 68; sex-change 136, 143, 145–147; sexualisation of abjection 37–42, 44n6; state of mind 38, 42; theory of 124; *see also* transsexual/transsexuality
sinthome 115
Socarides, C. W., *The Overt Homosexual* 21–22
Stengers, I. 96–97, 103

Stoller, R. J. 94, 100–103, 143
suicide risk 47–48, 85, 92n6, 116, 146
Sunflower Seeds 56
symbolic difference 17

theory and practice 106
therapeutic approach 10, 48–50, 53–56, 71, 80–81, 85, 89–90, 99, 115, 139, 152–153
Thomson-Salo, F. 1–4
tolerance 62–63, 65
Tompkins, S. 123
Torok, M. 122
transgender: identification 76–77, 80–82, 84, 89–91; identities and experience 77–79; individuals 76, 82–83, 85–86, 89, 91, 94, 140
trans identities 96, 114–115, 153
trans patients 63, 150, 152–153, 157
trans people 3, 66, 73, 115, 150, 153
transphobia 66, 150
transphobic position 4, 76–77, 84, 90
trans-receptive position 90
transsexual/transsexuality 96, 115, 140, 144–147; jouissance 115; madness 115; patient 140, 144–147
trauma/traumatic encounter 30, 33–35, 37–44, 44n3, 44n6, 48, 53, 63, 80, 90, 115, 124–125
Trías, E. 17
Tustin, F. 30, 32, 35–36, 40, 42
Tversky, A. 122

unconscious 2, 13, 16, 20, 22, 27–28, 30–32, 34–37, 39–44, 48, 50, 62, 68–70, 72, 78, 81, 86–91, 97–98, 103, 105, 114, 120–127, 134, 136, 139, 141, 143–144, 146–147, 155
uneasiness 68, 71
unobtrusive presence 42

Vila-Real, Â. 7–10

well-being and medical transitioning 86–87
whistleblowers 156
Winnicott, D. W. 23, 30, 32–36, 39, 41–42, 44, 82, 95, 144, 147
wondering mind 106–107
Woolf, V., *A Room of One's Own* and *Orlando* 12
World Health Organization (WHO) 67

Zolla, E. 12

For Product Safety Concerns and Information please contact our EU
representative GPSR@taylorandfrancis.com
Taylor & Francis Verlag GmbH, Kaufingerstraße 24, 80331 München, Germany

www.ingramcontent.com/pod-product-compliance
Lightning Source LLC
Chambersburg PA
CBHW070343270326
41926CB00017B/3952

9 7 8 1 0 3 2 8 7 1 8 6 8